David George – Vice President, Asset Protection, Dollar General Corporation

"The single most important tool to change organizational culture is one we have all had in our arsenal all along: language. The authors' "blueprint" and practical tools to guide us through different types of conversations to yield different results are so simple they're staggering. By understanding organizations as networks of commitments, new doors are opened that yield incredibly powerful, stimulating ways for teams to produce dramatically different results."

Ben Dominitz – Founder/Former CEO of Prima Communications; Vistage International Chair

"As a coach of CEO's and other leaders, I am confronted with the contradiction of instant and impersonal communication via electronic means, and the unchanging need for thoughtful and meaningful human connection. Chalmers and Vinay urge us to do more than exchange surface words, but to begin to think about our thinking, to use language (with all its verbal and non-verbal connotation) as a creative tool that can change relationships, paradigms, real-world results and the entire context of thinking. The notion that language can create is a liberating concept, allowing each of us to become artists in our own right, creating the prism through which we, and those we touch, live."

Carlos Salum - Founder – Salum International Resources; Leadership Performance Strategist; Professional Tennis Coach

"My experience with "language as creation" in corporate culture change processes is related to my work as an external consultant with Swiss private banks and multinational corporations for the past 15 years. I have learned that dialogue is the ultimate leadership skill – it's an invitation to look beyond profits – to surpass the banality of transactional interactions to create lasting contributions. This book provides a clear road map and set of tools for leaders to dramatically improve their thinking, their conversations, their organizational culture and their bottom line(s) – however these are measured."

In this book, you will discover an eye-opening organizational blueprint - coupled with a set of powerful, practical tools and pathways - for dramatically improving relationships, shaping workplace culture and driving breakthrough results.

How Extraordinary Leaders
Build Relationships,
Shape Culture and
Drive Breakthrough Results

Language and the Pursuit of
LEADERSHIP
EXCELLENCE

Second Edition

new
possibilities
press

naples florida

New Possibilities Press
8805 Tamiami Train North, Suite 311
Naples, FL 34108

info@chalmersbrothers.com; www.chalmersbrothers.com
vinay@leadingforbreakthroughs.com; www.leadingforbreakthroughs.com

Library of Congress Cataloging-in-Publication Data

Library of Congress Control Number: 2015912417

Brothers, Chalmers
Kumar, Vinay

Language and the pursuit of leadership excellence:
how extraordinary leaders build relationships, shape
culture and drive breakthrough results
(Chalmers Brothers and Vinay Kumar)

ISBN 13: 978-0-9749487-9-9

Printed in the United States of America
Cover Design and Illustrations by Mike Shotton
Produced by New Possibilities Press, Inc.

For

Betsy

Rachael

Ben

&

Caroline

———◦✕◦———

For

Sudha

Juhie

&

Tripti

CONTENTS

FOREWORD
by JULIO OLALLA

Human beings are creating and being affected by a series of crises of global dimensions:

- at the ecological level, we are experiencing increasing loss of biodiversity, environmental pollution, atmospheric contamination, extinction of native forests, global warming and many others;

- at the economic level, there is the increased (and increasing) accumulation of wealth by a very small percentage of the population;

- at the psychological level, we are witnessing a sustained increase in depression and youth suicide; and

- in our organizations, study after study shows a high index of lack of job satisfaction and a clear crisis of leadership.

However, there is another unspoken crisis, one that is transparent to us. This crisis, which is more than two centuries old and is at the origin of all the other crises, is the crisis of our knowledge. Modernity has focused our knowledge, and therefore our learning, almost exclusively in the material world, on the techniques and procedures for dealing with all things physical, leaving in abandonment values, purpose, emotions, spirit and meaning. As Ken Wilber would say, we are pointing only to growth for its own sake and have abandoned the awakening.

We have developed extraordinary technologies to increase the reach of our communications, but the quality and effectiveness of our communication has not grown. In the last century, our capacity to produce has multiplied many times; however, indices measuring our wellbeing have barely risen, and in many places have decreased dramatically. We are reaching a situation where this singular focus on only one type of learning and one type of knowledge - which is now considered to be part of the common sense of our era – is revealing its deep deficiencies and painful costs.

In a world obsessed with the search for technical effectiveness and productive growth, life reminds us constantly and painfully that even though these are important, there is a significantly larger challenge: to find meaning and satisfaction in our lives and in our work. We have confused "learning how to work" with "learning how to live".

I wholeheartedly believe that knowledge is indifferent to purpose and meaning, while wisdom is inseparable from them.

In other words, we are desperately searching for more information, more knowledge and more effectiveness, and we have finally forgotten why. In my work as a coach for over thirty years, I have worked with thousands of people in my public and organizational programs, people that were clearly effective and successful according to the standards of our times, but who nevertheless expressed lack of satisfaction, lack of purpose, lack of meaning in their lives. Clearly, the sole and unrelenting focus on technical effectiveness and high productivity is insufficient to achieve a good life, to create a better world.

Humanity has lived through huge transformations in history, including the world of the ancient Greeks, the Roman Empire and the Middle Ages . These transitions and transformations were not easy, as the main assumptions of these eras utterly collapsed. These collapses gave birth, of course, to new interpretations, new ways to understand ourselves, our relationships with others, our existence.

Today, our time invites us to recreate our epistemology, our ontology and our cosmology. It's a great opportunity! We have the possibility of participating in and catalyzing an evolutionary jump, and to do so being conscious of what we are doing. If we don't change the observer we are, the way we view our ourselves and our era, our actions will not change and we will continue to produce fundamentally the same results.

Question: What is the role of leadership in all of this?

One of the central roles of a leader is to break the transparency of that which has trapped us in a certain way of seeing, looking, understanding, and doing. In doing so, the leader generates a new level of purpose in our work and puts us in touch with new learnings which are not limited to the growth of our effectiveness in the technical domain, but that extend to the full range and scope of the human experience. Said in a different way, leaders create breaks, significant and unprecedented interruptions that lead us to learnings that were previously invisible and unthinkable. These types of leaders – the types of leaders we desperately need today – break our transparency, forcing us to fundamentally reexamine our way of looking at things.

This book will take us through rich and persuasive roads to create anew our understanding of leadership. It invites us to look at leadership and organizational life with a larger scope than we normally consider. If we, as human beings, build our reality in narratives and stories, as we claim we do, then leaders are master story tellers – and therefore, builders of reality. These narratives are not simply conceptual structures; they create meaning and purpose because they connect us emotionally. And in doing so, they predispose us to act in building the world in which the narrative is fulfilled, manifested, made real. And the new world that these leaders are pointing us to is a world of transformational possibilities opened up by including ourselves, our relationships, our culture, our consciousness, our moods and emotions, our beliefs and our spirituality in our learning.

Chalmers Brothers came 22 years ago to one of the training programs in ontological coaching and personal transformation in The Newfield Network, which I lead. He recently told me that "The program changed my life. Since then, I've been crystal clear that to work with leaders and their leadership teams is my joy and my passion – to be able to help them find a new way of seeing and understanding themselves, their organizations and their roles – knowing that they are in positions to influence and impact so many others gives me the strength to bring this message as far and as wide as I can". Chalmers has also shared with me that his mission in life is to shift the consciousness of a million people, to shift the way that a million people see themselves and their possibilities. This book is part of that commitment.

Vinay Kumar, also a Newfield program graduate, shares Chalmers' passion and enthusiasm for this work and its potential for leaders and organizations of all sizes and shapes. Together, they share these messages with leaders, managers and employees around the world.

It fills me with hope to know that more and more people are starting to realize that the materialistic, mechanistic and reductionistic paradigm in which we are living is collapsing. An extraordinary transformation of human consciousness is happening. And with it, dramatically more integral, pluralistic and systemic schools of thought are emerging – and these are beginning to affect all the domains of our existence.

This book is a contribution in that direction.

Julio A. Olalla
Boulder, Colorado, USA
2018

INTRODUCTION:
CHALMERS

My first book, *Language and the Pursuit of Happiness,* was published 10 years ago. Leadership excellence, conversations and breakthrough Results have unquestionably been at the center of my professional life since then. Over this period – week in and week out, month in and month out, year in and year out – I have had the great privilege of being in very regular conversation with thousands of thoughtful, innovative, successful leaders. These CEO's, business owners and senior leaders of all types come from an incredible variety of personal, educational and industry backgrounds and lead organizations of all sizes and shapes.

And although they have wildly different styles, approaches, strategies and skills – and work in incredibly different industries, markets and competitive environments – there are nonetheless commonalities, themes and foundational principles that have emerged and which this book is intended to share. There are certain frameworks, ways of understanding and tools which have been found to have enduring value and benefit, across the board, for those seeking to significantly improve real-world Results… and to sustain those improvements over time.

If you have picked up this book, it's quite likely that you are in a position of leadership and are interested in learning how to more consistently produce desired Results. If this is the case, please keep reading. I promise that what's within these pages will support you in being, doing and having a great deal more of what you're seeking to be, do and have as a leader.

If you have read *Language and the Pursuit of Happiness,* you will find review and reinforcement – as well as a new organizational framework and context in which to apply what you've learned – in the pages ahead. You will also encounter new distinctions in the areas of workplace culture, organizational conversations, leadership competencies, effective execution, moods and emotions, and body/biology. And if you have not read my first book, you will also be introduced – possibly for the first time – to a startlingly powerful way of understanding yourself, your colleagues and the ways you and they actually go about the business of producing Results.

Moving forward, when we use the word Results, think very broadly. Improved productivity is obviously a Result. As are improved profitability and higher levels of healthy growth.

But think about it – as a leader, what are some of the most important <u>other</u> types of Results that you would like to more consistently bring about within your organization? *Because the claim is this: these Results are the actual drivers of organizational productivity, profitability and growth.* A short list may include:

- A healthier and more powerful corporate culture
- Higher degrees of shared understanding and shared commitment
- Fewer "silos" and improved teamwork, cooperation and collaboration within and across functional areas
- Better accountability, coupled with fewer misunderstandings and "drops of the ball"
- Improved clarity, communication and listening
- Stronger talent-development and coaching skills
- Enhanced ability to facilitate healthy, constructive disagreement
- Greater retention of high-quality employees – and quicker identification of those who are not a solid cultural "fit"
- Higher levels of trust, as well as the ability to rebuild trust once it's damaged
- Improvement in the way your organization handles mistakes and learns (or doesn't learn) from them
- Improved innovation, agility and ability to thrive in an environment of relentless change
- Improvement in your public identity; the ways that you and your organization get perceived, or "show up" for others

- Healthier and more mutually-beneficial professional and personal relationships

- Better balance, reduced stress and less experience of "overwhelm"

- Higher levels of emotional intelligence and enhanced emotional well-being

All of these are types of Results, are they not?

And if you look closely, you can see ways in which they can all be said to be connected to each other, to be linked to one another and to influence each other... as well as to contribute to and impact overall organizational productivity, profitability and growth.

As a leader, you know this already. The intent of this book – in addition to sharing with you some powerful <u>new</u> distinctions, frameworks and tools – is to support you in more effectively <u>applying</u> and <u>using</u> what you already intuitively know.

Five Fundamental Competencies

I believe we can identify 5 core competencies that are required – not optional – for organizational success today and tomorrow:

- Functional

- Technical

- Conversational

- Relational

- Emotional

(We can certainly talk about whether this list should contain 4 or 6 or 7 competencies, but something like this is going on!)

Question: What competencies are often used as the basis for hiring people?

I have asked this question to literally thousands of CEO's over the past 10 years and the overwhelming answers are... Functional and Technical competencies. These are what get people hired. Is this your experience as well?

Next Question: As people advance in their careers, if they are ultimately let go (fired)... what are the most common reasons for this?

Having also asked this question many times over the years I can report that the overwhelming responses are... *deficiencies* in Conversational, Relational and/or Emotional competencies.

This book is intended to strengthen your Conversational, Relational and Emotional competencies because – as we shall see – it is precisely in these 3 areas that the most important leadership "work" actually takes place. It is precisely these 3 competencies that leaders and managers actually use in achieving and sustaining desired Results, including the unprecedented and historically never-before-achieved outcomes that we call breakthrough Results.

In some ways, Functional and Technical competencies have become the "price of admission" or the threshold for existence within a particular industry or market segment. It's increasingly evident that it's the Conversational, Relational and Emotional competencies that differentiate, that make the difference between good and sustainably great organizations.

These competencies – on top of a profoundly powerful framework and new way of understanding – are the focus of this book. Jim Collins, in his bestselling book *Good to Great* says "*Disciplined people who engage in disciplined thought and who take disciplined action – operating with freedom within a framework of responsibilities – this is the cornerstone of a culture that creates greatness.*" The book you are now reading is about **operationalizing** and creating such a culture and establishing such a framework within your organization.

Once we're talking about competencies, we are obviously involved with learning. And learning "about" is not the same as learning "to do" or learning "to be". In this book, we will be working with all of these. They are all valid and necessary parts of what I believe is our ongoing journey of growth, evolution and becoming. Changes out there begin with changes in here. And learning – in a number of different areas and in a number of different ways – is the key.

Special Acknowledgements

This book comes about out of my wonderful relationship with Vinay Kumar, a colleague and co-author in this work who has also become a great friend. It is through Vinay that I was introduced in a much bigger way to the Georgetown Leadership Coaching community and the Institute for Transformational Leadership. This generous community has deepened my understanding of the value and application of this body of learning, and I am tremendously grateful for these new relationships and the possibilities they represent.

I am also deeply grateful for the contribution and friendship of the following wonderful coaches, consultants and trainers: Sarah Happel, Francis Roman, Maureen Blackwell, Mark House, Joan Rooney, Penny Potter and Cary Larson.

During 2013-2014, I had the opportunity to lead two year-long "culture change" engagements – with this body of work as the foundation – within systems integration / technology companies in Northern Virginia. Vinay was instrumental in the creation of the program and its success at both of these organizations, and remains an integral part of what we call our SOAR Program. He is now also delivering SOAR (which stands for Success through Observer – Action – Results) internationally, and we continue to work closely together.

There are many ways to approach, understand and share the key distinctions, frameworks and tools that are within these pages. Vinay has been a constant "thought partner" in this process, challenging and probing and questioning all along the way, providing ideas, energy and a unique perspective that I have come to value greatly. This book simply would not have come about – or surely would not have come about now – without him.

Special acknowledgements would not be complete without also sharing with you the organization that first introduced my wife, Betsy, and me to the world of ontological coaching back in 1987. Chuck Smith, Mike Papania, Jeff Spring and many others have contributed greatly to my life and helped me change course when it mattered most. The company, Education for Living (Baton Rouge, LA) continues to be a wonderful source of powerful programs for people from all walks of life. I encourage you to explore what they have to offer.

The Impact and Influence of The Newfield Network and Julio Olalla

Twenty-three years ago, I was introduced to an organization and a man who changed my life, and who continue to impact and influence my work with my clients, my writing, and my personal life. I was fortunate to learn about The Newfield Network in the early '90s, and in 1995 I completed a year-long program called *Mastering the Art of Professional Coaching*. For me, everything has been different since then. The program was led by Julio Olalla, along with Rafael Echeverria, and virtually everything in this book – as well as everything in my first book – was taught to me by Julio and the other leaders at Newfield Network. Julio is a master coach and visionary, recognized worldwide as a pioneering force in bringing forth new ways of being, new ways of relating to each other and living together, new ways of understanding what it means to be human, what it is to learn, and the ways we human beings – no matter how different we may appear on the surface – are incredibly alike. Julio opened my eyes – and the eyes of all of us fortunate enough to be in that program – to a new world of possibilities and a new set of distinctions, tools and practices that are now the basis for my writing, as well as all the work I do with my training and coaching clients.

I am clearly a student of Julio Olalla, and a great many of the ways that I understand and explain things, frame topics and move through distinctions and tools were first taught to me directly by Julio.

I wholeheartedly encourage you to investigate The Newfield Network (Boulder, CO), now led by Julio's daughter Veronica, and the incredible, life-changing programs they offer. If you are interested in learning about yourself, your possibilities and new ways in which we can each contribute to making this a better world, Newfield is the place to start.

Suggested Approach to Reading this Book

Before going any further, I invite you to think about your role, your organization, your performance and your priorities as a leader.

With these clearly in mind, make a list that includes:

- What would you like to learn, or learn how to do better?

- For each of your key direct reports: What single area of improvement in his/her performance would have the biggest positive impact on your organization?

- What are 1 or 2 or 3 important new Results – possibly even breakthrough Results – that you are committed to achieve within the next 12 months?

Keep this list with you as you move through these pages. As you progress through each chapter, refer to your list and think about ways in which you can apply what you're learning and remembering. Take some notes. Enroll someone close to you in what you're up to as an "accountability partner." Identify ways you can share what you're discovering and noticing with your colleagues. Over time, initiate new conversations to discuss and explore these new possibilities.

Always, always, always be thinking: "How can I apply what I'm learning, what I'm noticing, what I'm discovering... *given the Results I say I want?*"

It's a privilege to share with you an incredibly empowering way of understanding leadership excellence, relationships, workplace culture and breakthrough Results... and even more importantly, yourself. Because, as you already know, this is where everything begins.

Chalmers Brothers
Naples, FL

INTRODUCTION:

VINAY

I was born in India where my dad worked as a civil engineer in the public sector and my mother was a homemaker. Most of my dad's family members worked in various civil service positions, while my mother's immediate family members were engaged in a family-owned business.

In 1969, at the age of 11, along with my sister and parents, I immigrated to the United States. Prior to my university education in chemical engineering, I held various blue-collar jobs including delivering newspapers, washing dishes at a pizza restaurant, cleaning offices and stripping floors after school where my dad worked as an engineer. Following my formal education, my first professional job was working as sales engineer for a major oil company.

For the next 17 years, I worked as a project manager at the U.S. Environmental Protection Agency, delivered Total Quality Management (TQM) programs and co-owned and operated a successful printing and mailing business.

Within these various organizations, I served in leadership and non-leadership roles. In addition, I have served on many committees and boards, and participated in various leadership forums. Along the way, as many of us do, I did some things well, and some things not so well. At times I succeeded because of myself and at other times, in spite of myself! To a great degree it was on-the-job-training and today I tell my friends that I earned my Ph. D. from the School of Life.

I have been fortunate to have had the opportunity to travel extensively to various parts of the world. Throughout my travels, observing others on their journeys, there is one thing I have consistently observed and thought about:

How is it that two people can grow up in very similar circumstances, have similar physical and mental capacities, similar opportunities, and yet one goes on to being successful, living a healthy joyful life… and the other struggles and experiences pain and suffering? In other words, how is it that many highly technically and functionally competent people, in spite of experiencing business and professional success, ultimately start to experience failure in their most important relationships, which inevitably also negatively impacts their business and all those connected to it?

Along my own journey, I too have experienced both success as well as failure and thus have often wondered if my success was accidental – my being in the right place at the right time – or was it something else?

Throughout my career, I often found employees, colleagues and friends reaching out to me to serve as a sounding board or thought partner. At this point in my life, I was also searching for a way to make a more meaningful contribution – and in 2012, this led me to join the Leadership Coaching Program at Georgetown University. It was in this program where I first came across *Language and the Pursuit of Happiness* by Chalmers Brothers, as this was one of our required readings. Here, I began to find some of the answers I was looking for. This was my first introduction to this body of work and to Chalmers.

I realize there are many external factors that also contribute to our quality of life and to what we are able to achieve, professionally and personally. Even so, I keep coming back to the question: What more could become possible and what more could we achieve if we could actually harness the power that is already within us? A story from Eckhart Tolle's book "A New Earth" comes to mind here:

A beggar had been sitting by the side of a road for over thirty years. One day a stranger walked by. "Spare some change?" mumbled the beggar, mechanically holding out his old baseball cap. "I have nothing to give you," said the stranger. Then he asked: "What's that you are sitting on?" "Nothing," replied the beggar. "Just an old box. I have been sitting on it for as long as I can remember." "Ever looked inside?" asked the stranger. "No," said the beggar. "What's the point? There's nothing in there." "Have a look inside," insisted the stranger. The beggar managed to pry open the lid. With astonishment, disbelief, and elation, he saw that the box was filled with gold.

This is how I have experienced the body of learning that we are sharing with you here. For me, through the course of the Georgetown Leadership Coaching program, my eyes began to open. I began to see and think differently and find some important answers in *Language and the Pursuit of Happiness*, as mentioned above. The distinctions Chalmers shares in that book began to help me see what had been in front of me all along, but because I had lacked the distinctions, I was unable to see. And now that I have learned the distinctions, I can now see what I didn't see before. I am much more aware of my own role in creating the experiences of my life, and much more able to purposefully design and bring forth peacefulness, stronger relationships and emotional well-being — for myself first, and now for others.

Having begun to experience the power of this work, I reached out to Chalmers and he graciously made a visit to TEOCO Headquarters in Fairfax, VA to visit with our founder and CEO, Atul Jain, and me. Atul's strong support and desire to bring this work into TEOCO prompted Chalmers and me to co-create a multi-month, leadership and employee development program we refer to as SOAR.

This program has since been delivered in the US, UK, Israel and India and it continues to expand into other parts of the globe, positively impacting more and more lives of our firm's leaders, managers and professionals. Since that 2012 beginning, we have also engaged many others in delivering this body of work, and they too are now successfully taking this work inside organizations.

For me, this body of work has provided many of the answers I had been searching for. And my sincere belief is that as you diligently begin to work with this knowledge and apply even just a few of the distinctions presented in this book, they will enable you to produce more of the results you want. These results — based on my experience and the experience of many others — include:

- Greater personal and professional effectiveness
- Increased levels of Emotional Intelligence
- Improved communication effectiveness
- Greater career, business, financial success
- Stronger ability to build, rebuild and strengthen important relationships
- Better physical and emotional health
- More self-confidence and greater ability to take on new challenges, deal with on-going rapid change, and move forward in the face of uncertainty.

As you begin to read this book, you will also come to see that much of this material is not rocket science and a lot of it will seem familiar. It's my prediction, however, that you are probably not using what you know as effectively and as fully as you could be. This material can appear to be deceptively simple. The key to experiencing the benefits, however, is to improve your ability to actually apply this material! At first it will take conscious effort and over time it will start to become second nature. As you continue on this path, you will begin to experience that while your growth and changes will be evolutionary, the net impact over time will be nothing short of revolutionary.

Here I want to acknowledge Chalmers Brothers, to whom I am deeply grateful for what we have created together, for the wonderful friendship that we have developed and now for our co-authoring of this book. In addition to Atul Jain, I would like to also acknowledge Alexis Kaltreider, TEOCO's Global Vice President of Human Resources and Resource Management, and Myron Radio, President of The R Group. Myron was the first person who opened the door and introduced me to the world of leadership coaching and development. Along with Chalmers, they and many others continue to be my strong pillars and for whose support I am deeply grateful. They include Mark Sachs, Penny Potter, Jean Frankel, Arvind Gupta, Joe Isaacs, Sarah Happel, Lewis Flax, Maura Fredericks, Joan Fletcher, Arun Lal, Francis Roman, Mark House, Cary Larson, Joan Rooney, Wendy Luke, Karen Mack, Philip Martin and many from my CBODN and Georgetown Leadership coaches community. Last but not least, I dedicate this book to my wife Sudha and my daughters Juhie and Tripti. I am grateful for their ongoing support and encouragement for the work I do.

With that, let us begin,

Vinay Kumar
Great Falls, VA

OUR STARTING POINT

*"I know of no more encouraging fact than the unquestionable
ability of man to elevate his life by conscious endeavor."*

- Henry David Thoreau

Given that you have picked up this book, it is quite likely that you are a leader
and are interested in improving your ability to produce significant, positive
and possibly unprecedented Results for yourself, your teams, your departments,
your functional areas and your organization. We will term these "breakthrough
Results" and they will be at the forefront of everything that follows.

*(Note: This book will focus explicitly on Results, the Actions required to produce those
Results, as well as the role each of us – as unique Observers – plays in this process. We
will capitalize Observer, Action and Results throughout to emphasize these aspects and
relationships.)*

With this in mind, you may ask: What is the most productive starting point for
this learning journey, this learning process, so that you are able to more effectively
and more rapidly move from where you are to where you want to be?

We suggest starting with self-awareness, improving your ability to notice what
you're currently doing, and the degree to which what you're currently doing is
working well… or not. One of the most fundamental objectives of this book is to
support you in becoming a more powerful, more competent Observer of yourself.

The focus here will be to help you begin to see yourself and the Actions you're taking – as well as the Results you're producing – in new ways. Without this awareness, we dramatically limit our effectiveness, as we end up focusing our time,
energy and resources in every area except the most important one.

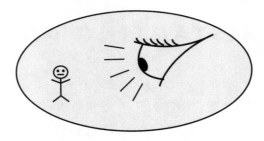

We refer to this graphic as the Big Eye. This is meant to indicate you taking a look at you, for this is where everything must begin. This focus on self-awareness is bolstered by some basic claims that we make here and that will serve to undergird the remainder of this book.

Eight Basic Claims

1. **You cannot change another human being.** Who has tried? Who has teenagers? A spouse or significant other? Now, we're not saying others don't and can't influence us… they certainly can, and they do. But at a most basic level, however, neither your spouse nor your colleagues (nor anyone) can change you. Only you can change you, if you choose to. *But you can't change what you don't notice.* Now, you may notice and choose not to change – great. Now you've got your eyes open. But if you don't notice, you don't even get to choose.

2. **Inner growth is a pre-requisite for outer growth.** Everything that is created by human beings begins with thought, with our own internal conversations. Therefore we claim if one is stuck on the outside – unable to produce desired breakthrough Results – one must first get unstuck and "break through" on the inside. We must be able to modify our thinking. Albert Einstein's quote *"We cannot solve our problems with the same level of thinking that created them"* comes to mind here. Our level of thinking, our way of thinking, our habitual patterns of thinking provide the starting point for seeing new ways forward and producing new Results we want to produce in our lives – at work as well as at home.

In order to produce Results we have not produced before we must think in ways we haven't thought in before, which goes hand-in-hand with taking Actions we haven't taken before. For now, consider: Who do you say you are? Who do you think you are? What do you think is possible? What do you think you (and your organization) have the ability to do? Do you think your responses to these questions – your thoughts – are connected with your ability to produce real-world Results? This book will strengthen your ability to take a new look here, and will provide you with a powerful framework and new set of tools for producing exactly these types of breakthroughs. It's these breakthroughs "in here" that enable you to produce those breakthroughs "out there."

3. **We're not hermits.** That is, much of what we do, produce and achieve is done, produced and achieved with and through others. Leaders (and everyone else, too) are always and already connected to other human beings, accomplishing Results with and through others. This is a given.

Think about it – we do work, family, Rotary Club, church, volunteering, PTA and soccer with and through people. So we can either be connected to others in such a way that it produces the Results we say we want, or be connected with others in such a way that it does not. Either way, we're still "dancing" with others. The key question is: Is the <u>way</u> you're doing this working for you, given the Results you say you want?

This is glaringly obvious for leaders and managers, is it not? A mid-level manager who had only been in his new job for a short while shared this at a workshop: "You know, I've only been in my new position for about 6 months, and I can tell you right now… this job would be so much easier… without these people!" What he didn't see is that if the people are taken away, he has no job as a manager. Guiding and managing and coordinating and collaborating with people <u>is</u> the job. This is what leadership, management and supervision are all about.

Furthermore, as we will see as we move through the pages ahead, there is a direct correlation between leadership effectiveness and the ability to establish and maintain mutually-beneficial, healthy and productive relationships, inside and outside the organization. Leaders do and achieve what they do and achieve in community with other human beings, and therefore they rely heavily on conversational, relational and emotional competencies to accomplish Results. The learning in this book will support you in further developing and strengthening these very competencies, along with many others.

4. **Change is permanent, so get used to it.** It's not just you and us, it's bigger than that. Relentless, ongoing change is the already existing background, the overarching context in which you are reading this book and in which absolutely everything we do occurs. And as you have very likely experienced, the pace and scope and reach of this relentless change is increasing.

As a leader, your orientation toward change has a dramatic and powerful impact not only on your personal effectiveness, but also on the performance of your organization as a whole. How you think about change, anticipate change, navigate change, respond to change and proactively induce change are all tremendously important factors influencing and driving the most important Results you are seeking to produce.

So again, we point to the importance and value of ongoing learning – for you as a leader and for everyone within your organization. Learning how to learn is crucial for individuals and organizations, today and tomorrow. Effective leaders are effective learners.

5. **If you always do what you always did, you always get what you always got.** If you want to produce new Results, with clients or customers or colleagues or team members, you have to take new Action. Obviously. And let's be clear – for those of us who do not wear hardhats and steel-toe boots to work – many of the most important Actions we take have nothing to do with our arms and legs. Said another way, the most important leadership and management Actions are not physical... there is something else going on here, and we'll take a closer look at it in this book.

We can actually add these two corollaries here: "If you always think what you always thought, you always get what you always got." And "If you always say what you always said, you always get what you always got." We will be exploring this in great detail moving forward.

Leaders must be able to see new possibilities and take new Actions to produce new Results. This again brings us squarely into the domain of adult learning: In order for you to take an Action at time period B that you didn't or couldn't take at time period A, new learning is required. The ability to continually learn is simply required for leadership effectiveness — now and for the foreseeable future. So whether or not leaders are able to instill a culture of learning, a culture of innovation, a culture of flexibility and agility within their organizations can mean the difference between that organization thriving, surviving… or becoming irrelevant and ceasing to exist.

6. **We're always at choice.** That is, we always have choices available to us, and we are constantly choosing and deciding as we deal with the issues of our lives. And back to the Big Eye — many of us are not very powerful Observers of the choices that we have available to us. Thus, a key objective of ours is this: To have you finish this book equipped with distinctions that will enable you to see more choices than you currently see, to expand your "universe set" of leadership choices, to equip you with a greater range of leadership options for taking effective Action that lead to achievement of your desired Results — in a wide variety of situations.

On the home front, we have children in their early 20's. If you have children, you too may find this interesting and familiar. We ask this question in workshops, and pose it this way: Depending on the ages of our kids, have we not said our version of this to them — "Pay attention to your choices, because your life is going to unfold, largely, the way it unfolds, based on the choices that you make." Virtually everyone nods, as they understand the power that comes with being conscious about the choices that we have and the choices that we make — as well as the possibilities that open up as a Result of having new, unprecedented choices.

Think about this: Every time in your life that things were screwed up, you were there! We are each the common denominator in our own situations. We are the ones who keep showing up, again and again. So let's take a new look at our choices, and where they are leading us. Let's flex the Big Eye right here. For it is our claim that we're not born winners or losers. Rather, we are all born choosers. Through the choices we make, we open possibilities and create our destinies, as individual leaders and for our organizations. So the choices we see and the choices we make matter a great deal.

7. **How you "see things" matters - a lot.** Is it possible that you and a colleague can look at the same thing or event or circumstance and yet see it very differently... and that this significant difference has nothing to do with your retinas? Of course. This happens all the time. We claim that the reason two people with very similar biologies "see things" differently is related to their thinking, their thoughts, their internal conversations and internal narratives.

How many of us know people for whom this is true: the way that they see a problem or a situation... is itself a big part of the problem! They way that they've framed it has paralyzed them. They're not framing it with 2x4's, of course. Something else entirely is going on. But the way they've done that has had the effect of dramatically shrinking their horizon of possibilities, and this is not trivial. So how we observe, how we see things, matters a great deal.

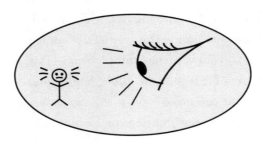

Therefore, in addition to supporting you in becoming a more powerful Observer of yourself, we have another objective here. *We are seeking to also support you in becoming a more powerful Observer of the way you observe,*

a more powerful Observer of the way you see things, as depicted by the graphic above. To begin taking a better look at how you look at things, so that this can be one of the universe set of variables on the table that you get to explore, should you decide you want to produce new and more powerful Results.

Our experience here is this: the ability to take a look at how you look at things is not simply one incremental step "up" from not being able to do that. Instead, it's an ocean, a quantum leap. It's a substantial shift in awareness to be able to look at how you look at things. But when you can do this, you will open avenues of possibility for yourself that are utterly off your radar screen if you can't – or choose not – to do this. They will be utterly invisible to you. Improvements here can dramatically expand your playing field and open unprecedented new possibilities and options for yourself and your organization.

8. **Much of this is simple but not easy.** Our prediction is that as you go through this book, some of this content will look familiar and will seem like a type of "common sense." This is because in some ways, it is. While you may not use the same terminology or the exact same ways of saying things as we do, when we cover certain topics we predict you'll think to yourself "I knew that!" Yet it's also our experience that while many of us "know" some or much of this intellectually, we often are not applying it in everyday life nearly as effectively as we could be. Common sense isn't always common practice.

This is the key – actual, real-life application, which takes conscious effort and commitment, over time. Learning "about" is not the same as learning "to do" or learning "to be." But if you go down this path, the path of conscious application and practice, we promise that the effort will be well worth it. Incrementally, day by day, you will deepen your understanding and awareness, creating the small shifts and small changes in thinking and behavior that – over time – will yield truly transformational Results.

Suggestions for Moving Through This Book

We have shared the body of learning that's represented in this book with many people over the years, in organizations and in personal settings. In virtually every situation, people are able to very quickly see – with remarkable clarity – how valuable these distinctions are and how beneficial these principles could be... **for other people in their lives!** For example, employees make it clear that their bosses are really the ones who could benefit greatly from this. At the same time, managers and leaders are incredibly quick at noticing how valuable it would be if their employees could only get some of this... and so on.

As you move through this book, our invitation is for you to keep the focus on how what you're learning may apply to <u>you</u>, as well as on the new possibilities and new options for taking effective Action that become available to <u>you</u>. This will give you the best starting point for moving forward.

Next, we will be sharing approaches and frameworks, tools and practices, ways of thinking and ways of taking Action, in the pages ahead. We will be offering interpretations and understandings, suggestions and ideas that have had profoundly powerful and positive impacts on us, as well as on a great many others. But we are not claiming that these are the "Right" ways of understanding and others who offer different approaches or frameworks are "Wrong." We aren't claiming that we have "understanding" and others who provide alternate interpretations have "mis-understanding."

We make this point out of our experience that in a great many situations, we have not collectively agreed on what constitutes right-ness or wrong-ness, truth-ness or false-ness, good-ness or bad-ness... but this doesn't stop us in the least from claiming to be Right and making others Wrong, or claiming to have the Truth and viewing what others have as False. We tend to throw these grids on top of many situations rather automatically, including situations in which these grids absolutely do not fit and absolutely do not help.

For example, is there really only one right way to increase sales or decrease expenses in a given situation? Is there only one good way to manage conflict, solve problems or on-board new employees? Or on the home front, is there only one right way to fold the towels, load the dishwasher, squeeze the toothpaste and unroll the toilet paper? Is it really good to drink red wine with steak and bad to drink the same wine with fish? Is it really true that everyone from the younger generation is this way and everyone from the older generation is that way?

Our invitation instead is to begin to orient ourselves with questions that are more directly connected to Results. That is, to instead ask the following sorts of questions as we view frameworks, consider interpretations and evaluate tools:

- What possible Actions and therefore, what possible Results come out of seeing things this way vs. that way?

- What does this way of thinking help me become more able to be, do and have… that this other way of thinking does not?

- What would happen if a great many people adopted this way or that way of evaluating and understanding? What would be the relationship impact and the collective impact on how we live and work together? On how we lead our organizations?

Always, always be thinking: How do these ways of understanding, these ways of thinking, these tools and practices impact my ability to actually achieve the most important Results I say I want to achieve?

So instead of the Right/Wrong, True/False, Good/Bad grids, we invite you to move through the pages ahead using the **Works/Doesn't Work** grid, posing for yourself questions such as the ones above, always considering how the offers we make may Work or Not Work… given the Results you say you want.

While we certainly don't claim that what's to follow is Right and others with different ideas and approaches are Wrong, we do claim that the concepts and distinctions presented within this book will allow you to lead more effectively, create better relationships and design your own life. They will enable you to produce more of the Results you desire and aim to produce. The invitation here is to use what works for you, given the Results you are seeking, and leave the rest.

Application

We invite you to establish a habit of flexing and strengthening your self-awareness, your Big Eye muscle. Over time, with enough time and practice, the muscle will become stronger and this will become a habit, something that you do ongoingly and in real time. As a starting point, the invitation is to engage in this practice for 5 minutes a day, every day.

<u>Activity:</u> Find a quiet place where you can sit without being disturbed. Get comfortable, breathe a bit more slowly and rhythmically than normal for a minute or two, and close your eyes. Once you've settled in, ask yourself:

- What types of thoughts are going through my head? Are they empowering me or disempowering me? Are they more about the past, the present or the future? And what are they about?

- Reflect on the previous 24 hours. What are the various conversations I engaged in and what were the outcomes they produced? What did I do or say that worked for me – given the Results I say I want? What did I do or say that didn't work for me – again, given my desired Results?

- What moods and emotions have I been experiencing over the past 24 hours? Did I spend more or most of my time being happy, sad, mad, irritated, peaceful, annoyed, ambitious… something else? Was it uplifting, energizing or the opposite?

- Physically, what am I feeling and where am I feeling it? Notice, for example, is my breath deep and slow, or is it shallow and quick? Are my muscles tight or are they relaxed? Which ones do I feel?

As you engage in this exercise, the objective is to simply observe and see what patterns you notice. The intent is to observe without judgment, without labeling anything you see as "good" or "bad" or whatever. Simply notice. (And one of the things you might notice is that it can be difficult to do this!)

Our suggestion for you is to establish a set time of day for this. For many people mornings work best. For others it's the evenings and for a smaller number, mid-day. The key is to establish a time when you can do this consistently and on an on-going basis. As we are reminded by Aristotle: *"We are what we repeatedly do. Excellence, then, is not an act, but a habit."*

CHAPTER 1

THE PATHWAY FOR PRODUCING BREAKTHROUGH RESULTS

"We keep searching out there for answers and pointing out there for blame... all the while looking through the very lens that is itself the source of our greatest potential for designing something new."

– Chalmers Brothers

We begin with a basic premise: As a leader, you are interested in and committed to achieving sustainable, positive Results for your organization and yourself. At a foundational level, your effectiveness as a leader – regardless of what industry or type of organization you may be part of – is directly connected to your ability to enable the achievement of desired Results.

We continue with three basic questions:

- How do you, as a leader and as a human being, actually achieve Results?

- What options are available to you, given that you sometimes produce Results that you'd rather not produce?

- What options are available to you when you find yourself "stuck" – having seemingly exhausted all options and not knowing what to do next?

How each of us frames and understands this very basic process greatly influences what we even see as possibilities for improving whatever we say we want to improve. This chapter introduces our favorite model for showing how leaders (and everyone, for that matter) achieve what we achieve, how we actually produce the Results we produce, as individuals and as organizations.

This is the simplest and also the most powerful way we know of understanding ourselves, our Actions and our Results. From here and through the remainder of the book, this way of understanding will be the framework and reference point we use in the journey from where you are today to where you choose to be.

This model, called the Observer – Action – Results model, was initially developed by Chris Argyris and Robert Putnam. It has appeared in articles and books by both and is a very influential model, having been adopted and modified and used by a great many practitioners. Let's take a look, as we build the model in stages:

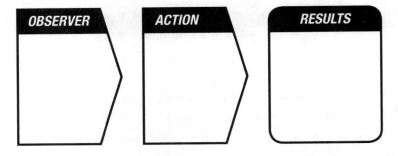

To start with, let's ignore the Observer part of the model and concentrate on only the Actions and Results. Can we agree that the Results we produce have a great deal to do with the Actions we do or do not take? Most of us would say, yes, our Results are strongly connected with our Actions or lack thereof.

Next, let's make sure we broaden what we mean when we use the term Results. For example, all of the following may be understood as valid, important types of Results that leaders seek to produce within themselves and/or their organizations:

- A healthier and more powerful corporate culture

- Desired levels of growth

- Improved productivity and/or profitability

- Higher degrees of shared understanding and shared commitment

- Fewer "silos" and improved teamwork, cooperation and collaboration within and across functional areas

- Better accountability, coupled with fewer misunderstandings and "drops of the ball"

- Improved clarity, communication and listening

- Stronger talent-development and coaching skills

- Enhanced ability to facilitate healthy, constructive disagreement

- Greater retention of high-quality employees – and quicker identification of those who are not a solid cultural "fit"

- Higher levels of trust, as well as the ability to rebuild trust once it's damaged

- Improvement in the way your organization handles mistakes and learns from them

- Improved innovation, agility and ability to thrive in an environment of relentless change

- Improvement in your public identity; the ways that you and your organization get perceived, or "show up" for others

- Healthier and more mutually-beneficial professional and personal relationships

- Better balance, reduced stress and less experience of "overwhelm"

- Higher levels of emotional intelligence and enhanced emotional well-being

So now our model may look like this:

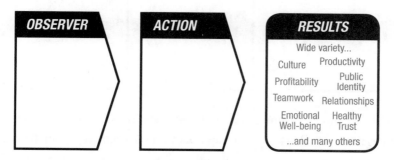

From here, we back up now to see that our Actions – or lack thereof – are always the influencers and drivers of our Results.

Depending on the type of job a person has – of course – the Actions he or she takes in order to produce desired Results may vary widely. For example, a backhoe operator may be seeking Results that include the successful, safe and timely loading of a certain pile of rubble into a waiting dump truck. And so the Actions he or she takes in order to achieve these Results would include operating the controls in such a way that the machine scoops and loads material safely and consistently till the load is complete within the allotted timeframe.

An underwater welder may be seeking Results that include the successful welding in a certain way of a certain joint on a bridge foundation, and so the Actions he or she takes include the appropriate use of scuba equipment, swimming and using the underwater navigation tools to locate the proper spot, followed by safe and proper use of the welding tools, and so on.

The Actions leaders take in order to produce the types of Results leaders are seeking are, in many ways, significantly different than those of the backhoe operator and the underwater welder. As we will see in the next chapter, the Actions of leaders are much less physically-oriented and much more rooted in their capacity to design and convene certain conversations.

So for now, we can say that both physical Actions and conversations are used by leaders to influence and drive Results:

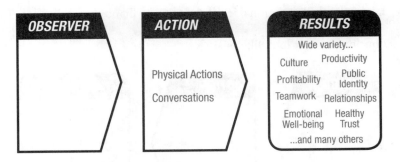

Now, once we produce some Results, we may assess these Results as either positive (+) or negative (-). That is, sometimes out of our Actions we produce Results we want, and sometimes we produce Results that we don't want. Again, this is true for individuals as well as organizations.

If we produce positive (+) Results, then we feel confirmed in the Action we took, and we'll probably take it again (see the far right side of the model below). And if we don't produce the Results we want, we can take another Action, and try again. If this doesn't work, we take another Action, try again. And so on, until we (hopefully!) do produce the Result we say we want. Chris Argyris has called this First Order Learning, and it's represented by the arrow suggesting more or new or different Actions, as shown below:

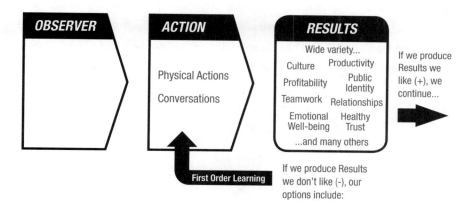

First Order Learning has to do with changing our Actions (which for leaders include changing our speaking, entering into new or different conversations) for the purpose of producing new Results. In some ways, First Order Learning represents our traditional approach to problem-solving. It implies that there is an objective problem "out there," and in order to solve it we must take Actions which are effective in producing some desired Result. It has everything to do with cause and effect.

Let's explore the Observer portion of the model now. Many of us have been in situations similar to this: You find yourself struggling with a problem, trying to figure out what to do, and it appears you've run out of options. You've tried several alternatives, none of which seemed to work, and you just don't see any more good possibilities left. At some point another person comes into the room, and in 5 minutes of conversation with you they offer a fresh new alternative, and you say "Oh, I didn't see it that way!"

Many of us have had this experience. We say that this occurs precisely because a new Observer has appeared – someone with a different view, a different perspective, a different way of looking at something. Notice how all the metaphors here are visual metaphors – they have a great deal to do with the Observer. They all point to a central claim of this model: ***Our Results have a great deal to do with our Actions or lack of Actions. This is well-known. What's less clear is that our Actions themselves have a great deal to do with the Observer that we are, with how we "see things".***

Now, when we use the term Observer, we aren't referring to a dispassionate "camera" or "visual scanning device." Instead, we are simply referring to each of us, as a functioning human being. The Observer that we are can be said to be composed of 3 separate but highly inter-dependent aspects or domains, as shown below:

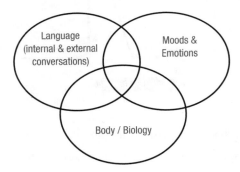

That is, each of us is can be viewed as a walking, talking bundle of congruency among three separate but strongly inter-twined aspects:

- Our physical body (includes our biology as well as our posture, our breathing and how we move through time and space)

- Our language (includes all of our thinking, our internal conversations as well as our external conversations)

- Our mood/emotional states (we will make some basic distinctions later between moods and emotions)

So the Observer – each of us – may be understood with the graphic below:

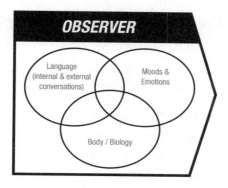

Now back to the model: What we don't often notice is that the way we observe, interpret, listen – the way we see things – comes <u>before</u> we take any Action. That is, the way we frame a given situation tends to create a particular "starting point" set of possibilities. Now, we may not know exactly which Action we will ultimately take, but we <u>do</u> know that it will come from this set of initial possibilities. Others, who frame the situation differently, see other sets of possibilities, which lead to other Actions.

Just because you (or any of us) may have exhausted all the possibilities you see doesn't mean there are no possibilities or options left. It just means that from the way you see things, the way you're thinking, the way you've constructed the situation, the story that you've built, from <u>your</u> perspective, through <u>your</u> beliefs, there are no possibilities. This is so for each and every one of us. No exceptions.

We claim here that we are each unique Observers. We are each unique thinkers, listeners, meaning-makers and interpreters of situations. We bring unique sets of beliefs, concerns and stories to the table… and so what we see, the way we observe, reveals more about us than about what's out there. ***What's important to notice is that many of us do not notice this!*** Back to the Big Eye, to our self-awareness. Many of us do not notice that we're observing in a particular way in the first place. We think we're seeing things objectively, "as they really are." And as we will demonstrate through the upcoming chapters, we offer that nothing could be further from the truth.

We live in an interpretive world. We are each "seeing things" through our own unique filters or lenses, which of course have nothing to do with wire mesh or polished glass. This is fundamental for leaders to notice and understand, and it will be a central theme within the chapters ahead.

The Grand Canyon looks different from the river than it does from the rim. Where you stand matters. The Observer portion of this model makes this explicit. If we don't like the Results we have produced or are producing, we can now take a look at how we look at things. We can become an Observer of the Observer that we are, and do so on purpose. If we don't like our current Results, we can bring our way of observing into the equation. We can flex the Big Eye muscle, and become conscious Observers of our particular way of observing. Chris Argyris has called this Second Order Learning, and it's represented by the arrow pointing back to the Observer, as shown below:

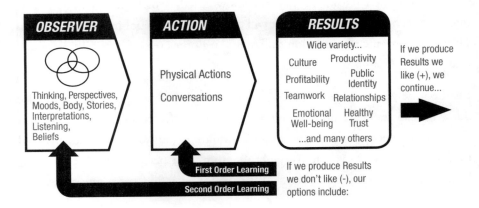

We agree with Chris Argyris that Second Order Learning holds the possibility for truly transformational learning, for making profound shifts in the Results we produce. It is here that we become conscious of the impact that our particular way of observing has on our Actions. From here, we are able to be much more conscious in designing new Actions that have historically been unavailable (unseen or viewed as impossible) to us. By bringing our own perspective, our own way of seeing things, into the mix, we open possibilities that simply would not have existed under "the old way of seeing things." It is this fundamental position of openness that serves as the foundation for new possibilities and breakthrough Results.

Of course, the whole notion of Second Order Learning makes no sense at all if we think the way we see things now = the way things truly are! The whole idea of taking a look at how we look at things is of very little value if we're convinced that we see things "objectively" and "realistically" already.

It takes more courage to take a look at how we look at things than it does to simply try new Actions. We claim that in one sense, the Actions a given person takes are all more or less the same. They're all coming from the same place, the same point of view, the same Observer, the same perspective. But if/when this person finally looks at how he looks at things, he then sees that he has, indeed, had a particular "point of view" all along. Not <u>the</u> way to see things, but simply <u>a</u> way of seeing things.

Moving forward here requires courage for most of us, we believe, because it involves fear for most of us. Not fear of being eaten by a tiger, but real fear nonetheless. This is because when we choose to look this way, at some level we know that we've expanded the playing field a bit, and that we're getting closer to the real stuff – the actual stories, interpretations, meanings and beliefs – that are underneath a lot of our Actions. We know we're getting closer to an area that has more to do with who we say we are and how we say we "be" – and far less to do with any of the particular things we may be doing.

Summarizing, we can say that if we <u>do</u> produce the Results we want (+), we usually continue taking those Actions that produced the effectiveness or the desired Result. However, if as an organization or as an individual we <u>don't</u> produce the Results we want (-), we have three primary options:

1. Assume the negative Results were caused by factors outside our control. Do nothing. Obviously, this is not a very powerful orientation!

2. Change our Actions, including our speaking (called First Order Learning). This is usually included in our traditional problem-solving models and approaches.

3. Change the way we look at things. Call into question the Observer that we are (called Second Order Learning). For us, this is the place of truly

transformational learning and of greatly expanding our possibilities for Actions that lead to unprecedented – breakthrough – Results.

This basic Observer – Action – Results model represents a profound shift in how we understand the role that each of us plays in producing what we produce for ourselves. We have found it to be an excellent foundation for leaders at all levels who are seeking a way to create and sustain significant improvements within their organizations.

Moving forward, everything else in this book will point you to the Observer that you are… or to the Actions you are taking… or to the Results you are producing… or to the processes of First Order Learning or Second Order Learning… as we seek to build a framework and provide you with distinctions and tools that will improve your effectiveness as a leader, as well as the performance of your organization.

Summary of Key Points

This book is all about supporting you, as a leader, in producing breakthrough Results. This chapter offers a simple yet powerful model for framing and understanding how each of us actually achieves Results in the world.

The Observer – Action – Results model supports leaders (and everyone) in understanding the factors impacting our ability to actually achieve breakthrough Results.

Think very broadly when using the term Results. Everything from your individual productivity to your public identity to a certain team's cohesiveness to the degree of shared understanding to the type of corporate culture you have to the nature of your most important relationships can be understood as different types of Results.

The Results we produce are a function of the Actions we do or don't take, and how we do or don't take them. This is well-known. In cases where we end up not producing desired Results, we can take another Action, and try again. And if this doesn't work, we can take yet another Action, and try again. Chris Argyris and others have called this First Order Learning.

As a leader, a great many of your most important Actions are not physical. They are conversational.

In some cases, we exhaust all the alternative Actions we see as possible and still haven't produced the desired Result. This doesn't mean that there are no more possibilities – it simply means that from our particular perspective, there are no more. Here we move into the Observer portion of the model.

Each of us is a unique Observer, seeing and interpreting and understanding the world in our particular way. Should we find ourselves not producing desired Results and exhausting all ready-at-hand alternative Actions, another type of learning is available. This is called Second Order Learning, and it occurs when we call the Observer we are into question. It involves taking a look at how we look at things, and it holds the possibility for transformational learning and the opening of unprecedented new possibilities.

Second Order Learning requires more courage and more emotional strength than does First Order Learning because you are now involved more with who you say you <u>are</u> than any particular thing you may or may not be <u>doing</u>.

The ability to achieve breakthrough Results is dependent on your ability to take a look at yourself in this way, to observe the way you observe and to open yourself to purposeful, conscious changes in these areas. Breakthrough Results involve new choices at the level of how you are interpreting, how you are thinking and how you are seeing things; that is, at the level of the Observer that you are. *Once these changes are made, new options and new possible Actions simply appear – and once they do, they often appear to be obvious.*

We live in an interpretive world. When we can see our interpretations as interpretations, we can break free from them and then purposefully author more powerful interpretations – those that can open new possibilities for effective Action and the achievement of unprecedented – breakthrough – Results. And who we think we are, what we think is possible, and what we think we can do are all interpretations. This is crucial for leaders to notice and to understand, and it will be a central theme in the chapters ahead. The distinctions you will learn in this book will support you in seeing more choices for moving forward, organizationally and personally, as well as in achieving literally unprecedented Results.

Application

1. As you began this book, you were invited to bring to mind and list 1 or 2 important Results that you are committed to bring about within the next 12 months. You were also encouraged to identify what you'd like to learn, or learn how to do better, moving forward. With these in the background, reflect on situations where you have hit a wall, you are feeling stuck, and you don't know what more to do to move forward. Capture as specifically as you can:

   - What you're seeking to produce

   - For the sake of what (why) you're seeking to produce it

   - What's at stake if you don't?

   - What you have tried so far

   - Where you seem to be stuck

2. Think of 3 people with whom you can share what you captured above. Ask them what they see and how they see it, and what they would do in order to move forward. As these individuals share, listen carefully. Ask probing questions to understand how they frame the situation, how they see it and what they would do. (What you're doing is bringing other Observers into the conversation). Notice what you notice and learn as you listen.

CHAPTER 2

WHAT EXTRAORDINARY LEADERS DO

"To get to the next level of greatness depends on the quality of the culture, which depends on the quality of relationships, which depend on the quality of conversations. Everything happens through conversations."

- Judith E. Glaser

Let's start with a basic question: What do extraordinary leaders do? Think about it. Of all the things excellent leaders do, day after day, year after year, what would you say are the top 1 or 2 or 3 on their list?

You may also think of your own role as a leader, and this tongue-in-cheek question: What do you get paid to do? Framed differently, what is your fundamental job as a leader?

Before you respond, frame the questions this way: Of all the many things extraordinary leaders do, if you could boil it down to the 1 or 2 or 3 most important, most critical, most foundational aspects… what would those be?

With your responses in mind, let's review a sampling of responses we have received over the years from thousands of CEO's and business owners:

- To guide and grow the organization
- To lead by example
- To establish and maintain a productive culture
- To establish and implement our strategy
- To set the vision and enroll people in it
- To get things done

- To build and maintain productive, beneficial relationships
- To ensure that the 3 broad areas of Operations/Administration, Sales/Marketing and Customer Service/Delivery are operating effectively and not becoming "silo-ed"
- To hire the right people and get them in the right seats on the bus
- To make sure the bus is going in the right direction
- To make sure everyone and everything is aligned and going in the same direction
- To get everyone on the same page
- To anticipate and manage change
- To make sure we stay relevant
- To build effective teams and get out of the way
- To create structures of accountability
- To create an environment of innovation and adaptability
- To oversee the development of our core business processes
- To make sure we stay in business
- To sell
- To ask the hard questions
- To inspire
- To coach
- To motivate
- To mentor
- To groom the next generation of leaders
- To make the tough decisions
- To think
- To keep the lights turned on

- To mobilize and deploy resources effectively
- … you can likely think of many more.

Can you see yourself in some – or many – of these responses? Does your list contain your version of some of these? It's quite likely that it does, and even more so if you're in a position of senior leadership – regardless of what industry you may be in or how large / small / complex / straightforward / centralized / decentralized your organization may be.

Workplace Application: *You may find value in leading this conversation with your direct reports. That is, ask them to share with you what they believe are the 1 or 2 or 3 most important, most critical, most central aspects of their jobs. By teeing it up this way, what you may find is that what you think they get paid to do may not be exactly what they think they get paid to do! Experience tells us that this may be a very valuable way to spend the first 15 minutes of a Monday morning staff meeting.*

Three Themes

Before continuing, we'd like to share with you three themes that continually surface when sharing and discussing leadership priorities in this way. While this certainly is not the only way to view and frame these responses, it's our intent to introduce these now as a way to guide and illuminate broad sets of priorities in the pages that follow.

The three themes around which a great many responses to the "What do you get paid to do?" question cluster are:

- Relationships
- Culture
- Execution

Let's look at each of these in greater detail.

Relationships

Try to imagine for a moment a leader whom you consider to be exceptional and highly effective... who has maintained this effectiveness over time... and who is also unable to build and maintain healthy, productive relationships. Difficult, isn't it?

Also for a moment consider the degree to which many organizations today have lessened the importance of position-based hierarchy and increased the use of cross-functional teams and highly collaborative processes. It quickly becomes clear that leadership at all levels involves accomplishing Results with and through others.

Thus, we claim that regardless of industry, exceptional leaders establish and maintain healthy, productive, mutually-beneficial **relationships** inside and outside the organization. We further claim that creating and maintaining such relationships is simply required for sustainable leadership effectiveness.

Meg Wheatley, best-selling author of *Leadership and the New Science*, says it this way: *"In organizations, real power and energy is generated through relationships. The patterns of relationships and the capacity for them are more important than the individual tasks, functions and positions we perform."*

The content in this book is absolutely about supporting you, as a leader, in establishing and maintaining powerful, mutually-beneficial relationships.

Culture

Do organizations have a culture? The overwhelming response in workshops to this question is Yes, absolutely. Does this culture impact Results – in a wide variety of ways and areas? Yes again. If you don't agree, try having a brainstorming conversation around a table of deeply resentful, deeply cynical people! We claim that an absolutely essential aspect of effective leadership is the ability to purposefully create and sustain positive corporate **culture**.

Peter Drucker, world-renowned author and leadership thought-leader, authored an expression that succinctly captures a very powerful truth: "**Culture eats strat-**

egy for breakfast." In layman's terms, what does this mean? It means that no matter how logically sound or analytically intelligent and well-thought-out your strategy may be... if the human beings inside the organization do not commit, communicate and collaborate effectively and solve problems and adapt and learn from each other over time... the desired Results of the strategy will simply never see the light of day. And committing, communicating, collaborating, solving problems, adapting and learning are all functions of – and drivers of – what we and others have come to refer to as workplace culture.

Another writer, Patrick Lencioni, author of *The Five Dysfunctions of a Team* and *The Advantage* (among other excellent books) offers a powerful distinction that can also reinforce this point. He talks about the difference between <u>healthy</u> organizations and <u>smart</u> organizations, and offers that the health of an organization is much more associated with its culture, with the ways that human beings relate to, communicate with and collaborate with each other. He concludes that this is a far more important driver of sustainable bottom-line Results than the intelligence of the key leaders or the content of the particular strategies that are developed. He further claims that healthy organizations virtually always get smarter over time, and not the other way around.

Culture and strategy are certainly related, and strategy is also important for organizational success. This book, however, is purposefully oriented toward supporting you in building, shaping and sustaining a powerful culture, as we agree with the following key points (adapted from the *Cultural Blueprinting Toolkit*):

- When culture and strategy collide, culture wins.
- People are loyal to culture, not strategy.
- Strategies can be copied, but no one can copy your culture.
- Culture creates competitive differentiation.
- Culture provides resilience in tough times.
- Cultural miscues are more damaging than strategic ones.

Execution

And thirdly, we claim that leaders get paid to **execute** – to actually get things done, to make things happen, to produce real-world Results – and to do so with and through others. In fact, culture and execution can be understood as the subjective and the objective, the soft and the hard, the intangible and the tangible… different yet equally important dimensions of organizational life.

This book provides an incredibly powerful framework and a set of proven, practical tools for dramatically improving quality of execution – collaborative Actions that people engage in for the sake of producing desired breakthrough Results.

What Would a Camera See?

Back now to the question "What do extraordinary leaders do?" and your list of responses (as well as the longer list provided).

Pretend a camera is outside your office window, filming you as you're "building a powerful culture", "creating structures of accountability", "getting the right people on the bus", "motivating", "implementing the strategy." What would the camera actually see you doing? What would a camera see as it films a leader "leading by example", "setting the vision", "creating alignment among all teams and processes", "mentoring", "establishing powerful and productive relationships", "grooming the next generation of leaders?"

Think about it. What is the human being who is doing all of this actually doing? When you are engaged in these most fundamental, most critical leadership acts… what are you actually <u>doing</u>?

With a bit of reflection, we come to this observation: A camera would see you engaging with people, talking and listening. In other words, extraordinary leaders talk and listen. Extraordinary leaders design, convene and participate in effective conversations, conversations that produce certain Results and not others. This often is so close that we miss it. It's so obvious that we don't see it. (Some people we've worked with have said it this way: I get paid to have effective conversations!)

As a leader you are a conversational engine, getting done whatever it is that you get done by virtue of the conversations you design and convene, as well as conversations that you avoid – what we refer to as missing conversations. Missing conversations are conversations that we're not having now – but if we were having them, better Results could be achieved.

Workplace Application: *Consider the various conversations you have been engaged in over the last 24 hours. What did they produce? Did they move you toward your desired Results? Did they lead to strengthening of relationships and teamwork? Or did they lead to something else, something that you weren't seeking to produce, such as friction, misunderstanding, disengagement? Reflect for 5 minutes and consider how many conversations you (and others) engage in and spend hours in, simply because previous conversations did not produce desired Results! What is this costing your organization? Also consider your missing conversations, understood as conversations which if designed and convened could lead to better outcomes. And what's it costing you to not have those conversations?*

We're frequently asked if whether or not there are physical aspects to leadership. To this, let us ask you: Can you be a strong leader without the ability to lift 100 pounds over your head? Of course you can. "Strong" is a metaphor, having nothing at all to do with physical strength here. Can you be a powerful leader from a wheelchair? Of course, and we have historical examples all over the place.

Here's an everyday example – a surgeon friend says, "I've got something going on in my right index knuckle and I've been a bit concerned about it for a few months. Well, I finally had it looked at last week and found out that it is the beginning of arthritis. Now I'm really concerned. I'm 42 years old, and I'm concerned." Why is he concerned? Because he gets paid to cut, to extract. Fine motor skills. Gigantic physical dimension to that job. We are not suggesting that as a leader, you have no physical dimension to your job. The invitation, however, is to look a bit more closely at the relative difference in importance between the physical and the conversational.

A story comes to mind here. A 9-year old boy accompanies his dad to work on "Take-Your-Child-To-Work-With-You" day and he's naturally all excited. Dad is a senior VP of a major manufacturing company, and he too, is looking forward to having his son spend the day with him. At the office, the son stays with his dad all morning, shadowing and accompanying him to meetings, being introduced to his colleagues and being with him in his office. They go to lunch together in the cafeteria and afterward, put on hard hats and safety goggles for a tour of the factory floor in the afternoon. Then back to the office they go as the dad wraps up his day.

At dinner that night, Mom notices the little boy being a bit dejected and not nearly as talkative as she thought he'd be, given the big day he just had. "What's wrong?" she asks. The little boy hesitates, then finally looks up at his dad through sad eyes and says "Dad, you don't DO anything!" What he had experienced, of course, of his dad's role as a senior leader is the conversational nature of his job. Conversations during meetings, on the phone, over lunch, in the hallways, on the factory floor, via email, via texting.

Many of us were taught "It's not so much what you say that's important. It's what you do." Well, as leaders, a great deal of what you do is actually accomplished out of what you say, how you say it, where you say it and when you say it – as well as what you don't say. Not knowing what to do – in a great many leadership and management situations – actually means that you don't know what to say, or how to say it.

We are dealing squarely now with the Actions required for successful leadership, as shown below:

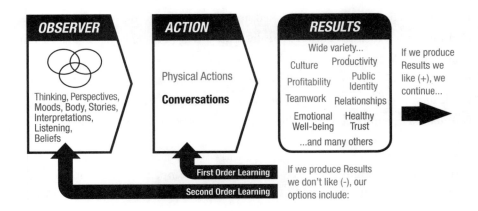

Because of the centrality of conversations for leadership effectiveness – and deeper than this, the centrality of conversations for understanding and improving organizational performance – we claim that there is great value in taking a closer look at language, which we will do in Chapter 3.

Conversations and Organizations

As the following graphic shows, every organization, no matter how big or how small, can be understood as human beings coordinating Action for the purpose of achieving desired Results. And this coordination of Action takes place through some particular types of conversations. **Every organization, no matter how simple or complex, can be viewed as a network of conversations, relationships and commitments.** By acquiring new distinctions in this area and by being more purposeful about the conversations we enter into and how we have them, we can dramatically improve both the objective (getting things done) and the subjective (mood, atmosphere, relationships) dimensions of our lives – at work as well as at home.

We will be moving into all of this and more in the upcoming chapters.

For now, consider this partial list of important conversations and the different types of leadership and organizational Results that they produce:

- <u>Conversations for Orientation/Context-Setting</u> – For the purpose of building and sustaining shared understanding of the organizational "come from" (organizational and/or team purpose, values, standards and roles) and the organizational "go to" (vision, goals, objectives, performance targets). Include on-boarding processes for new employees, as well as ongoing conversations to sustain high levels of shared understanding throughout the organization. Conversations to create organizational context, constructively and consciously shaping the organizational "environment" or culture to enable decentralized decision-making with strategic intent.

- <u>Conversation for Relationship</u> – For the purpose of deepening relationships and laying the groundwork for future conversations in which carefrontation (much more on this to come) and healthy, respectful disagreement may be needed. Typically include self-disclosure and sharing, often in areas not directly related to current roles within the organization. May also include acknowledgement and recognition of others' positive contributions. These conversations may be viewed as mutual "trust deposits" made among members of a team or organization.

- <u>Conversations for Innovation/Speculation</u> – For the purpose of generating ideas and possibilities in order to address concerns, solve problems or take advantage of opportunities. Forward-looking, these ensure the organization remains relevant today and is able to grow and prosper in the future. They include brainstorming and other creative-thinking processes that produce alternatives and take advantage of diverse backgrounds, perspectives and ways of thinking.

- <u>Conversations for Coordinating Action/Implementation</u> – For the purpose of accomplishing Results with and through others. Of central importance, these may be viewed as the "essence of execution" as they involve the basics of collaborative Action: setting direction, enrolling others, making requests and offers and managing promises and commitments.

- <u>Conversations for Progress/Completion</u> – For the purpose of declaring satisfaction or dissatisfaction, checking in at regular intervals within projects or assignments to analyze and evaluate Results; also repeated at completion. These conversations include giving and receiving feedback, listening to multiple perspectives, and understanding the potential implications on future efforts and related processes. They also include declarations of acknowledgement, recognition and celebration… or conversely, declarations of complaint, requests for change, and possibly even termination.

- <u>Conversations for Celebrating / Recognizing</u> – For the purpose of sincerely acknowledging the positive contribution of others, as well as creating, uplifting and establishing more productive and positive moods and emotions. Directly connected to whether or not an organizational culture is characterized by "commitment" or simply "compliance." In upcoming chapters we will discuss more directly how moods and emotions dramatically impact the quality of important workplace interactions and whether or not desired Results do – or don't – get produced.

- <u>Conversations for Coaching / Mentoring</u> – For the purpose of supporting people's professional and personal growth, and increasing their ability to see new possibilities, take new Actions (behaviors) and produce new (sometimes unprecedented) Results.

- <u>Conversations for Accountability</u> – For the purpose of ensuring that commitments are kept and managed according to established criteria and standards, and to ensure that important relationships are kept "clean".

- <u>Conversations for Handling Breakdowns</u> – For the purpose of effectively dealing with often-unexpected "breaks" in the transparency that often accompany routine behavior. For successfully dealing with situations in which threats or problems or challenges (or opportunities) suddenly and unexpectedly arise.

- <u>Conversations with Ourselves</u> – We don't just talk with others, of course. All of us also talk to ourselves. This is the voice in the head, and it's what we commonly refer to as our thinking. These internal conversations have a great deal to do with how we "see things", and they serve to orient us toward – and away from – certain possibilities, Actions and Results. Much more on this in the pages ahead.

Conversations and Emotions

We also claim there is no such thing as "un-emotional" conversation – that is, a conversation that takes place without any emotional flavor or emotional context. While it's true that we don't all have to be psychologists to be effective leaders, it's also the case that without some degree of "emotional intelligence" we will dramatically sub-optimize what's possible. Much more on this to come, but for now, consider the extent to which moods and emotions impact the following fundamental organizational activities (which, as we now know, actually occur via a series of particular conversations):

- Leadership
- Coaching, talent development and performance management
- Customer satisfaction (Interestingly – one of the most fundamental goals of organizations of all sizes and shapes is to produce customer satisfaction, is it not? And producing satisfaction where it didn't exist before is an emotional shift. So we can say that one of the most fundamental goals of business is to produce an emotional shift!)
- Sales
- Strategic planning
- Marketing
- Teamwork and collaborative Action
- Innovation and creativity
- Learning and adaptability

Consider again the significant shift in many of today's organizations away from formal hierarchy and toward a dependency on cross-functional teams and highly collaborative processes.

Can you see how dramatically the moods and emotions of the people (the unique Observers) involved in these processes impact the quality of the interactions and the ultimate Results that get produced? Emotions have a dramatic impact on organizational performance, and we have all experienced these impacts firsthand.

Conversational, Relational and Emotional Competencies

Before we move into the next chapter, let's revisit the three themes of relationships, culture and execution as fundamental areas of focus for effective leaders. Given this way of understanding leadership and organizations, the value and importance of conversational, relational and emotional competencies becomes clearer.

While these competencies are obviously related to each other and impact each other, we distinguish them broadly as follows:

- Conversational competencies may be understood as the capacity to design, convene and participate purposefully in conversations that produce meaningful and positive Results for the organization and the people involved. Given that leaders get paid to have effective conversations, and that organizations can be understood as networks of commitments, the value and importance of this competency is clear.

- Relational competencies involve your ability to form and maintain healthy, productive, mutually-beneficial relationships inside and outside of your organization. They also involve your ability to purposefully repair, rebuild (as well as to significantly change and sometimes end) important relationships with direct reports, colleagues, customers, suppliers, partners... as well as those with your significant others and family members.

- Emotional competencies are all about becoming aware of your own emotional patterns, as well as those of others, and the impact these patterns have on your perceptions, interpretations and evaluations – as well as on the possibilities you see or don't see, the Actions you take or don't take, and the Results you produce or don't produce. They also include your ability to purposefully design, shape and influence your own moods and emotions, as well as those of others.

Much of this book is devoted to providing you with a framework and set of tools for further strengthening these very competencies. Given the conversational nature of leadership, it is these competencies – much more than technical or functional competencies – that deserve our focus and attention.

Summary of Key Points

Extraordinary leaders, at a foundational level, engage in effective conversations. Leadership is fundamentally a conversational competency. As a leader you may be understood as a conversational "engine."

The Actions of leaders are primarily conversational (vs. physical). For example, you can obviously be a world-class, strong and powerful leader without the ability to lift heavy weights or run fast.

Three fundamental types of Results – that dramatically impact organizational performance, regardless of your organization's size, industry or level of complexity – are:

- Relationships
- Culture
- Execution

The job of the leader involves ongoing attention to, focus on and responsibility for these three dimensions, which can be understood separately yet are highly inter-related and inter-dependent.

Leaders produce Results through a set of particular conversations, which can be purposefully designed and convened.

Leadership effectiveness also involves what has come to be called "emotional intelligence", given the dramatic impact of moods and emotions on virtually all important business processes. Increasingly, given the nature of today's organizations, the role of the leader involves the ability to 1) become aware of moods and emotions (his/her own and those of others) and their impact on perceptions, interpretations, behaviors and outcomes, and 2) purposefully shape and influence moods and emotions – in him/herself as well as others. Specifically, this involves designing moods and emotions that are more empowering and lead to better outcomes.

For the sake of supporting you and improving your ability to build strong relationships and a productive culture – as well as your ability to produce breakthrough Results – the rest of this book is intended to enhance three core leadership competencies:

- Conversational
- Relational
- Emotional

While it may be the case that we often hire people based on functional or technical competencies, it is demonstrably true that leadership effectiveness – particularly the higher up one progresses – depends on these. They are simply required for sustainable leadership success.

Application

Let's start with this question: Which goals are more likely to be achieved, private goals or public goals? Public goals, as we know. With this in mind:

1. Reflect again on the 1 or 2 or 3 most important Results you are committed to bring about within the next 12 months, as previously identified. Think also about what you've previously declared you'd like to learn or learn how to do better as you move through this book. As you go through the pages that follow, we encourage you to reflect and consider how you can apply what you're learning and noticing to support you in achieving these very Results.

2. Next, we encourage you to identify a person (or people) to support you in your learning process and your movement through this book. Be clear on how what you'd like to be, do or have moving forward is different from what you're being, doing or having now. Enroll them (via conversation, of course) in what you're up to and establish an ongoing framework for periodic sharing, reflection, feedback and application. View this person (or people) as your "accountability partners."

Given the conversational nature of leadership, we offer the following for your consideration, reflection and practice:

3. **Effective Conversations**: In the context of your desired outcomes, which conversations would you say are currently effective? That is, which ones are moving you forward, toward the Results you say you want? What do you notice about these conversations that makes them effective? Consider the people involved, the mood (your own and of others), the context, what is said and how it's said. Can you put your finger on what it is about these conversations that makes them effective? Reflect and put your thoughts about this in your notes.

4. **Ineffective Conversations**: Which conversations do you participate in that you say are ineffective? Consider the number and subject matter of conversations you are involved in that are for the purpose of "cleaning up" previous conversations that did not produce desired Results. Consider how much time and energy you are spending in such conversations. Think about and document what you think is contributing to the ineffectiveness, as well as what could make these conversations better.

5. **Missing Conversations**: Still thinking about your desired Results, can you begin to identify some conversations that are currently missing? These are conversations that are not now occurring… but if they were designed and convened, would have the possibility of moving you forward. For each of these missing conversations, complete the following preliminary outline:

   - **Desired Result**: What would the conversation be designed to produce/create? Be as specific as you can here.

   - **Leader**: Who should convene/lead the conversation?

   - **Participants**: Who should participate in the conversation?

   - **Mood**: What do you believe could be the most appropriate mood for this conversation, given what it's designed to bring about?

   - **Potential Obstacles**: Given your experience, what do you see as some possible obstacles or barriers to success within the conversation, and how can you break them down or navigate around them? Be as specific as you can as you anticipate these.

- **Context and Approach**: Given what you've captured so far about these conversations, describe your plan for establishing the initial context as well as moving through the conversation. What will you say up front to "set the stage?" What approach do you believe could have the greatest chance of yielding the desired Results?

6. Share and discuss your reflections, notes and priorities with your Accountability Partner(s).

CHAPTER 3
THE POWER OF LANGUAGE

"Between stimulus and response there is a space. In that space is our power to choose our response. In our response lies our growth and our freedom."

- Viktor Frankl

The previous chapter explored the centrality of conversations for leadership effectiveness, and claimed that in a fundamental way, leaders are conversational engines. The actual Actions leaders take to produce Results are conversations.

Because of this, we now claim it is absolutely important to take a look – and for some readers, perhaps, a new look – at language. And this takes us to the notion of paradigms.

An Invitation to Try On a New Paradigm

Let's tee up this new look at language by asking these questions: What are paradigms? What do they have to do with leadership and the most important Results we produce in our lives?

Keeping it simple, we say that paradigms may be understood as ways of thinking, believing and taking Action. They are ways of understanding, sets of beliefs, frames of reference from which we "see the world," take Action and produce the Results we produce. They may also be understood as involving mental models and "filters" through which we observe and through which we determine and conclude "how things are" and what they mean to us.

Our paradigms obviously impact the Results we are able to produce, as they influence the Actions we take that lead to those Results. There is also a deeper impact here which is not so obvious at first and yet is crucial to understand: Our paradigms directly and powerfully influence and shape the "universe set" of possibilities and opportunities that we even see in the first place! Individuals with different paradigms are different Observers (see graphic below). They see different things, and interpret and evaluate what they see differently. And these are often key differentiators, separating those who take more effective Action and produce more powerful Results from those who do not.

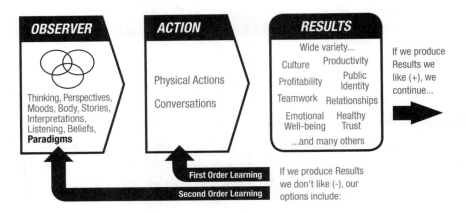

Said differently, by consciously adopting new paradigms or updating existing ones, we have the opportunity to purposefully shift how we see things, opening avenues for possibly unprecedented choices, Actions and Results.

As we know, we have paradigms in virtually every human domain and endeavor: science, religion, politics, leadership, teamwork, manufacturing, customer service, medicine, engineering, homebuilding, sailing, art, raising children, being in relationships. The problem here is not that we <u>have</u> paradigms, of course. We need them and they serve us greatly. The problem is that if we're not mindful, our paradigms can go from "a" way of thinking, believing and taking Action... to "the" way of thinking, believing and taking Action. We can go from having paradigms to our paradigms "having us." And this dramatically limits what we may call our **horizon of possibilities**. For those of us interested in breakthrough Results, this is important to notice... because seeing new possibilities is always the first step in purposefully producing new Results.

So going back to language... ask 100 people, ask 1000 people, ask 100,000 people: "What is language? And what is language for?" What will the great, vast majority answer with? We have asked these very questions to thousands of leaders around the globe and the number one response we receive is that language is "a tool for communication" or some variation of this. In fact, this is such a widely held paradigm about language that most people don't see it as a paradigm at all – they see it as a definition, as a fact, as The Truth about language.

We offer that it's a paradigm, an interpretation, a particular and obviously widely-held way of understanding language. Certainly we label, we describe and we communicate using language. But this is only half the story, only one side of the coin.

We claim this: If language is a tool, it's a tool we cannot put down. It's not like all the other tools we use. It's the one we need, for all the other ones. This one is qualitatively, subjectively different. What follows will be quite familiar to readers of *Language and the Pursuit of Happiness*, as it is a central focus of the first few chapters. For new readers we provide this overview.

We offer a different view, a different paradigm. At a fundamental level, we claim that *language creates and generates, it does not simply describe and communicate.* And this, as we shall see, opens up entirely new possibilities for leaders at all levels. This interpretation – this shift in paradigm, this new way of understanding language – changes everything. Everything that we will share with you in the pages ahead is built on this new understanding.

Overview – This Generative, Creative Understanding of Language

Let's start with a few examples:

If you ask John "Will you have lunch with me tomorrow at 1 o'clock?" and he replies "Yes", you and John have just invented a tomorrow at 1 o'clock that five seconds ago was not going to happen. You aren't describing anything. You're making something happen.

Think about every time in your life you said the word "Yes." Think about every time that word came out of your mouth. Question: If all of those times you had said "No" instead, would your life be different? Absolutely, positively it would. It would be different in significant, meaningful ways. The simple act of saying "Yes" moves you in the world this way, and not that. It opens these doors and closes those.

One of our favorite ways to show how language generates and creates goes like this: Two baseball umpires were sitting around talking, and one says, "Old Joe, he's a great umpire. There's balls and there's strikes, and he calls 'em like they are." The second umpire then says, "Yeah, Joe's a great umpire… there's balls and there's strikes, but he calls 'em like he *sees* 'em." Just then Joe walks up and says, "You're both wrong… there's balls and there's strikes, but they ain't *nothin'* till I call 'em!"

Can you see that Joe literally declares them into being? The act of calling them makes them what they are. And we can be sitting in the left field bleachers, screaming "ball four, ball four" and guess what? If the umpire says "strike three," the batter's out. The umpire has the authority to make certain declarations (to say certain things). And when he or she makes these declarations, the world is different than it was before.

If you are married or have ever been married, consider this question: Is it different being married than not being married? With just a little reflection, we can conclude that definitely, it's different being married than not being married! It's different legally, socially, sexually, emotionally, financially – it's different. Question: How did we go from being not married to being married? How did that happen? Answer: Somebody said something… "I do." And in that moment, it's different. And it's not trivially different or marginally different. It's really different.

We speak ourselves into the world. Let's repeat this: We speak ourselves into the world. And it's not trivial. We are not saying that we don't describe with language. What we're claiming is that describing and "communicating" is not all that we do. And for those of us who get paid to have effective conversations, this whole other "not all that we do" is worth looking at!

A few additional examples:

How was the United States of America created? What is in the archives, under the glass, right next to the US Constitution? The Declaration of Independence. This country was declared into being, was it not? Now, there was work to do after that declaration, yes. But the claim is this: Without that declaration, it doesn't happen.

Think about your organization, as well as all organizations. Question: How was your organization created? How are all organizations created? With a little reflection, we come to see that organizations are also declared into being. And somewhere in the file cabinet we can find it: "... we shareholders hereby declare... par 100... ABC company... " and while on August 1, the company does not exist – on August 2, it does.

Think about an argument you've had in your life, one that was significant. It escalated, it was not fun for either person. Possibly this was when you were a teenager, or when you were a younger adult in your first job, or even just recently. Or think about an email you recently received that may have rubbed you the wrong way. In the heat of that moment, you quickly typed out a response and hit send, replying to all.

At some later point, however, after the argument or after you sent your hasty email, you began to calm down. You began to reflect on what you had done, and as you're calming down and reflecting this thought slowly trickles into your mind: "You know, as I think about it now, I actually wish I hadn't said that..." Have you ever had this experience? Virtually all of us, if we're being honest, have.

So the question is: Why do we ever think this? Why do we ever think to ourselves or say out loud "I wish I hadn't said that"? Because we realize we produced a Result back there, we didn't just describe. And now we see it's not a Result we intended to produce. A diminishment of possibilities is a Result. A shift in context is a Result. A change in the nature of an important relationship is a Result. Are they not? They're not physical, but they're utterly real.

The Connection Between Language and Learning

We live in a time of ongoing, relentless change, do we not? Given this background of relentless change, on a scale of 1-10, how important is learning for your organization? On a scale of 1-10, how important is learning for you as an individual? We've asked these questions to thousands of leaders and the answers always come back "It's a 10." While we will focus directly on the phenomenon of learning in a later chapter, for now let's tee up one or two key points.

As a leader, you have obviously been both a teacher and a learner in your life. Question: Independent of subject matter – learning to ride a bike, learning to repair an important relationship, learning to lead a company in times of change – what would you say are some pre-requisites for learning? What would you say needs to be in place to optimize the learning situation? Again, having asked this question for many years we find responses that include:

- Willingness to listen
- The ability to connect the learning to a desired future outcome
- Good communication between learner and teacher
- An environment conducive to learning
- Willingness to fail
- Willingness to practice

You can probably come up with others. We agree with these and also often get one more response, one that we feel is truly central to our ability to learn. A particularly powerful pre-requisite for learning is something many of us call "open-mindedness." Agree? Of course, we know that open-mindedness is a metaphor, it's not about physically having our heads popped open.

We connect open-mindedness to language in the following way: People who are open-minded live, ongoingly, in certain types of internal conversations and internal narratives. And they do not live in other types of internal conversations and internal narratives. You change those internal conversations, and you change the degree of open-mindedness. Those internal conversations are not by-products of the phenomenon of open-mindedness… they are producing it!

We have identified a close cousin of open-mindedness, a pre-requisite that we feel is directly connected to our ability to learn, regardless of subject matter. This pre-requisite is a powerful language step. It's when the learner thinks, or says out loud:

"I don't know".

In this way of thinking, declaring "I don't know" does not describe a state of affairs. It produces something. And what it produces we call a context for learning. With everything else being the same – same teacher, same curriculum, same physical environment – when the learner thinks or says "I don't know", something is now present that was not present 5 seconds ago. And that something we call an openness for learning, a context for learning. Not physical, but obviously real.

We all know this. How many of us have ever tried to teach someone something when the learner thought they already knew it? How much learning takes place? Not much.

Given the importance of learning in a time of change, and given the impact of "I don't know" on our capacity to learn, we invite you to take a look at "I don't know" two different ways – one corporate, one personal.

On the business side, how do you treat people in your organization who say "I don't know"? This is a culture question, is it not? Is it OK, in a public forum, for employees to answer an inquiry with "I don't know"? Now "I don't know, and I'll find out by Tuesday" and now it's Wednesday – different game entirely. This involves making commitments, which we will cover later. Here, we are only talking about the first time it becomes apparent, the first time the subject is covered. Because broadly speaking, our claim is this: If one of your desired Results is a sustainable culture of creativity and innovation, and if you repeatedly slap people's hands or embarrass them when they say they don't know something, you're going to have a hard time achieving that Result! Those Actions are simply incompatible with that Result (remember Observer – Action – Results).

Many of us grew up in corporate environments in which it was absolutely not OK to say "I don't know." Or at least it was our strong interpretation – based on our experiences and observations – that it was not OK to do so. As a leader, we invite you to consider the message from an oil filter company named Fram. Depending on your age, you may remember quite clearly the Fram oil filter TV commercials, which always ended the exact same way: the crusty mechanic would wheel around, look the camera dead in the eye, and say "You can pay me now, or you can pay me later."

Paying me now, in this sense, is finding out now that somebody doesn't know. Now, while we're all still sitting around the table, before the meeting adjourns. Paying me later is cleaning up the train wreck that happens because somebody didn't know, they didn't feel safe enough to acknowledge not knowing, they got up and they did what they <u>did</u> know... and now you have to deal with it. The cost/benefit of "paying me now" is usually a very attractive cost/benefit, is it not? What does it really cost? And what negative future consequences may be avoided altogether by doing so?

If you want this degree of openness in your sphere of influence, you may have to be overt and explicit. That is, you may have to say something like this:

"All right everyone, before we move into our regular Tuesday project management meeting agenda, I'd like to clarify a thing or two with everyone. Are we all clear that it's utterly OK if you find yourself at one of these meetings not knowing something? That it's not a character defect? Just wanting to be very clear with everyone about this... in fact, moving forward, I have a request. If you ever find yourself not knowing something during any of our conversations, I request that you let me know 100% of those times, so we can deal with it. OK? OK. Now let's proceed..."

Will Rogers has a great quote attributed to him that seems appropriate here: *"Everybody is ignorant, just in different subjects!"*

Is this not your experience? Think about it – when you're working on a team or having a meeting, are there often not pockets of deep, deep expertise among the members? Of course. And are there not also often areas of utter blindness? (Meaning, situations in which not only do we not know something – we don't know that we don't know!)

When we say or think "I don't know", what we're really saying or thinking is "I know that I don't know. I am aware of the limits of my competency." This, we call ignorance (vs. blindness). And we say it's the threshold of learning, not the opposite of learning. It's the necessary jumping off point from which learning can begin.

On the personal side, taking a look at "I don't know" may involve this question: Given the age that you are now, and the levels you've achieved organizationally and socially, do you give yourself permission to be a beginner at anything? Because you declare beginnerhood into being. You speak it so, just like the umpire.

If language is only a passive tool for communicating or describing how things are, the last few paragraphs make very little sense. But if language also has a creative and generative dimension to it, we claim there is value in paying attention to how we're wielding this tool. The reason conversations bring about real outcomes and actual new Results – for leaders and for everyone else, too – is because language itself has this generative and creative dimension.

Four Basic Claims About Language

Let's expand our discussion of this way of understanding language by covering four basic claims:

1. We live in language.
2. Language creates and generates.
3. Language conveys commitment as well as information.
4. Language provides us access to breakthroughs.

1. We Live in Language

Our experience is that this expression "we live in language" is not an everyday expression. So what does it mean? Here's how we like to frame it: Do you have a little voice inside your head? The one that right now may be saying, "What's he talking about?" Well, that's the one we're talking about! Many people we have met have shared with us that they also frequently have a "debate team", an "inner critic", an "itty bitty shitty committee!"

There is an expression attributed to Mark Twain, although we're certainly not sure whether or not he ever said it. Yet we love this expression, as it points wonderfully to the phenomenon we're seeking to explore. The expression is: "I'm always in conversation, and sometimes other people are involved!"

Is this not your experience? We say it's all of our experience – we are all doing it. No exceptions. This apparently is part of being a human being. Yes, it's true that we are physical beings. We are obviously also emotional beings. Here, we add that we are also linguistic beings, beings who live in an ongoing internal dialogue.

This brings us back to the initial claim from Chapter 1, that we are each a unique Observer, and the Observer we are is composed of these 3 separate but obviously inter-related domains.

Because we live in language, because our internal narrative is seemingly always with us, this is what we do: Each of us is confronted with events every day... events at work, events at home, events at the customer's location, events in the car, events at Rotary, events with friends, events at the beach and events in the shower. And as a human being, we very quickly:

1. Make up stories about these events

2. Hold our stories to be The Truth

3. And forget that we made them up!

Now, when we say stories we are not talking about fibs or fabrications, purposeful manipulations or self-deceptions. We are simply talking about interpretations, explanations we form as a function of the way we see things.

Now this is not a problem, in and of itself. But because we forget that we made it up, we begin living as if our story, our interpretation, our explanation, belongs to the event. And nothing could be further from the truth. We say the event belongs to itself and your story belongs to you, and my story belongs to me. We aren't just *reading* these stories, we *wrote* them. To summarize, we say:

<u>EVENT</u> IS NOT EQUAL TO <u>EXPLANATION</u>!

Let's take an example. Say your child, who is a senior in high school, comes home one day and announces to you "I'm stupid." "What are you talking about?" you ask. "I'm stupid..." "What are you talking about, what happened?" Finally your child answers: "I got an F on my English mid-term."

In this story, what's the event? The F on the test. What's the explanation? "I'm stupid." Question: If that child lives in that conversation, that interpretation long enough, is that a descriptive thing or a creative thing? It's creative.

Now let's back up from the F and the test and think more broadly – is it the <u>events</u> of your life, or your <u>explanations</u> about those events, that are more influential as to the actual Actions you end up taking in the world? It's the explanations. And out of the actual Actions you end up taking in the world, you produce Results in the world, do you not? Yes. In a tremendously wide variety of areas. And the explanations are the springboards, not the events. And out of any given event, how many possible explanations are there? Infinite.

This is a major distinction and a major observation, one that is crucial for truly redesigning ourselves and opening new possibilities for effective Action. The key question is not whether or not your story is "right" or "wrong"; rather, the more powerful question is **"Is your story – your interpretation, your explanation – _working_ for you? Is it allowing you to produce the Results you say you want?"** Because if it's not, you can learn – with time and practice – to begin authoring new stories, more powerful interpretations, ones that serve you more than your old ones.

As we can see below, these stories, interpretations, explanations and narratives serve to orient us, influencing how we see things and shaping what we even see as possibilities in the first place. And out of this initial orientation and set of possibilities influenced by that orientation, we select a possibility, make a choice and take an actual Action in the world. And of course, our Actions – including our conversations – lead to Results, in a wide variety of areas.

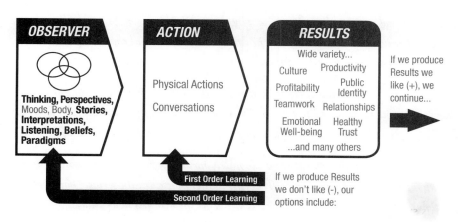

But none of this makes any sense at all if you don't see yourself as making up interpretations and explanations in the first place.

Self-awareness is the key. Back to the Big Eye. It's the absolute starting point for making any meaningful changes or improvements in our lives.

The moment we begin thinking that our explanation of what happened <u>is</u> what happened, we stop listening. And we close ourselves to all the benefits of Second Order Learning. We become so terminally certain that we close down new possibilities and new opportunities that new explanations could reveal. This frequently has a negative impact on our effectiveness, our ability to innovate and adapt, as well as our professional and personal relationships. In these situations, we don't see what we're doing – we just seem to find ourselves "stuck." And closing down possibilities for improved effectiveness and improved relationships without seeing what we're doing is certainly not a Result many of us would purposefully produce for ourselves.

As you reflect on the various people you know or have interacted with during your career, can you identify any who did not see themselves as making up explanations and interpretations? Have you met people who claimed to somehow have access to how things "really" are? People who were "sometimes wrong, but never in doubt?" Here's what they might sound like:

"Jim, you misunderstand. That's not my 'interpretation' of what happened at the board meeting. I was there and I'm telling you, that is specifically and exactly what happened at that meeting!"

"Priya, I am telling you that there is no way that is possible for me. I tried selling before and it didn't work out. Clearly I am just not cut out for it and there is no way I could ever do that again. After all, I am an engineer and we're just not built to sell."

"Shlomi, can't you see that there is no way I could ever speak in front of a large audiences? I am just not wired that way. It's something only those extroverted folks can do. Being an introvert, I am just not meant to get up and speak in front of people."

"Benny, I am telling you that there is absolutely no customer loyalty anymore. All they care about is price, price, and price. It doesn't matter how great the service, how great the solution. They just don't care. So if you want to get the business now-a-days, you just got to beat the competitors' prices. That is The ONLY way to get ahead these days. Period."

Or how about this exaggerated version:

"I arrived here at the event early enough to meet a lot of you over a brief cup of coffee. Even in that short amount of time, it's obvious to me how each of you are necessarily influenced by your age, your race, your sex, your degree of travel or non-travel when you were young… by your educational, cultural and work histories, and how these necessarily serve as filters through which you perceive reality. I, on the other hand, am somehow blessed with cosmic objectivity, and was somehow born unfettered in this regard, and unburdened by all the cognitive, emotional and cultural filters that clog you up. My eyes are – amazingly – more like clear panes of glass, allowing me access to native reality in such a way that it yields cosmically objective viewpoints. How excellent for me that I was somehow born and blessed with such a gift!"

As you know, this is BS. Everyone is interpreting, no matter what. No exceptions, ever.

One of our teachers in this work said it this way: *Everything that is said, is said by someone.* Well, of course. Someone who was born somewhere. Someone who was born in some culture, and in some time period, somewhere. Someone who was raised by individual human beings, each of whom had standards, values, beliefs, life experiences, moods and emotions… just like us. Exactly just like all of us.

Let's be clear here. We're not talking about whether or not you're doing this or not. That question is not on the table, because you're doing it now and you've been doing it your whole life. We all have. We are all Mark Twain. The only thing we're talking about now is self-awareness, the Big Eye: Do you see yourself as doing this? Do you see yourself as making up explanations, and taking Action based on them? That's the only question we're dealing with now. The value and impact of self-awareness here simply cannot be overemphasized. *Because if you do not see yourself as doing this now – making up explanations and taking Actions out of them – and you couple that with not producing some important Result that you say you want… then the option of authoring more powerful interpretations will simply never occur to you!* It will be off your radar screen, because if you don't see yourself as doing this now, there's nothing to update. There's nothing to shift, nothing to modify.

And what you will have done in that moment is take off the table a spectacularly powerful set of leverage points for opening new avenues of possibility for bringing about truly unprecedented – breakthrough – Results. You will have removed from consideration the opportunity to take a look at how you look at things.

55

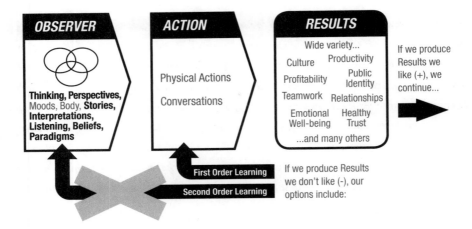

As depicted above, you will have taken Second Order Learning out of play, leaving you with only First Order Learning at your disposal. And Second Order Learning is a type of learning that a great many other leaders have found to be very powerful in producing significant breakthroughs.

The Impact of Moods on Explanations

Do your explanations have anything to do with your moods? Absolutely. (Think about those 3 circles inter-connected). And back to the Big Eye, back to self-awareness – many, if not most of us, are terrible Observers of our own moods. We often don't even see them as moods. We see them as "the way things are." It was taught to us this way: If you do not see yourself as having moods, you don't have them... they have you. And they will shape and color your interpretations, and you'll never see it.

Consider for a moment – in many instances, those close to us (spouses, partners, close friends) are better Observers of our moods than we are! What do many of us say when a spouse or partner asks "Why are you in that mood?" Think about it... we often respond with "What mood?"

We think to ourselves "I'm not being pessimistic, I'm being... *realistic!*" I'm simply objective, unburdened by all the filters that have you clogged up. I'm just a conduit for native reality, streaming in. I'm simply reporting out!"

We repeat – we are all interpreting. (More on this to come in a later chapter). We don't have objectivity – we have objectivity "in parentheses." We are each interpreting, explaining, making meaning based on all the things that we know make us each unique. This isn't good or bad, right or wrong. It simply is. This acknowledgement is our starting point. This self-awareness is the required first step toward a more conscious, productive and powerful way of leading our organizations and living our lives.

Many readers may recall this analogy: We live in language like a fish lives in water. A fish is born in water, lives in water, water all around, water everywhere. Question: When would a fish first know that it was born in water and lives in water? Answer: When you take him out! Until then, if you asked him "How's the water?" he'd likely respond with "What water?" We are born in language and live in language. Language all around, language everywhere.

The internal (our thinking) and external (our out-loud conversations) are such an integral part of the "soup" in which we exist, that we don't see the extent to which they are <u>already</u> shaping our interpretations and influencing our Actions. Becoming a more powerful Observer of ourselves and what we're "up to" in language is fundamentally important.

It is only when we can see our interpretations as interpretations, that we can break free from them. From this point forward, at any given time and in any given situation, we can consciously and purposefully generate new thinking and new ways of seeing. We can consciously and purposefully author new and more powerful interpretations that can better serve us, given the breakthrough Results we are seeking.

The invitation and opportunity here is to begin looking <u>at</u> language, rather than simply living <u>through</u> it.

Events, Explanations and Coaching/Mentoring/Guiding

In workshops, we ask people "How many of you do coaching, mentoring, guiding or counseling… formally or informally… with adults or kids?" and virtually every hand goes up. Think about it. In that role, isn't a large part of our job helping the other person separate event from explanation, and to adopt a more powerful explananation than the one he or she may now be operating with?

Our job as a coach or mentor is to help the individual let go of one explanation and begin operating with another, one that would lead him/her to Action A (and not Action B) and therefore achieve Result A (and not Result B)... given that Result A is the one he or she has declared is desired. This is easy to see about other people, of course. The challenge – back to the Big Eye – is to begin to more clearly see it about ourselves.

Events, Explanations and Productive Meetings

Question: If you find yourself at a meeting, either arguing or at cross-purposes with a colleague, is the argument typically centered around events or explanations? Typically, it's about explanations. And how many times is it the case that we haven't even agreed on what the events are, what the objective facts are?

In *Good to Great*, Jim Collins claims that powerful leadership teams have the ability to constructively confront the "brutal facts." This is what we're pointing to here.

Here is a tool or a practice we have found to be very valuable. If you are at a meeting and you feel the meeting is "wallowing" and is no longer very productive, intervene in this way:

"Stop, stop, let's stop, everyone, for a moment. I would like us to definitely continue the conversation, but with your permission I'd like to introduce a new ground rule for the remainder of our meeting. The new ground rule is this: starting now, I'd like everyone here to operate with hyper-vigilance, hyper-awareness, as to when you and others are stating facts, vs. stating opinions. OK? What this means is that as we move ahead in the conversation, I may say something like 'Jim, I hear what you're saying... but are you saying that's a fact? Or is that your opinion?' We'll have space for that, a context for each of us doing that, as we continue this conversation."

What this will allow is the opportunity to expand the conversation to include questions and dialogue around *"How did you go from Event A to Explanation B in such a different way than I went from (now I know) same Event A to Explanation C? What did you infer that I didn't infer? What did you deduce that I didn't deduce? What standards did you use to draw that conclusion that I obviously didn't use? What assumptions did you make that I didn't make?"* This is a profoundly more productive conversation. But not if we can't separate events from explanations.

The late U.S. senator Daniel Patrick Moynihan famously once said *"You're entitled to your own opinion, but you're not entitled to your own facts!"* We agree.

The ability to stop a meeting in its tracks and re-set the context is a profoundly powerful and important conversational competency, is it not? And having this understanding of events and explanations enables just this sort of shift.

Going forward, we will be sharing with you additional empowering distinctions that will support you seeing new possibilities, generating new thinking, taking new Action and creating new Results. That's what this entire book is all about.

2. Language Creates and Generates, It Does Not Simply Describe

Building on some of our previous examples, we further claim that language creates and generates in four areas of particular importance to leaders. These include:

- Relationships
- Moods and Emotions, and Culture
- Public identity
- Context

Relationships

We claim that the vast majority of our relationships are not physical. They are conversational. They're truly constituted out of the conversations we have and how we have them. Change the conversations, and you change the relationships. Stop the conversations, and you stop the relationship. Start new conversations, and you start new relationships.

Think about it this way: How did your relationships with your clients, your customers, your direct reports, your suppliers, your backers – how did they all start? With conversations, of course. And over time, if you and Customer A gradually begin having deeper, more meaningful and more personal conversations, we will say that your relationship with Customer A gradually becomes deeper, more meaningful and more personal. If your conversations with Customer B remain "strictly business" and "arm's length", we will say that your relationship with Customer B remains at this level. Not good or bad, of course. Just different. And if asked about the two customers, we would likely report that our relationship with Customer A is "stronger," or that we simply feel "closer" to Customer A. Well, of course we do. We talk about different things.

The poet David Whyte has a great expression that comes to mind here: *"Our conversations are not about our relationships. Our conversations are our relationships."* We agree. After all, where do your relationships live? Where are they? Can you touch them and put them in a box? No, because they live in the "space" between us, in the inter-subjective space of our conversations.

Moods, Emotions and Organizational Culture

In addition to relationships, we claim that language has a great deal to do with generating moods, emotions and workplace culture. We know people have moods. (Remember our 3-circle model). Do organizations also have moods? Yes. Do departments within organizations also have moods? Yes again. Whether we call it culture or mood or "environment" or "atmosphere" or "vibe" – we are discussing the non-physical but very real background or context in which all the organizational activity takes place.

For example, if lots of people within an organization or department have what we can call "bitching and back-biting" conversations when someone fails to keep a commitment, does this have anything to do with the mood of that organization or department? We say yes, and to such an extent that we can't separate the conversations from the mood. (We characterize these negative gossip conversations as "recreational character assassination!") It is demonstrably true that the prevailing mood or culture of an organization allows certain conversations to happen. This is fairly well-known. *But it is equally true that by having certain conversations, we perpetuate the mood.* Causality is two-way, because language creates. For leaders, this is a fundamental observation.

What if when a person initiates this type of conversation, people started responding in a new way: *"I decline your invitation to participate in this conversation. I can't do anything about your situation anyway. I think Jeron is an adult, and he can handle it. So why don't you bring it directly to him?"* We claim that if enough people began inventing and practicing these sorts of conversations, the mood of the organization or department would shift. A new mood or culture would be designed. What we're doing is reversing the causal element – and making it much easier to deal with this thing called organizational mood or workplace culture.

Many of us know intuitively that workplace moods are powerful, important and have a dramatic impact on the quality and types of daily employee interactions that occur, as well as on the tangible, bottom-line Results that get produced. But it's also the case that we often don't know exactly what to do in order to bring about the shifts in the moods and culture that we desire. Many of us may have come to the conclusion that charismatic leaders – by virtue of the force of their personality (in other words, "magic") – are able to purposefully shape and design moods and culture... but the rest of us? We know it's important, but how do we actually do it?

We invite you to consider – the conversations you **Require** and the conversations you **Prohibit** can be spectacular leverage points for purposefully shaping culture. The tools we need to shape moods and culture are not shovels and fertilizer, of course. What's needed is discernment in generative conversations. We can have a conversation about conversations. We will be moving into commitments and accountability very deeply later in the book, but for now consider: Are there conversations you could be or should be requiring, given the Results you say you want? Similarly, are there conversations you could be or should be prohibiting, given the Results you say you want?

There is also a third category of conversations to explore here – that of **Missing** conversations. As mentioned earlier, missing conversations are those that have not historically been taking place, but if they were, the possibility of new Results would emerge. Our experience is this: You don't have to be the sole generator of these. That is, very good things can happen by writing the phrase "Missing Conversations?" on a flipchart and convening conversations about this with your direct reports. This can be an eye-opening and valuable conversation.

As a leader, you may even post such sheets around the office and encourage your employees to write down what they consider to be missing conversations, and then have conversations about what they're seeing and suggesting. This can also be a wonderful way to give voice to the people at all levels in the organization while providing a forum for everyone to contribute to meaningful improvements.

Public Identity

We also claim that language creates and generates our public identity. Let's explore. We know the public identity of your organization is its reputation in the marketplace, its "brand", it's image. For yourself as an individual, what is meant by public identity? Similar to organizations, it's your "personal brand". It's how you get perceived, how you "show up" for others, how other people see you.

Now, is it possible that the way you see yourself isn't the way others see you? Yes, of course it's possible. In fact, more than possible, it's quite likely... some would even say it's virtually guaranteed! This isn't right or wrong, good or bad. It just is. Given this fact, let's ask a couple more questions: Do you know how you're being perceived, by the most important personal and professional constituencies in your life? And is it what you want? Is it working for you?

Because the world does not interact with who you think you are. That is, people do not interact with your personal, private conversations about yourself. Instead, they interact with who they perceive you to be, with how you "show up" for them, how they see you. And you can either be aware of this or not.

There is power in becoming aware of how you are being perceived. As we claimed earlier, we are not hermits. We do what we do with and through people. Leaders and managers accomplish all important Results with and through people, not in a vacuum or alone on a remote island. Because of this, your public identity impacts which opportunities become available to you, and which ones don't.

So, what's this got to do with language? We say that given the conversational nature of leadership, a significant portion of your public identity is generated out of your conversations, the things you say and how you say them, the ways you listen and participate in conversations, the ways you make and manage commitments, the ways you come up with and share your opinions and how consistently you state facts… all of this generates and influences your public identity.

So again, do you know how you're being perceived? Is it possible that your ability to achieve significant and positive new Results may improve out of conversations designed to provide you with this information? Might these be important – but missing – conversations? These new feedback conversations might be important new Actions that could lead to a new process of self-reflection and learning on your part… leading you then to new future Actions and different future Results.

Who is responsible for your public identity? You are, of course. You may have heard this expression: If you can't measure it, you can't manage it. How can you possibly take responsibility for something for which you have no data? And as a leader, if you're interested in getting feedback about your public identity, it is very likely that you are going to have to request it. Very few organizational cultures support spontaneous, non-contextualized sideways (much less upward) feedback. The invitation here is to request specific feedback from specific people in specific areas, for then you can be better equipped to purposefully design a more powerful public identity – should you so choose.

Requesting feedback may look like this:

"Steve, I'd like to request your feedback in a few areas, if you don't mind. Here's what I'm interested in… at our Monday morning staff meetings, please pay attention to how I set the initial context for the meeting. What I'm hoping for is ambition, with a bit of urgency thrown in about the Johnsonville project. Also please pay attention to how I handle the guys from Toledo, as I think there still may be some residue from the issue with Tom last year and I want to be sensitive to that. Finally, keep an eye on how I manage the overall agenda, as one of my goals for this year is to tighten up our meeting structure and do a better job of overall agenda management. Here's how I'd like the feedback – in my office, in private, within 24 hours of the meeting. Do you accept?"

Another way of requesting feedback may be to simply to ask: *"Steve, can you please share with me 1 or 2 things that you feel I ought to be doing more of or doing differently in order to be a better, a more effective leader?"*

We have seen valuable feedback structures which are quite simple, such as what's come to be known as Start / Stop / Continue. In this approach, in regular meetings, leaders and direct reports share views on what each feels the other could Start doing… Stop doing… and Continue doing, given the collective Results the organization is seeking.

Now, we are not suggesting that you open yourself to feedback from everybody and anybody and about everything. With respect, it may be that some people are not competent to give you certain types of feedback in certain areas. But some people are! It's not all or nothing.

This topic of feedback is particularly important for leaders. When leaders' careers are derailed, it is often because of deficiencies in conversational, relational and emotional competencies that they are unaware of, that they are blind to. None of us wakes up in the morning with the conscious intent of damaging our career or limiting our future opportunities for advancement and success. But it is often the case that the higher leaders progress within their organizations, the less likely it may be that they receive candid feedback in the most important areas. In some ways, this may be understood as an example of the "bull in a china shop" – causing negative impacts, damaging relationships, limiting effectiveness… while being utterly blind to these Results.

On the home front and on a lighter note, many of us don't even have to request feedback from our spouse or partner… it's right there, as soon as we arrive! In all seriousness, though, is this not a valuable person to have in your life? With this feedback, you're no longer the "bull in a china shop." Now you're awake. Now you are aware of how your words and Actions are being interpreted, you are aware of how you are being perceived – at least by this one individual. Now you get the gift of being able to consciously choose something else – or not – tomorrow.

If you are interested in learning more about getting feedback and how to make improvements in this area, we suggest an excellent book by Marshall Goldsmith. It's entitled *What Got You Here, Won't Get You There.*

Context

We claim that language also creates and generates context. While it's not physical, it's very real and it's very important. Let's start with an example.

Let's say Randy and Chalmers work together at a large company. They are friends, their wives are friends, they socialize together, and they play on the same softball team. Randy joined the company 4 years before Chalmers did and Chalmers is now a first-year analyst on one of Randy's projects. Regarding public identity, Chalmers thinks he's basically an A player, maybe an A minus on a bad day. In reality, he's a C, barely holding on, and Randy says:

"Chalmers, I've got to have a conversation with you and I'm not exactly sure how to have it. My concern is that you may over-react to some feedback I'm going to give you, and you may think our friendship is in jeopardy. Our friendship isn't in jeopardy now and never will be. But there are some blind spots in your work. I'm calling them blind spots because I don't see you working on them, and I know you well enough now to think that if you saw them, you'd be working on them. But because I don't see you working on them, I'm concluding that you don't see them.

I have another concern – you're telling me at softball that you want a long career here. My concern is that unbeknownst to you, you're doing things that are not going to let that happen. So I'm not sure of the best way to have this conversation… all I know is, we have to have it, because I care about your success, as well as the success of this project."

The invitation here is to **speak into your concerns** as a way to purposefully create context. As we stated above, context is not physical, but it's utterly real and it impacts how you will be listened to, how you will be interpreted. We're not saying to make up new concerns. The move to make – the new conversational competency to develop – is to speak them if you have them, and to do so with sincerity.

Everyone in a long-term relationship knows this: Conversations of self-disclosure are powerful. How different is it for you to share with your spouse "Honey, I'm upset with you about X or Y…" than your simmering in silent resentment about it? How different is the dinner table? How different is the car ride? The bedroom? Think about your historical norms of self-disclosure at work. As a leader, the invitation here is to move the needle toward a bit more business-appropriate self-disclosure, for the sake of consciously producing more powerful contexts for your most important and most challenging conversations. These possibly unprecedented contexts may lead to possibly unprecedented interactions, understandings, Actions and – of course – Results.

Outside the military, leadership has gone from "command and control" to "inspire and enroll." Would you agree? And authenticity and sincerity are enrolling. Most of us have a good BS detector. We also have authenticity detectors. When we experience authenticity and sincerity in our leaders, it enrolls us, and shifts how we listen. Creating such a context – on purpose – is a key conversational competency.

We claim this: If your con<u>text</u> is strong enough, you don't have to be impeccable with the con<u>tent</u>. That is, if the "space" you create on the front end is strong enough, you don't have to be perfect with your choice of words and how you move through the actual content of what you want to say. Are we clear that in the above example, Randy had not gotten to the actual, job-specific content about what Chalmers was or wasn't doing well on the project? All of this is context.

How hard was this conversation for Randy? Think about your experience in similar situations. To this, we ask these questions in workshops: *How many of us have ever benefited from constructive or corrective feedback during the course of our careers?* Every hand goes up. *And how many of us have ever avoided giving it?* Almost every hand goes up. *In these cases, who are we serving?* We're not serving the other person. We're serving ourselves.

We agree with many others who have observed: *Ambitious people want to hear the negative feedback.* Let's repeat: *Ambitious people want to hear the negative feedback.* Now, do they want to hear it in a space of respect, safety and trust? Absolutely. But they want to hear it. For leaders at every level, and for everyone in the business of talent development, context is key. The ability to have what may have historically been "difficult" conversations – and to have them well – is tremendously enhanced by the ability to purposefully set context. And by speaking into your concerns, sharing them authentically with the other person, you are practicing and improving an essential conversational competency.

Remember one of our earlier basic claims: If you always do what you always did, you always get what you always got. This is obvious to most of us. What we can now add is this – As a leader, one for whom the creation of context is important: If you always say what you always said, you always get what you always got. Speaking into your concerns is a predictable way to establish a context of authenticity.

One of the most powerful organizational contexts we have learned is called **"carefrontation."** Have you heard of this term, or something similar? If not, when you hear this term, what comes to mind? What does is seem that this term means? We characterize it this way:

- Confronting done with care and respect
- Challenging the other in a healthy and supportive way
- I care more about you than having my hands not sweat...
- I care enough about you to enter into a conversation with you that I'm not sure where it's going to go and how it's going to go...
- I care more about you than staying in my own physical comfort zone...

In the best-selling book *Good to Great*, Jim Collins shares characteristics of highly-effective leadership teams. If you've read the book, you may recall his descriptions of teams whose interactions involved healthy, respectful disagreement. Robust, authentic dialogue. He shares that one of Intel's philosophies was "Disagree, then commit." While he didn't use the term carefrontation, we see obvious parallels.

In Patrick Lencioni's best-selling book *The Five Dysfunctions of a Team*, one of the key dysfunctions listed is "Fear of Conflict." Again, we can see the power of a context of carefrontation to enable team members to move past this fear and into the authentic dialogue that characterizes powerful, effective teams.

The invitation here is to adopt your version of carefrontation as the context for your most important – and most challenging – conversations. And speaking into your concerns is a proven and powerful way to begin strengthening your ability to do this. Once again, this is a conversational competency. And as with all types of learning, it takes time and practice.

Another way of understanding context is this: How many of us like to know "why" we are being requested to do something? Or "why" X or Y is now required? Or "why" X or Y is now the new priority?

Context has everything to do with the "why." As a leader, helping your colleagues understand the "why" is powerful. Simon Sinek has a wonderful TED talk entitled "*How Great Leaders Inspire Action – The Power of Why*" in which he makes this very point. An organization in which a shared understanding of "why" exists – from top to bottom – operates at a very different level from one in which only the "what" and "how" are understood. Many organizations are seeking ways to bring about decentralized decision-making with strategic intent. Helping everyone understand "why" is purposefully creating a context that enables this valuable type of decision-making to take place.

Human beings are apparently addicted to meaning; that is, an event occurs and we immediately go about the internal process of determining its meaning for us and our organization. And the context in which we place a given event or circumstance dramatically impacts this meaning-making process. (All of this happens in language, of course. We aren't physically placing anything anywhere). What's the main problem with short sound bites on TV? Lack of adequate context. Which often leads, of course, to wildly different explanations of the same event.

Organizationally, context has to do with the organizational "come from" and the organizational "go to". We will move into this more deeply in a later chapter, but for now we can say that an organization's mission, values and standards – as well as its goals, objectives and performance targets – constitute the context in which all the Actions and transactions – the organizational content – takes place. The context is the background that shapes the meaning of events and circumstances, and the extent to which it is widely and deeply shared within the organization is directly related to the type of culture the organization possesses.

Just because you don't purposefully shape the context of an important meeting or conversation, does that mean that meeting or conversation doesn't have a context? Just because you don't purposefully shape the context of your organization, does that mean the people within your organization are operating without a context? Of course not. We always and already are operating out of contexts, no matter what. These just may or may not be conducive to the Results we're looking for! Clearly, conscious and purposeful context creation is a conversational competency of the utmost importance for leaders.

3. Language Conveys Commitment As Well As Information

A third basic claim we make is that language is Action, to speak is to act and to put things in motion. And with our language we convey commitment, as well as information.

We will cover commitments more directly and in great detail later, but for now we point to the way in which our requests, offers and promises (commitments, agreements) are the "tools" we use for coordinating Action with others and producing Results with others. As we introduced previously, the following graphic captures how organizations – no matter how simple or complex, large or small – can be understood as human beings coordinating Action. That is, people making and managing commitments with each other.

The fundamentals of collaborative Action – how we actually achieve anything in groups of more than one – are language tools and conversational competencies. We can use these well or use these poorly, but we are using them now. And the ways in which we use them shape and impact our 3 key types of organizational Results for which leaders of all types are responsible: relationships, culture and execution.

Clearly, these types of Results are related… and it's becoming increasingly clear to many of us that what have traditionally been understood as the "soft skills" are the actual drivers of bottom-line performance in many of today's organizations.

4. Language Provides Us Access To Breakthroughs

We also claim that with language, we make visible that which was previously "invisible" to us. And when we can see what we couldn't see before, we can then do what we couldn't do before. Many of us have heard this expression, and we agree: "You cannot intervene in a world that you do not see." Another related expression is "What the mind does not know, the eyes do not see".

So what exactly are we saying?

Language has the power to enable us to see with "new eyes" the same territory we've been covering, the same organization we've been leading, the same market we've been operating in, the same team we've been a member of, the same relationships we've been part of. It's precisely this expanded perspective, this widened view, this larger "horizon of possibilities" that is the basis for creating literally unprecedented – breakthrough – Results.

We are talking now about the power of distinctions. And these distinctions live in language. Once we acquire new distinctions, they enable us to see, to listen, to feel, to taste, and to smell that which we could not see, listen to, feel, taste and smell before.

Some examples:

Let's say John is a regular guy, he walks out of his house last night, looks up and he sees "a bunch of stars." That's it – a bunch of stars. Today, John has a conversation with Ann, who happens to be an amateur astronomer, and she says "John, some of those aren't stars – they're planets. And these planets have a more reddish or yellowish hue, and they look slightly different to the eye. And some of those are what we call nebula, which are remnants of apparently incredibly powerful explosions, millions of years ago and many light-years away. These have a slight "halo" or ring that you can actually see if you look for it. And some of those are man-made satellites, and they look slightly different, and they can be seen to track, ever so slowly, across the night sky…"

John walks out tonight, looks up at the sky again, and what now might he see? He might see planets, nebula, and satellites. Question: Where were the planets, nebula and satellites for John, last night? They were "invisible" – to him. Stars, planets and nebula are linguistic distinctions in the domain of astronomy. And when we acquire these distinctions, what we can then see when we look around with our biological eyes is different.

Another example: A professional forester has distinctions in the domain of trees and plants that a layperson does not have. This means that what the professional forester observes in the forest is absolutely not the same as what most "regular" people (people without these distinctions) would observe. The forester may go for a walk and see healthy pin oak trees, or poplar saplings that are suffering from amillaria root rot, or American sycamore trees with Anthracnose disease. The rest of us most assuredly do not see this, but the forester does. And the reason is: He or she possesses distinctions we simply do not possess. So he or she can see things, in the domain of trees, that we are blind to, that pass by totally unnoticed by us.

And because the forester <u>sees</u> what we don't see, he or she can <u>do</u> what we can't do. He or she can effectively treat the amillaria root rot. We cannot. (We don't even see it to begin with!) In this case, we claim the forester has more power – defined as capacity for effective Action – in the domain of trees than we do. So acquiring new distinctions = improving our capacity for seeing new possibilities and taking more effective Action in a given domain. This is important to notice.

So we make this fundamental claim: *We look with our eyes, but we observe through our distinctions.*

We could go on and on. A mechanic looks under the hood of a car, and does not see what we see. An obstetrician looks at an ultrasound reading and sees what we do not see. A hitting coach looks at a person taking batting practice and sees what we do not see. A chemist and a physicist look at the same slide under the microscope and they see different things. Western-trained and Eastern-trained physicians look at the same patient and they do not see the same things. A race car driver listens to the motor running and doesn't hear what we hear. A commercial fisherman puts one hand on the net in the water and feel what we do not feel. Why is this? Because each is observing (or listening or feeling) through a different set of distinctions. And these different distinctions enable these different Observers to see different possibilities, take dramatically different types of Action, and produce dramatically different Results, in each of these given domains.

Building a shared vocabulary of empowering, commonly-used distinctions is a key leadership competency.

What we see, when each of us opens our biological eyes, has more to do with what's "in here" that with what's "out there." As Albert Einstein reminds us, *We see the world not as it is, but as we are.*" What we listen (interpret), when sound waves enter our ears, has more to do with what's "in here" than with what's "out there." What we feel, when the clutch vibrates beneath our feet or the fishing rod bends in our hands has more to do with what's "in here" than with what's "out there." The differences have to do with the different sets of distinctions with which each is operating.

The starting point for achieving breakthrough Results is to begin to see new possibilities. This is precisely the power of new distinctions – to enable you to begin to see possibilities for effective Action that may have been "off your radar screen" previously. And out of these new possibilities we begin the process of orienting ourselves, taking a stand, enrolling others in our new vision of what's possible, using new tools as we coordinate Action and produce Results with others.

The rest of this book is all about sharing with you new distinctions in the domain of leadership and organizational effectiveness that will enable you to take a walk through your organization – the same organization you may have been part of for years – and to see things you've never seen before. Then by seeing what you haven't previously seen, you can begin to do what you haven't previously done… achieving Results you haven't previously achieved.

We realize that many people before us have shared some variation of this same core message. It's our hope that our particular way of framing this powerful understanding can contribute to your overall effectiveness as a leader and the performance of your organization… as well as to the "quality of your journey" as a human being. From an ancient proverb we read:

"Be careful of your thoughts, for your thoughts become your words. Be careful of your words, for your words become your Actions. Be careful of your Actions, for your Actions

become your habits. Be careful of your habits, for your habits become your character. Be careful of your character, for your character becomes your destiny."

Summary of Key Points

Extraordinary leaders design, convene and have effective conversations, so learning about language is very valuable.

The widely-held view that "language is a tool for communication" or "a way of labeling things so we know what we're talking about" is only half the story. Like two sides of the same coin, we agree that language does have a descriptive side that labels, describes and communicates. This aspect of language is fairly well-known and well-understood.

We offer that language (our internal conversations / our thinking, as well as our external conversations) is also profoundly creative and generative. And it is this creative and generative understanding of language that opens new possibilities and enables leaders to bring about a wide variety of unprecedented Results.

We live in language. We each have the "little voice" inside and these internal conversations – what we've come to call our thinking – are also profoundly creative and generative.

We are each continually confronted with events, in every domain of our lives. Because we live in language, once these events occur, we:

- Make up stories (interpretations, explanations) about these events
- Hold these stories to be The Truth
- And we forget that we made them up!

A fundamental distinction to possess is that events do not equal explanations. We invite you to replace the traditional "right/wrong" orientation for explanations with the "Works/Doesn't Work" or the "Powerful/Un-Powerful" orientation. That is, we invite you to always consider whether your explanations work or don't work… given the Results you say you want.

When we can see our interpretations as interpretations, we can then break free from them. We can examine them in terms of the possibilities that each opens or closes. This freedom enables us to purposefully and consciously generate new thinking, new ways of seeing, and new possibilities for Action that can lead to desired Results.

We look with our eyes but we observe through our distinctions. Similarly, we hear with our ears but we listen through our distinctions. And these distinctions live in language, and give us access to utterly unprecedented observations, possibilities and opportunities for producing breakthrough Results.

Language is directly connected with learning, and our ability to continue learning throughout the course of our lifetimes is obviously crucial to our success. Acquiring and practicing new distinctions is a key aspect of learning. And the first step in learning, the "threshold" for learning, is our ability to declare (internally or externally) "I don't know." This declaration is a profoundly generative, creative act. Far more than describing a state of affairs, it produces what is called a context, or an opening, for learning.

Through language we create and generate our relationships, moods and emotions, context, and public identity. Through the power of distinctions, which live in language, we gain access to breakthroughs. Sharing new, enabling and empowering distinctions in the domains of leadership effectiveness and organizational performance is the central focus of this book.

Most of our relationships are not physical; rather, they are conversational. Change them, and the relationships change. Stop them, and the relationships end. Start them, and we start new relationships.

Workplace mood and culture have a great deal to do with the conversations that are required and those that are prohibited. The "tools" we need to shape culture and mood are conversations, and improving culture and mood is a conversational competency.

It is demonstrably true that culture impacts the conversations people do or don't have at work. It is equally true that by purposefully changing the conversations, the mood and culture can be shaped. Causality is two-way.

Leaders can often find highly effective solutions to workplace performance issues by convening a conversation designed to surface "missing conversations." And one conspicuously large type of missing conversation has to do with building shared understanding of standards (more on this later in this book).

As a leader, your public identity – how you "show up", how you are perceived by others – is greatly shaped by your language, your conversations, how you speak, how you listen, and how you make and manage commitments.

Language also creates context, and the ability to purposefully create or shift context is a key leadership competency. By "speaking into your concerns" you can bring about a context of authenticity, and authenticity is an enrolling space. Helping others understand the "why" – as opposed to only sharing the "what" and the "how" – creates a richer and more powerful context for a variety of organizational undertakings. If your context is strong enough, you don't have to be impeccable with the content and you'll still be able to produce solid Results and preserve and strengthen the relationships involved.

One of the most powerful organizational contexts is known as carefrontation. It enables authentic, robust and healthy disagreement that actually strengthens – not diminishes – relationships. And it is precisely these types of conversations that leadership teams within sustainably great organizations participate in. Creating and sustaining context is the key. It's not physical, but it's very real. Context creation is an incredibly important leadership (and also emotional) competency.

Language conveys commitment, not just information. By understanding your organization as a network of conversations, relationships, and commitments (human beings making and managing commitments), you can open dramatically new possibilities for intervening and improving performance in a wide variety of areas.

We look with our eyes, but we observe through our distinctions. Acquiring new and powerful distinctions enables us to see what we didn't previously see, opening the door for us to begin doing what we couldn't previously do… and being what we couldn't previously be. This book is all about sharing with you distinctions that will enable you do see new possibilities, take unprecedented Actions and bring about breakthrough Results.

Application

Here are some suggested exercises to support you in applying the distinctions we have covered in this chapter.

1. Given that leaders accomplish a great majority of Results with and through others, identify 1-3 individuals (who may or may not be direct reports) that can support you in achieving the 1 or 2 or 3 most important Results you've previously identified. Then, given the power of language and conversations, think of 1 conversation that you can design and convene with each of these individuals in order to further strengthen these important relationships and move you toward your desired Results. Once identified, we encourage you to take Action and engage in these very conversations.

2. For one week notice the language others are using and what it's creating and generating. Notice what they say, how they say it (which includes tonality, body language, facial expressions) and the impact that has on their relationships, moods and emotions (their own and that of others), their public identities, and overall Results. Share your observations and what you're noticing with your Accountability Partners.

3. After completing exercise number 2, for the following week, pay attention to your own language. Notice what you tend to say and how you tend to say it, and whether the Results created and generated are positive or negative, according to your standards. Always keep Results in mind. Circle (+) or (-) depending on your view of each.

At home:

Son	+	-
Daughter	+	-
Significant other	+	-
Sibling	+	-
Mother	+	-
Father	+	-
Extended family member	+	-
Friend	+	-
Member of the community	+	-

At work:

Your direct reports	+	-
Your superiors (if applicable)	+	-
Your peers	+	-
Your colleagues	+	-
Customers	+	-
Suppliers	+	-
Members of a professional group	+	-

4. Identify one direct report, one person at your level and one superior (if applicable) – who know and care enough about you to give you honest, candid feedback about your public identity and your performance at work. In the spirit of carefrontation, ask each person to share with you 1-2 specific things you could be doing more of, less of or differently in order to become a more effective leader. Capture what you learn and discuss with your Accountability Partners.

CHAPTER 4

LISTENING, HEARING, BELIEFS AND RESULTS

"Many 'active listening' seminars are, in actuality, little more than a shallow theatrical exercise in appearing like you're paying attention to another person. The requirements: Lean forward, make eye contact, nod, grunt, or murmur to demonstrate you're awake and paying attention, and paraphrase something back every 30 seconds or so. As one executive I know wryly observed, many inhabitants of the local zoo could be trained to go through these motions, minus the paraphrasing."

— Robert K. Cooper

A Key Distinction for Leaders: Listening vs. Hearing

Extraordinary leaders are in the business of effective conversations. And organizations can be understood as networks of conversations, networks of commitments, networks of relationships. Bottom-line organizational Results are produced as a direct consequence of the Actions within these networks. Because of this, we claim that acquiring some distinctions around listening and hearing is important for leaders. These distinctions can serve to strengthen your conversational, relational and emotional competencies.

Let's start with some examples here. Have you ever given 10 people instructions, only to have 7 do it one way and 3 do it another? Have you and a colleague ever been in the same meeting, heard the same announcement, and after the meeting you shared and discussed what you both heard and you quickly realize that you both reached very different understandings of what just happened? In fact, your understandings are so different that you wonder for a moment if you both were in the same meeting!

Continuing, have you ever been in a situation where you said something with the best of intentions and in a way that you thought was perfectly clear… but later discovered you had been totally misunderstood? Or have you ever had the experience of totally misunderstanding someone else?

79

How do we explain the above situations (and countless other versions and varieties of these)? What's going on? Is it the case that someone was listening and someone else was not? Was someone getting it "right" and someone else getting it "wrong?" Was someone understanding and someone else mis-understanding? Was one person smart and the other not so smart? Or is there another way, perhaps a more powerful way, to look at this phenomenon? Toward this end, we offer the following key distinction:

LISTENING and HEARING are two entirely different things.

Let's explore. Listening and hearing are both real, they both exist, but they are not the same thing.

- Listening and hearing are two different phenomena. The names or labels we use here are not important. We could call them tacos and burritos, beer and wine, salt and pepper – but let's be clear: one of these is a biological phenomenon, and the other is a linguistic phenomenon.

- We choose to say that hearing is biological – it has to do with a bone vibrating by an eardrum, and when this happens we have the biological experience of hearing. Hearing, defined this way, involves physics and biology, sound waves and how our bodies are. People who are hearing impaired have a different biology than those who are not hearing impaired.

- We then say that listening is linguistic, it lives in language. Listening is active interpretation, active internal storytelling. Listening is definitely not passively receiving objective information, but instead has everything to do with building a story, a narrative, and interpretation about what was said and heard. Listening is where meaning gets generated, and meaning matters.

- Another way of framing it is: Listening = Hearing + Interpretation. And we interpret events, situations, what people say, what people do, visual inputs, auditory inputs, sensory inputs… first we get some biological input, then we interpret it. And this has everything to do with our listening.

- The way that each of builds interpretations has more to do with us, than with the words that were spoken by the other person. And what we are able to distinguish and discern and create meaning about in the first place – as the sound waves enter our ears – has to do with the distinctions we posses.

Listening has to do with the Observer, with how we interpret and see things, as shown below:

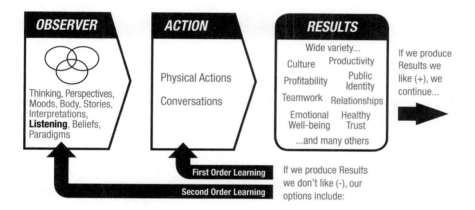

Listening is profoundly generative and creative, serving as one of the key ways that we orient ourselves toward certain Actions and Results, and away from others. We live in an interpretive world, and listening = interpretation.

Let's look at an example. Let's say Vinay is a regular guy, and Chalmers invites him to the Boston Symphony. During the intermission Chalmers asks, "Are you enjoying the show? What do you think of the symphony?" Vinay responds by saying "I'm enjoying it, the music sounds nice." Let's now say that Vinay actually begins violin lessons, and through the next 6 months of lessons he's introduced to cellos, flutes, oboes, xylophones, saxophones, clarinets, trumpets, French horns… all of the different instruments in a typical orchestra. At another symphony event months later, Vinay talks about "… how the clarinet soared" and "… the subtlety of the oboe" and "… the way the French horns set the stage for the trumpets."

What changed? Vinay's newly-acquired distinctions in the domain of musical instruments enabled him to listen – interpret and understand – in ways that he could not before. The same sound waves may have been entering his ears (he may have been "hearing" the same thing) but his listening, his interpretation, is dramatically different.

In the previous chapter we explored the power of distinctions, and made the claim that *we look with our eyes, but we observe through our distinctions.* We can now also claim: *We hear with our ears, but we listen through our distinctions.*

And we repeat: Building a shared vocabulary of new and empowering distinctions – in the domains of leadership effectiveness, teamwork and organizational performance – is a key leadership competency.

Let's continue – Have you ever had the experience of forgetting people's names? How about forgetting someone's name 5 seconds after you first met them? In this case, you are literally just ungrasping their hand from the introductory handshake and you have the unpleasant realization that you do not know what their name is! You look frantically for the name tag, and it's not there...! Many of us have had this experience.

What's going on? There are many ways to look at this, from "not paying attention" to "didn't really care" to "thinking about something else." We don't disagree, but would offer it in a different way. We say that in these cases, we are often *listening to the wrong conversation*! We're so busy listening to our own internal conversation that we don't even hear their name at all. We're lost in "What will she think about my hair?" or "I wonder how the Braves'll do tonight" or "I'm getting pretty hungry" or "That's Sheila, from down the street, she's the one who's been doing X or Y" or "I hope I don't look stupid" or whatever.

Our favorite explanation for this event is this: Anytime 2 people are in a conversation, there are actually 3 conversations going on. One is the public conversation – the external conversation that a tape recorder could faithfully record and play back for us later, capturing our spoken words. The other two conversations are, of course, the private ones – the ones that each person is simultaneously having with him/herself. We can say that the external conversation is what we're *hearing*, while the internal conversations say more about what we're *listening*.

We invite you to treat listening as a sport, as a competency – not as a character attribute. If you are a golfer, you are likely familiar with the term "swing thought." For golfers, a swing thought is something you say to yourself, such as "head down" or "tempo, not speed" or "left arm" (or any number of other ones) that has the effect of centering you, grounding you and helping you be successful in the shot.

We invite you to adopt and practice a swing thought for every introduction and every important conversation. As you're approaching the person – not the tee box – say to yourself "Quiet" or "Be Here" or anything else that can help you get out of the internal conversation and into the external one. With practice, you can get better at this. Without practice, you cannot. Declare yourself a beginner in this area, tee it up for yourself and simply start practicing.

As listening is not passive receipt of objective information, we can say there are "modes" of listening. Notice that listening with the intent to respond is different than listening with the intent to understand. How many of us, while we're listening to someone else, have already started to construct our response in our head and the other person is still talking? This is very common, of course. The other person is about halfway through and we are saying to ourselves "As soon as he/she shuts up I can say what I want to say... once you be quiet I'll be able to make this very good point... come on, come on, hurry it up...". And it's very possible that we totally miss what the other person has to say, and that what we want to say may not even be relevant by the time we speak! The first step to begin listening with the intent to understand is to notice – notice the automatic-ness with which we begin to create stories, and then quiet the voice. With practice, this can absolutely be done. Without practice, it cannot.

Another mode or way of listening is what we call listening to make wrong. Here, the listener already knows a thing or two about the topic, and is poised, ready and waiting for the chance to pounce on the speaker and make the speaker wrong about item A or item B or whatever. The whole orientation of the listener is toward spotting and leaping on opportunities to make the speaker wrong. Obviously, this manner of listening greatly influences how the listener interprets what is said. It also has the listener totally miss a great deal of what's said, as so much of the internal conversation is busy elsewhere. (As many of us have experienced, a person who listens to make wrong, over time, usually also achieves "full jerkhood" in the world! In other words, people who consistently listen to make wrong usually end up with a very negative public identity. Language creates and generates, and people who listen to make wrong very often create a public identity of "jerk.")

Often, what may also prevent us from listening more deeply with the intent of further understanding is a belief. This belief is: To seek more information about something = to agree with it. It takes strength to listen with openness to ideas that are different from the ones we currently hold, to create a space for the other person to feel free enough to share with us. Again, practice is everything. Maybe upon further listening we still don't agree with Jill, but we can certainly be more well-informed in our disagreement.

We human beings appear to be creatures that must make sense of things – have you noticed this in yourself and others around you? It occurs in every situation, at home and at work and everywhere in between. We do not simply experience events and circumstances and that's the end of it. No, for us, that's just the beginning. From some event as our starting point, we then actively go about making sense of it, we then actively make meaning and add significance and construct interpretations and stories.

Have you ever known someone who tended to make up un-powerful interpretations? For example, some event happens to John and the story that he builds around it has the effect of paralyzing him, of limiting his choices, of _not_ moving him toward effective Actions. Has this ever happened to you? Our experience is that this occurs for all of us, at one time or another. This has everything to do with our own particular listening, our own particular way of interpreting. Fernando Flores has summarized the power of listening in this manner: **"The key is to stop producing interpretations that have no power."**

This distinction between listening and hearing has some important additional implications for leaders:

- Human beings do not have a brain-to-brain data link by which a "message" or "information" is directly sent from one person to the other. Human communication is all about interpretation and shared meaning. The model of effective communication that many of us grew up with

– in which we see a Transmitter, a Signal, and a Receiver – is woefully inept for understanding human communication. It may work well for digital communication, TV and radio, where we can say communication is effective if the Receiver can replicate the Signal 100%. But that model is terrible for human beings, because it says nothing about shared interpretation and shared meaning.

- Your listening and the listening of others (how you and others in your organization are interpreting) is dramatically impacted by your and their moods and emotional states. On the other hand, your hearing (the passage of sound waves into your and their ear drums) is not.

- It's not so much what is <u>said</u> that's so important in many situations – it's what gets <u>listened</u>. What's important is the interpretations that get produced, regardless of what you had to say to get there. You cannot check the box "Success" at the end of the meeting just because you said exactly what you wanted to say, exactly how you wanted to say it. No – you can only check that box if all the listeners present produced the interpretations you wanted them to produce.

- You are 100% responsible for how you listen. That is, you are 100% responsible for your interpretations. You are the author, you are making them all up, you and you alone. And you've been doing this your whole life.

- While you are 100% responsible for how you listen, we then say that you are partially responsible for how you "get listened." That is, you are partially responsible for how others interpret what you are saying. Do you accept this? If you do, we may now inquire: How do you go about ensuring that you did achieve the Result called shared understanding?

- A helpful conversational competency is the practice of "checking someone's listening" or "checking for shared understanding." Many of us do this fairly regularly and fairly well, and many of us can certainly improve here. At the end of the meeting, the move to make may be to check in with people to see if their interpretation, their understanding is what you were hoping for. And when you say "Lee, I'd like to check your listening" or "I'd like to check your understanding" you are not accusing Lee of not paying attention. That's not the context here. The context is that Lee is a unique Observer, he is not you, he is interpreting you, and he cannot not interpret you! (You aren't connecting to Lee or anyone else in the room via a direct brain-to-brain data transfer mechanism…). In doing so, you will be using your awareness of this distinction – that listening is not the same as hearing – in a way that can improve your ability to achieve shared understanding and more desirable Results.

- This practice of checking others' listening while you are still at the meeting – that is, before everyone gets up and starts taking Action – usually has a very productive cost/benefit. The old Fram oil filter commercial comes to mind again here: "You can pay me now, or you can pay me later." Paying me now involves checking people's listening now, here at the table. Paying me later involves cleaning up the mess that happened because you thought you had shared understanding and shared meaning… but in actuality, you didn't. And now you must deal with the consequences of Actions taken and Results produced from this lack of shared understanding.

- Is it possible to listen for what's not being said? That is, to listen for the underlying concern that the speaker may not have articulated directly? We say yes, and while some people do this intuitively well already, we can also learn to improve in this area.

To start with, assume that everyone to whom you are speaking is "speaking out of some concerns." In other words, assume that in every conversation we have, we are operating with some concerns in mind, some concerns that we would like to see addressed… but that we may not have articulated explicitly. Listening in this way enables you to say, during the conversation "… OK, I think I understand what you're saying, Tomas, but let me ask… is your real concern that you think we may lose this customer?"

This is a key point – you do not have to be 100% accurate with your inference here in order for this to be a productive move to make. The simple act of going here – asking about the background concern – may be the catalyst for the other person to respond with "… No, Vinay, I don't think that's it. But I think it might be that I'm not sure Janet is fully competent to do the job we're asking her to do…" or something along these lines.

Getting closer to the real concern is always the goal, and listening for what's not being said is a conversational competency that can absolutely support you in getting there. So of course, listen to what others are saying and how they're saying it. But save a bit of attention for an "auxiliary" antenna that is always on the lookout for unspoken, unarticulated concerns.

Listening, Beliefs, Actions and Results

Broadly speaking, why do people listen so differently? What makes one person interpret this way, and another person interpret that way? One common-sense answer to this question is: our life experiences.

Most of us have an intuitive understanding that our life experiences absolutely influence how we "see things" (which by now, we understand to mean how we listen, how we interpret, which occurs in language, not via our eyes). Everything from our age, race, sex, bus driver, travel, no travel, school, major, significant incidents or events we were involved in, sports, you name it. All of these impact how we tend to listen, how we tend to interpret situations. But here is a key question: Is it possible for two people to have the exact same *experience*, but draw from it two very different *beliefs*?

We say the answer is yes, and it happens all the time. And it's not so much the experience itself that influences how we interpret or listen later on. It's the belief we draw as a Result of that experience. And this belief lives in language, it's a story we created which, from this point forward, tends to influence or shape how we interpret and orient ourselves toward some Actions (and away from others).

A story comes to mind about this very thing. A TV program from several years ago showcased a woman from a town in New York who was experiencing significant depression and was withdrawing from her family, friends, and community. She enjoyed fishing, and so as a last resort they decided to organize a big fishing trip to the Florida Keys for her. They chartered a boat and off they went.

Lo and behold, she hooks a very large barracuda. A barracuda is a large, fast-swimming torpedo-shaped fish that has a mouthful of extremely sharp teeth. Somehow, as she was fighting the fish, she was straining against the rod and the fish just shot out of the water like an arrow, heading straight towards her. The fish slammed into her leg, and the sharp teeth cut a very deep, very serious gash on her thigh. An emergency situation ensued, with Coast Guard helicopters airlifting her out for emergency, life-saving surgery.

When she recovered and was able to talk to her family, she said that her recovery instilled a belief in her that there was still something more to live for, something left for her to do with her life. Two years later, in a follow-up, she was fully active and engaged in her life, family, church, and community. She was "back." Her level of happiness, her well-being, the quality of her journey had obviously shifted.

Now, is it possible that she could have adopted a different belief as a Result of that accident and her hospital stay? We say yes, it's very possible. Other possible beliefs may include: "One more bad thing to happen to me, I guess I'm snakebit" or "I told you we shouldn't have taken this trip, nothing good would happen." Now, this is not to minimize the seriousness of clinical depression or to say that depression can be overcome by a fishing accident. But it is important to notice that it wasn't so much this lady's *experience* that influenced how she interpreted things later on; rather, it was the *belief* she created (in language) as a Result of her experience.

We are each the authors of our own beliefs, and they absolutely influence how we listen, how we interpret words and Actions that haven't happened yet. (**And this is somehow not taught to us at an early age!**) From our interpretations, we act. And from our Actions, we produce Results.

Obviously, beliefs have everything to do with the Observer that we are, with how we see things, how we interpret events and how we orient ourselves in the world.

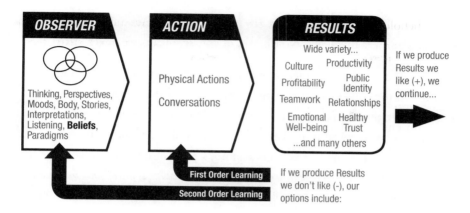

And let's be clear – we aren't just talking about beliefs related to religion or church or spirituality. We have beliefs about everything. Men, women, money, tall people, short people, skinny people, fat people, long-haired people, short-haired people, African Americans, Caucasians, Asians, Native Americans, unions, management, Fords, Chevys, imported cars, Canadians, neighborhoods, oak trees… we even have beliefs about beliefs!

We're not saying that it's somehow wrong to have beliefs, or that certain beliefs are wrong while others are right. We are saying that the huge numbers of beliefs we have, in the incredible range of areas in which we have them, absolutely impact our listening, absolutely influence how we interpret situations.

We are saying that our beliefs open and close possibilities, and that we often don't see this. We tend to look *through* our beliefs, and often do not look *at* our beliefs. Beliefs may be viewed as part of the lenses of a pair of glasses through which we see the world. We say that sometimes, it's worthwhile to take the glasses off and look at the lenses themselves.

The more powerful question may be "Are your beliefs serving you, moving you toward the Results you say you want?" as opposed to "Are your beliefs the right beliefs or the wrong beliefs?" For example, if you have a belief that you will never learn how to manage the department well, or that a key customer is unrealistic about delivery dates, these beliefs strongly influence how you interpret situations involving issues in the department or with delivery dates for the customer. And these interpretations, in turn, strongly influence the Actions you take or don't take, which create the Results you produce or don't produce. Specifically, beliefs that include "I can never…" almost always lead us to *in*-Action, to *no* Action, in the particular areas involved. No Action, of course, means we never learn.

Consider this example: A gentleman named Stan was in a personal coaching session with Pat. In the course of conversation, Stan declared that what he really wanted was a committed relationship with a woman. That was his desired Result. He had been divorced awhile, was in his late 40's, was tired of the single/dating scene, and was now ready for a committed, monogamous relationship with a woman. Pat understood and said *"That's great, let's take a look…what are some of your beliefs about women?"* The very first thing out of Stan's mouth was "Well, you can't trust 'em"… upon which Pat stated *"I think this may be a good place for us to start!"*

Can you see that Stan's belief that "you can't trust women" will not lead to the Result he says he wants, that of a committed, partnering relationship with a woman? Regardless of whatever experiences he's had in the past, this belief is what's in the present and is what will influence how he interprets and listens in the future. He may start a new a relationship with a woman, she will be 2 minutes late from some errand, he'll notice it and say *"See, I told you I can't trust you"* and the relationship dance will start down a road that probably won't lead to the Result he says he wants.

Once we adopt a belief, we can find it difficult to alter it, update it, or let it go. Many of us have had this experience. And many of us don't see that this is happening, because we don't see them as beliefs in the first place – we see them as "the way things are", as attributes of reality.

We've heard this story about a man who has very strongly-held beliefs about "women drivers." Anybody who knows him is aware that he thinks that as a group, women should not be allowed on the road because of their inattention to what they're doing, lack of knowledge about rules of the road and highway etiquette, and other problems with safety, proper speed, and general competence. He's driving down the road one day and gets behind a vehicle moving very slowly and hesitatingly thru a downtown area. Immediately he's fuming and thinking *"those x&*%#!! women drivers, can't they ever get it right… wouldja look at that, no bleeping idea what she's doing…"* The car finally pulls over and the man passes by, looking over to see who was driving. To his great surprise, he sees a man, not a woman, behind the wheel.

Let's imagine now that each of us is this person. Do many of us, upon this realization, think to ourselves *"Hey, here's some evidence to the contrary of my beliefs. Here's a great opportunity for me to be lots more open and possibly update my beliefs about women, etc"?* No! Instead we say *"Hey, that guy drives like a woman!"*

For relationships, important conversations that are often missing are those about beliefs. What are our beliefs about discipline? About customer service? About teamwork? About money? About sex? About having children? About child-raising? About what constitutes a healthy relationship? About the role of men and women? About spirituality and religion? Having these conversations is different than not having them. You will produce different Results and different relationships by having these conversations than you will by not having them. We create out of what we speak.

Where do many of our beliefs come from? Where did we get them? (And do we ever update them?) For many of us, our beliefs were given to us by our parents or whoever was involved in our childhood. Certainly our cultural, religious, or spiritual beliefs have a great deal to do with when and where and how we were raised. Now, we may certainly adopt new beliefs as we grow and learn and change, but the ones we change *from* usually have their roots in our childhood and the society in which we were raised.

We adopted many beliefs from our parents, as well as from other influential adults who may have participated in our childhood and early adulthood. And it's likely that when our parents and those other influential adults were just starting out, they adopted many of the beliefs of their parents or elders. But at some point in life, we get to say "These are <u>my</u> beliefs." A key question for all of us is: When do we get to do that? That is, when do you get to declare which beliefs are yours, regardless of those of your parents or former bosses or teachers or anyone else?

Our experience is that different people do this at different times during their lives. We know young people who have definitely adopted their own beliefs by age 25, and we know older people who still have not done so. We know people who, once they come up with beliefs, seem to be able to update them when confronted with new information, while others do not. Interesting. It's an important question –

are your beliefs working for you? Are they allowing you to achieve the Results you say you want? And do you see them as *your* beliefs in the first place?

In Peter Senge's *The Fifth Discipline Fieldbook*, Rick Ross outlines what is called The Ladder of Inference. In many ways, what he is offering serves to reinforce what we've been discussing here – and it all happens in language:

> *"We live in a world of self-generating beliefs which remain largely untested. We adopt those beliefs because they are based on conclusions, which are inferred from what we observe, plus our past experience. Our ability to achieve the Results we truly desire is eroded by our feelings that:*
>
> - *Our beliefs are <u>the</u> truth.*
> - *The truth is obvious.*
> - *Our beliefs are based on real data.*
> - *The data we select are the real data.."*

He goes on to say that very quickly, we climb up what Chris Argyris calls a "ladder of inference" (remember going from Event to Explanation?). According to the author, this is a very common mental pathway of *"increasing abstraction, often leading to misguided beliefs."* This ladder is summarized below, in order of when the steps occur:

1. *Observable data and experiences occur; some "event" occurs*
2. *I select "data" from what I observe; some details and Actions; (I miss other details and Actions)*
3. *I add meanings (cultural and personal)*
4. *I make assumptions based on the meanings I added*
5. *I draw conclusions*
6. *I adopt beliefs about the world*
7. *I take Actions based on my beliefs.*

And, of course, we produce Results – including the qualities of our workplace culture, the nature of our most important relationships, the effectiveness of our most important processes and the productivity of our teams – based on the Actions we take.

Kevin Ashton, in his excellent book *How to Fly a Horse: The Secret History of Creation, Invention and Discovery*, has this to say about beliefs: *Confidence is belief in yourself. Certainty is belief in your beliefs. Confidence is a bridge. Certainty is a barrier.* We agree wholeheartedly.

Finally, Stuart Heller, in his book *Retooling On The Run: Real Change for Leaders With No Time*, offers this powerful way of understanding the impact of our beliefs on our lives: *"The power of belief shapes your actions, your experiences, and your results. Believing involves the whole body. Your beliefs are not found only in your thoughts, they are found everywhere, even in the subtle shapes of your posture and in the dynamics of your movements. Your habitual ways of reacting to people, events, and feelings tell the story of your beliefs. If you are to make the changes you desire, you must harness the power of belief. As you believe, so you behave. As you behave, so you become. As you become, so becomes the world."*

Listening and Being Present

In our workshops, we ask leaders to identify and discuss 1 or 2 ways in which they can improve their listening. In a great many cases, the conversation turns to improving their ability to "be present" with others. Let's conclude our chapter on listening by exploring the phenomenon of being present and its impact on our listening, our relationships and our Results.

First, let's be clear – being "present" has nothing to do with where your feet are! It's a metaphor, of course. But it's pointing to something of critical importance for leaders, who get paid to have effective conversations. In this way of understanding, being present has to do with the degree to which we can lessen or quiet the internal conversation for the sake of focusing fully on the external conversation, the conversation we're having with the other person.

Have you ever had the experience of being genuinely listened to? Many of us have, although it's not a very common occurrence. These are usually memorable occasions, precisely because they are so rare. Here is a claim: The person who gave you that experience was not caught up in a big internal conversation at the same time they were talking with you. That other person had somehow quieted the inner voice, quieted the internal dialogue, so as to be much more fully present with you. The capacity to do that – on purpose – is required if we are to improve our ability to be present with others, and is a key leadership competency.

Question: When you are at your best – whether at work or at play, whether alone or with others – often, what's going on upstairs? That is, when you are at your best, whatever that means for you, what are you saying to yourself? What's the degree of internal chatter you're experiencing? For most of us, it's very little. For most of us, when we're at our best, there is a noticeable lack of internal dialogue occurring. We're focused on the other person, we're in the "flow", we can be said to be more fully present than at other times. The invitation here is to create more of these experiences!

In our workshops, we ask leaders *"Who here has ever tried a meditative practice of any sort?"* and many hands usually go up. *"When you first started, was it easy or hard?"* Virtually everyone reports it was very hard. *"Who here has ever had an unsolicited thought?"* Everyone laughs and hands go up – because we all have. And when your intention is to quiet the internal voice, to lessen the internal dialogue, those unsolicited thoughts are noticed with remarkable clarity.

We focus on the power of language and conversations for leaders in this book, and *Language and the Pursuit of Happiness* obviously was also centered on this generative, creative understanding. However, we believe it's also important to periodically "give it a rest." That is, for leaders and for all of us, the ability to regularly quiet the internal conversation, to rest in silence, to experience some stillness, brings with it an entirely different type of power. Now, there are many ways to accomplish this, are there not? Some people find it on a bicycle, some people find it running or taking a walk. Some people find it in sitting meditation, others practice this in yoga or riding a motorcycle. Or skiing, dancing or gardening.

You may consider this a type of rhythm, in which first you're externally focused and in lots of conversations, making things happen in your organization and in the world, and then you're internally focused and silent. Then you're externally focused and talking, thinking, pushing, enrolling, achieving Results… followed by a period of internal focus and stillness. And on and on and on, an ongoing cadence or rhythm alternating back and forth, inward then outward, silent and still, then active and engaged. A great many people have found tremendous value in some version of this. Think about it this way: Human practices that do not add some kind of value or benefit tend to die out over time. This practice is ancient, of course, and we notice it's still around and going strong.

There are many resources available for those seeking to deepen their practice and experience in finding your version of silence, your variety of stillness. We ask leaders who have been practicing awhile and experiencing some success in this area to share their experiences, and virtually all report that when they re-engage they are better, more grounded and centered and more able to be authentic and present with others. They report being more comfortable in their own "skin" and more able to declare "I don't know" and move into learning easier and more comfortably than before. We invite you to explore this powerful avenue in your continuing development as a leader.

Background Conversations That Impact Our Listening

All of us grow up in what are called background conversations. These are societal conversations, or beliefs, that you and I did not invent personally. They were here when we got here, and we just picked them up. And in our work, we have observed one particularly powerful background conversation, especially for Americans. This background conversation, this belief, is:

I'm Right

Notice this about yourself? About others? Our kids, at very young ages, were talking about the right way to do Lego and the right way to play the made-up game and the right way to ride the wagon. Incredible. And we know we didn't explicitly teach them that. They just picked it up from being alive in early 21st century USA.

Chalmers' friend and colleague Mark tells a personal story to help illustrate this. He and Chalmers both used to work for the same international consulting firm. The firm had a strong commitment to ongoing learning and education / training, with a full campus training facility. Thousands of people from across the world spent many hours training at this facility.

Mark and a friend were at the social center (the bar) and ended up in conversation with a young lady from South Africa. It was about the same time as Apartheid was ending and lots of changes were occurring there, and the conversation had to do with whether or not we were receiving true news reports and what it was really like to be there, and so on. She then told them she had been in America a few weeks, visiting several states and sightseeing around our country.

Seeing that she'd been in the U.S. long enough to see a few things, having visited different areas and spent time with different people, Mark asked her what she thought about America and Americans. Her immediate response was *"You Americans are so arrogant!"* Mark and his friend were surprised and taken aback. *"What do you mean?"* they responded. *"You think you live in the only great country in the whole world,"* she stated. Mark and his friend looked at each other, looked back at her, and in unison replied *"We do!"*

What this exchange illustrates, we believe, is how the I'm Right conversation is often very present for Americans (although versions of it are also clearly present within other cultures), and we don't see it. It's not so visible to us, but it becomes very visible to someone who does not come from this culture, this background conversation.

We tend to listen so as to make our beliefs right, and this definitely includes our beliefs about ourselves. We love being right, and it shows up everywhere. What prevented the male driver from seeing data that was different than his beliefs about female drivers was his commitment to being right. What prevented the gentleman from creating the healthy relationship with a woman that he said he wanted was his commitment to being right. What often prevents many of us from exploring new possibilities or being open to new avenues or taking new Action... is our commitment to being right.

Let's make a few distinctions here – Being right, in this context, is not the same as being correct. If you're typing Vinay's blood for a blood transfusion tomorrow, please do it correctly. If you're fixing the brakes on Chalmers' car, the car that is used to drive his family around in, please fix the brakes correctly. Two plus two equal four today, it will equal four tomorrow, it's always going to equal four. We're not talking about these situations.

We're talking here about a stance, an orientation, of being righteous, being convinced that your way of doing something or your way of looking at something is cosmically, Objectively Right, and anyone who does it or sees it differently is just plain Wrong. What's the right way to get married? The right way to get buried? The right way to manage a conflict? The right way to deal with new opportunities? The right way to raise kids? We could go on and on. Is it possible that what's right for you and your company, you and your life, is wrong for someone else's company and someone else's life?

Would you agree that there are many ways to do many things, and still produce positive Results? Of course there are. There are many ways to take Action in many situations and still produce good outcomes, all the while still staying within ethical or legal or procedural guidelines. This is our focus here.

If we think the way we listen, the way we interpret, the way we "see things" is Right, and your way happens to be different, what does that make you? It makes you Wrong. And how many of us find ourselves gravitating toward people who constantly make us wrong?

"Oh, I just love being with John because I get to be made wrong all the time. Yes, I love being with him and I love how it feels to be made wrong every time I have a different perspective than he does. It makes me want to spend so much time with him. Oh, how excellent it feels to be made wrong at every turn!"

How ridiculous. But notice how quickly we tend to make others wrong, how we come from this background conversation of I'm Right; and if I'm Right, and you happen to have a different view, then you must be wrong. What else could you be?

Most of us will not voluntarily be with, work with, associate with people who constantly make us wrong. At some point we take our toys and find another sandbox. We wonder why our spouse or kids walk right by and don't want to sit on the couch next to us, or why our colleagues never invite us to join them for lunch. Maybe they're tired of being made wrong.

Another distinction: I'm Right Done Well is not the same as I'm Right Done Poorly. I'm Right Done well = assertiveness and self-confidence, as well as the ability to hold yourself and others to a standard. I'm Right Done Well = discipline and self-discipline, and is essential for effective leadership. Physically, this energy is "up and out", pointing and leaning forward, seeing opportunities and going for them. In fact, I'm Right Done Well is so important that we say this: If you know people aspiring to assume positions of leadership, and they don't have any I'm Right Done Well, they will have a very difficult time.

On the other hand, I'm Right Done Poorly is assertiveness and self-confidence... overcooked. Gone 'round the bend. Way, way too much. What do we call assertiveness and self-confidence that's way overdone? Arrogance. *"Why am I surrounded by such stupid people?"* Here, the person is so assertive and so self-confident that they're utterly unable to see that maybe, just maybe, someone else might have something useful to contribute. Maybe, just maybe, someone else might have a valuable perspective to share. Same energy, just done poorly. So leaders absolutely need I'm Right Done Well. But not I'm Right Done Poorly.

Another example or two relevant for leaders at all levels – Humbleness Done Well is openness and inclusiveness, the ability to work as part of a team and the ability to genuinely consider others' ideas and contributions. Humbleness Done Poorly is living your life a walking doormat. You never stand up. Again, same energy – done well or done poorly.

How many of us would say that Skepticism Done Well is healthy? Leaders we talk with nod their heads in agreement, that it is indeed healthy (and valuable) to have a healthy skeptic or two on the team. On the other hand, what do we call Skepticism Done Poorly? Skepticism that's overcooked, gone around the bend? Cynicism. Active, enrolling resignation. *"Let me enroll all of you as to why nothing we do will ever make a difference."* Totally different, is it not? Same energy, just done well or done poorly.

On the home front, and especially with close relationships, we see a related background conversation tend to show up. This background conversation is:

I'd Rather Be Right Than Be Happy

Our experience is that many of us will definitely give up our happiness for the sake of being right, and it shows up – it reveals itself – in our language. *"Honey, how many times have I gotta tell you, the toilet paper comes over the top, not under the bottom"* or *"the right way to load the dishwasher, the big plates have to go on the left... Now I've gotta re-do it..."* or *"the right way to clean the floor"* or *"Look, I've told you, my remotes have to be on this table, stacked in order of size, or the whole setup is ruined"* or whatever. Or we have to have the last word in a conversation, and when we really look at it, it's for the sake of being right. Or *"I hear what you're saying, but the reality of the situation is..."* Get ready, because someone is about to be right.

How committed are you to being right? What are you willing to give up in order to be right? Because there's a cost.

Let's clarify a bit here – for most of us, "I'd rather be right than be happy" is not running around as a fully formed thought that you can easily see with a bit of self-reflection. No, it's much more subtle. But because you keep having the conversation you're having about the dishwasher, this is the choice you're making. We "back into" this one. Because you keep having the conversation you're having about the toilet paper, this is the choice you're making.

Also, "I'd rather be right than be happy" does not mean you'd rather be right than skip giddily down the sidewalk, smiling and laughing. No, it means "I'd rather be right than have a nice dinner at home" or "I'd rather be right than have this kind of relationship with my sales manager." Make sense? It's about choosing to be right over another valid outcome, usually having to do with the quality of a relationship or the nature of an experience with someone else.

Many of us have heard this expression: **You can be right, or you can be in relationship, but not both.** And this has been our experience, and the experience of a great many leaders with whom we've worked.

If a colleague continually makes you wrong – in areas where there are legitimately more than one path forward – just because your view is different from his or hers, what are you likely to do? If this occurs regularly, recurrently, what do you think you will ultimately do? Think about situations in which people make other people wrong, not for months but for years. Are there people in your life – at work or in your family – who have made other people wrong for years and years? We ask this question in workshops: In these situations, almost always, where do these people end up? And the overwhelming answer reported is… they end up alone. A south Louisiana expression that captures this perfectly is: Welcome to the loneliest bayou there is… Bayou' Self!"

If you're ever in a conversation and you feel that the energy is no longer excellent, the flavor and tone of the conversation is no longer positive, we invite you to adopt a new practice. If your Big Eye is working well (that is, if you have some capacity for self-awareness) in that moment, ask yourself this question in real time, while the conversation is occurring:

For the sake of what am I about to say what I'm about to say?

In other words: Why is this very next thing about to pop out of my mouth? And if we're honest, it's often that we want to be right. That's why. Now we get to choose: How committed are we to being right? What are we willing to give up in order to be right? We will absolutely produce different Results in our lives, at work as well as at home, depending on how we orient ourselves in these situations.

Being Right Done Well produces achievement, commitment to high standards, discipline. Being Right Done Poorly produces a public identity of arrogance and "make wrong." Being Right Done Poorly makes good people want to go away. Being Right Done Poorly damages relationships and the company culture, increases unwanted turnover and diminishes innovation and creativity. And many of us are not very good Observers of this phenomenon, of this background conversation that impacts our listening, our interactions and our Results.

I'm Right, Listening and Distinctions

Chalmers' friend and longtime coach Mike Papania has also shared with us a powerful connection between I'm Right, listening, and distinctions. **We often make people wrong who don't have the same distinctions we do**.

For example, a husband asks his wife *"Honey, go in the garage and get me that Phillips screwdriver, will ya?"* She doesn't know tools, goes in, searches the best she can, and comes back with a hex-nut driver. *"Were you not listening?"* he says. *"How many times do I have to say it?"* Or she asks him *"Honey, will you get me that taupe shawl-collar cocktail dress from my closet? It's right by my Capri pants."* He's utterly lost and comes back with goodness-knows-what, and it's *"That's what's wrong with our relationship...you never listen!"*

This is very powerful to begin to observe, our tendency to make others wrong simply because they do not have the same distinctions we do. It impacts our relationships at all levels, personal and professional, with adults and with children. It impacts our teamwork, our productivity and the quality of our journey in many ways.

Interestingly, we can see that we often also make ourselves wrong because we don't have the distinctions others do. Many of us tend to have this experience and then live in all sorts of negative conversations that, upon reflection, simply do not serve us. We can stop being so hard on ourselves simply because we didn't see something that someone else saw. What's possible is to accept that in this moment, we don't possess these distinctions... declare ourselves beginners... and move into new learning.

Summary of Key Points

Listening is not equal to Hearing. Hearing is biological. Listening is linguistic. Listening = Hearing + Interpretation.

Through our listening we orient ourselves toward (or away from) certain possibilities and Actions. Building shared listening – shared interpretation, shared meaning – is a key leadership competency.

Human beings do not have a brain-to-brain data link. Human communication is all about interpretation and shared meaning.

Your listening and the listening of others (how you and others in your organization are interpreting) is dramatically impacted by your and their biology, posture, distinctions, social history, moods and emotional states, beliefs, concerns (values), standards, and ways of making meaning. On the other hand, your hearing (the passage of sound waves into your and their ear drums) is not.

It's not so much what is <u>said</u> that's so important – it's what gets <u>listened</u>. What's important is the interpretations that get produced, regardless of what you had to say to get there. You cannot check the box "Success" at the end of the meeting just because you said exactly what you wanted to say, exactly how you wanted to say it. No – you can only check that box if all the listeners present produced the interpretations you wanted them to produce.

You are 100% responsible for how you listen. That is, you are 100% responsible for your interpretations. You are the author, you are making them all up, you and you alone. And you are partially responsible for how you "get listened." That is, you are partially responsible for how others interpret what you are saying. Do you accept this? If you do, we may now inquire: How can you go about ensuring that you achieve the Result called shared understanding?

Many of us are not very powerful Observers of the way we listen. We interpret "transparently" to ourselves; that is we don't see ourselves as interpreting at all. From our individual perspectives, we think we're "getting it like it is." Nothing could be farther from the truth. We tend to listen in such a way to make ourselves, our stories, and our moods "right."

A powerful conversational competency is the practice of "checking your own listening", "checking others' listening" and "checking for shared understanding." By not practicing this, you will very likely end up dealing with the consequences of Actions taken and Results produced from this lack of shared understanding.

Is it possible and important to listen for what's not being said? That is, to listen for the underlying concern that the speaker may not have articulated directly or clearly? We say yes, because everyone to whom you are speaking is "speaking out of some concerns." Getting closer to the real concern is the goal, and listening for what's not being said is a conversational competency that can absolutely support you in getting there. So of course, listen to what others are saying and how they're saying it. And also save a bit of attention for an "auxiliary" antenna that is always on the lookout for unspoken concerns.

Being "present" has nothing to do with where your feet are. It has everything to do with the degree to which you can quiet your internal dialogue and in so doing, be "with" the other person in a qualitatively different way. Meditative practices are excellent ways in which to improve in this area. Adopting a lifelong "rhythm" of external focus and making your agenda happen... followed by internal focus and quieting the internal dialogue... followed by external focus and enrolling people to support you in what you're up to… followed by quiet and stillness and silence… can be a wonderful avenue to improved listening, as well as a healthy emotional life.

Application

For all the items below, keep in mind the 1 or 2 or 3 important Results that you are committed to achieving during the next 12 months, as well as the areas in which you declared you are seeking to learn or learn how to do something differently or better.

1. For one week, **practice checking your listening**. In your own words, share with the speakers what you are interpreting out of what they're saying. You may say something like "What I'm understanding is…" or "What I think you're meaning is … Is this what you meant?" Look for degree of shared understanding. See what you notice.

2. For another week, **practice checking others' listening of your speaking**. Ask them to share with you in their own words what they are interpreting out of what you're saying. You may say something like *"I want to make sure I am communicating clearly. So would you mind sharing with me, in your own words, what you heard me say?"* Look for degree of shared understanding. See what you notice.

3. For another week, **notice** each time you find yourself "wanting / needing" to be Right. For each situation, **ask yourself**:
   - How important was it for you to be right?
   - In order to be right, what were you willing to give up?
   - If you held firm in being right: What did you gain? What did you lose? Was it worth it?
   - If you didn't hold firm: What did you gain? What did you lose? Was it worth it?

4. Write down some of the first of your beliefs that come to mind. Separate those that empower you – those that serve you – from those that don't. Always keep in mind your desired Results. Practice changing those beliefs that

are not serving you. If possible, share what you're noticing with your Accountability Partner(s), and see where those conversations take you.

5. Periodically find a comfortable place to sit and **practice being quiet**. Treat this as an exercise to improve your ability to be present with people. Start for periods of only 2-3 minutes and work up from there. Sit comfortably, close your eyes, slow your breathing, relax… and when the thoughts invariably enter, simply ease them aside – knowing you'll have plenty of time to deal with them later – and return your attention to just breathing, just sitting, just being. What do you notice during these times? Does this noticing lead you to new Action? If so, what?

CHAPTER 5

LEARNING HOW TO LEARN

"In times of change, those who are prepared to learn will inherit the land, while those who think they already know will find themselves wonderfully equipped to face a world that no longer exists."

- Eric Hoffer

Note: While this entire book is made possible because of our great fortune in meeting and learning from Julio Olalla and others at The Newfield Network and Education for Living, this chapter in particular draws very directly from Julio's work. Julio is the first person who ever suggested to us that dramatically new ways of understanding the phenomenon and process of learning are of crucial importance for all of us – for all human beings seeking to live and work together peacefully and productively. We encourage you to explore all of Julio's writings, programs and contributions in this field.

In Chapter 2 we briefly touched on the phenomenon of learning, as well as its impact and importance for organizations and individuals in times of ongoing change (such as we are experiencing now and are anticipated to experience for the foreseeable future). We also made a clear connection between learning and language; specifically, the way in which declaring "I don't know" – either to ourselves our out loud – creates an opening, a context for learning... regardless of the subject matter.

In this chapter we will go further and explore additional ways of understanding learning that can directly support leaders in more effectively creating and sustaining a workplace culture of innovation, creativity, adaptability and growth. Readers of *Language and the Pursuit of Happiness* will recognize many of these key concepts, as they were also introduced there. For new readers, we provide this exploration as we cover key aspects of learning, key dimensions of learning, that have proven to be helpful to leaders and teams of all sorts. The invitation here is to explore the ways in which you or your teams can benefit by incorporating these understandings, principles and practices into your key conversations and workplace processes.

When you make a conscious decision to enter into the types of learning we will cover here, you are purposefully intervening on your existing Way of Being. Depending on the nature of the learning, you may be directly impacting, shifting or updating your beliefs, your interpretations, your ways of understanding and ways of seeing things. You may be acquiring distinctions that enable you to walk into your organization and literally see patterns, positive behavior and negative behavior that was previously invisible to you. You may also be directly impacting your traditional emotional patterns, as well as your physical body. When you decide to engage in these types of learning, you are working directly with the Observer that you are, as shown below:

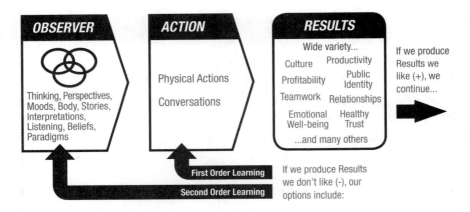

This is critical to notice: Learning in these areas – what has come to be known as Second Order Learning – opens us up to avenues of possibilities and options for new Action that are utterly invisible to us previously. It introduces an expanded "universe set" of options that serve as the starting point for making new choices and taking new actual Actions. And given that we are interested in producing and sustaining positive – and sometimes unprecedented – new Results for ourselves and our organizations, this is not a trivial claim.

This type of learning goes beyond utilitarian learning for the purpose of acquiring additional functional or technical know-how, for example. It goes far beyond simply adding additional layers of knowledge on top of what we already have. Here, we introduce the possibility of truly transformational change, as the learning is at the level of how we are "being" in the world. And this changes everything, since being precedes "doing" (taking Action) and "doing" drives "having" (achieving Results).

What we are inviting you to try on is a reversal of the traditional, widely-held message that virtually all of us have been bombarded with since we were conscious enough to watch TV, listen to the radio or read the advertising pages in a newspaper. Today's advertising and marketing industries, in a great many fields, are actively courting potential consumers by consistently reinforcing and promoting a particular link between having, doing and being. It may be explicit or implicit, out loud or in the background, but the linkage can be summarized as:

This widely-held orientation may be understood as: If you *have* this, you can then *do* that... which then causes or allows you to *be* whatever. One example might be: If you have this particular automobile, you can do things like drive fast and hug the road and cruise beautiful, scenic highways with your partner... which will enable you to be happy, or satisfied, or fulfilled. Another might be: If you have this particular suit, shirt and tie, you can do things like run meetings effectively and generate the respect of your peers... which will enable you to be successful, secure or confident. We could go on and on. This promise may be out in the open or somewhere in the background, but in our culture, it is there. It's ingrained in and underneath a steady stream of messages that we've gotten for many years. It's so pervasive and so built-in that it moves to the background of our thinking as one of the "givens," one of the "facts." It's often totally taken for granted

Now, there's nothing wrong with advertising and marketing, of course. We are simply pointing out the broad background or context in which our way of understanding and positioning learning is offered.

By focusing on learning at the level of our Way of Being, we operate with a different understanding of the relationships among being, doing and having. We introduce the possibility of bringing to awareness entirely new sets, classes, domains or categories of Action. We open a doorway that leads to enhanced awareness and new ways of understanding ourselves and what we are capable of, as well as the ways in which we may have been limiting our own progress and getting in the way of our own success.

Specifically speaking, what we offer in this book includes learning that dramatically expands leaders' range of possible Actions, especially in areas related to relationships, organizational culture and effective execution. By starting with your Way of Being, and by enabling you to take all new Actions from your new Way of Being, you become far more able to produce these types of desired Results.

Here, you will acquire the ability to much more purposefully and much more effectively have specific conversations that drive improvements in your most important relationships, as well as your organization's culture and levels of teamwork and productivity, as depicted below:

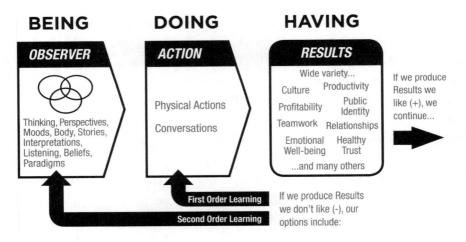

Many organizations today speak of core competencies; that is, of a set of skills or Actions or attributes that absolutely must exist in order for the organization to succeed. Many of us have come to this observation: maybe, for today and tomorrow, the "mother of all core competencies" for individuals and for organizations, is **learning how to learn**.

Learning is tied to language in some obvious and not-so-obvious ways. In addition, learning has a great deal to do with our bodies, not just with our heads, as well as with our moods and emotions. This chapter offers a powerful way to look at the process of learning, especially in a way that is relevant for adult learning, for the types of learning that occur within organizations, for learning in areas not confined to formal education.

Changing Our Model of Learning

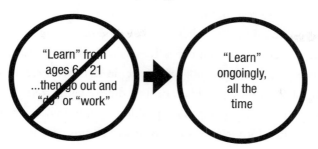

One way that we've shifted is in how we think about <u>when</u> learning occurs. Most of us are probably familiar with the circle on the left. This is a very traditional view, going back many years. This view says that in the early part of one's life, the learning takes place. This learning is adequate for whatever may be coming later in life. Once we're through learning, we then go out and "do" or "work" or "raise a family" or "live." At this point, we apply the learning – which we acquired earlier, and which is assumed to be adequate for what's coming later – in doing our jobs and living our lives.

Many of us have already embraced the right hand circle, the part of the model that offers that purposeful learning must occur ongoingly, all the time, through-out one's life. The line between our doing and our learning is now very blurry. In order to continue doing what we need to do, we must continue to learn. In fact, the expression *lifelong learner* has appeared on the business landscape, particularly in industries in which rapid, disruptive change is the most obvious. Many of us fully understand that our desired Results, in many domains, depend on our ability to continue to learn, to adapt, to re-invent, as we do what we do.

The Learning Formula

Let's explore a bit. For example, how many of us now, or at some point in our lives, learned how to ride a bike? Virtually everybody. So how did we learn to ride a bike? Did anybody read the book *How To Ride A Bike*? No! We learned by doing it, by shifting our weight from one side to the other, from leaning and turn-ing and pedaling, from training wheels and falling and trying again, with help and a friendly push. In other words, we learned to ride the bike by riding the bike.

We don't disregard that a type of learning occurs when we read something, and that in many ways the reading may be the first step. But look at us, in real life. How many of us would say we're better leaders, better managers, better parents, better swimmers, better speakers, better teachers, better carpenters, better architects, better campers, better doers of what we do than we were 10 or 20 or 30 years ago? And how did we get this way, how did we get better? We learned, by actually leading, managing, parenting, speaking, swimming, camping, teaching, by putting our bodies into it, by doing. And we call this practice.

To us, one of the best, and certainly one of the most simple definitions of learning is this:

Learning = Doing the thing (whatever is to be learned), while not being able to do the thing.

That is, learning to ride a bike = riding a bike while not being fully able to ride a bike. Learning to be a better manager = managing while you're not yet a "better manager." Learning to be a better parent = parenting while you're not yet a "better parent." We further claim:

Learning = Time + Practice.

We get better, we learn by practicing, by doing. It's not magic, it's cause and effect. So let's be clear – while learning about X or Y by reading may a important first step, we claim that without time and practice, learning does not occur.

Additionally, to reach a level of mastery and gain significant levels of competency, we see that the amount of practice and time which are often involved bring another element to light: the element we call **rigor**. Rigor may be defined here as "practicing even when you don't really feel like practicing!" In many situations, we can see very clearly that:

Learning = Time + Practice + Rigor.

A couple of other ways of looking at this come to mind here. First, a saying attributed to Vince Lombardi, the legendary coach of the Green Bay Packers: *Practice doesn't make perfect... perfect practice makes perfect.* And another one which is attributed to our friends at Newfield Network (as well as others): *Practice makes perfect... so be careful what you practice!*

These point to the notion that whatever we do over time, we get really good at. We get very competent, very effective at. Now, these may or may not be Actions which produce the Results we say we want, but we get really good at them anyway!

Learning About is Not the Same as Learning To Do

What would you have to observe in the real world before this statement would ever come out of your mouth: *"Bill learned auto mechanics."* Most of us would say that we'd have to observe Bill fixing a car, and that no matter how many books we have seen Bill read, we'd never say that he learned auto mechanics without his actually fixing a car, without doing the work. We may say *"Bill read 12 books"* but not *"Bill learned auto mechanics."* Now, of course, you may go pick up your car from Bill and find that he really did <u>not</u> "learn to do" auto mechanics!

Consider other examples from our everyday lives: *"John learned how to handle tough customers"* or *"Priya is managing that situation better"* or *"Sami didn't learn that X is needed before Y will occur."* In these and many other cases, we already know that learning and Action are connected. We have some notion already that learning has to do with an assessment that a person can take some Action, produce some Result, at time period B that they could not take or produce at time period A. When we see that, we say that learning has occurred. When we don't see it, we say that it hasn't.

Thus, we claim that learning <u>about</u> and learning <u>to do</u> are both real phenomena. Both are valid and both happen in the real world. But these are two very different phenomena, two very different things. Different Results get produced when we learn about something than when we learn to do something. We take different Actions (physical Actions as well as language Actions) in order to learn about something than we take when we're interested in learning to do something. This clearly moves us toward view of learning that has to do with Action, and away from the primary metaphor for learning being that of a lonely scholar, poring over a lamp, late at night, with books piled up everywhere.

Learning and Embodiment

Many Eastern traditions have long embraced a model of learning that many of us may just now be coming to understand. In this way of thinking, learning may be said to happen in steps or levels, as shown below:

1. Intellectual understanding. Learning "about" something.

2. Practice. Gaining experience. Doing.

3. Embodiment. Actualizing the learning. Being.

Many of us in the industrialized West tend to equate learning with Step 1, emphasizing this in many ways, and somehow forgetting the practice, the experience, the embodiment parts. Many of our schools tend to reinforce this, as do many of our organizations. In addition, the way learning is often portrayed by the mass media tends to also reinforce this. We'll talk about barriers to learning shortly – what many of the different barriers seem to have in common is that, in the end, they keep us from practicing.

The key, for us, is the interpretation that learning must include the body, that indeed learning occurs – in a tangible, physical way – in the body. New findings in the area of neurobiology tell us that every time we take a new Action, do a new thing, that new neural passageways are being activated and new (microscopic level) structures are being formed. Our brains and bodies are apparently incredibly plastic, able to be reshaped and malleable to our environment and Actions. We are literally becoming somebody new, out of the Actions we take in the world. We are producing a new structure, out of which new Actions are then more able and more likely to spring.

Rafael Echeverria captured this perfectly and powerfully in a workshop when he said: **We act according to how we are, and we do. <u>And</u> we also are, according to how we act.**

The Chilean biologist Humberto Maturana has led pioneering new work into the nature of living systems, into which human beings obviously fit. A key conclusion he's drawn is that living beings are closed systems and that we are structurally determined; that is, what's possible for living beings has to do with the structure we possess. How we respond to what our environment serves up for us has everything to do with us... and not so much to do with the environment. The environment is simply a trigger.

A second major conclusion is that human beings' structure is not fixed and permanent, that new Actions (including new conversations) on our part have an impact on our physical structure. If we change our structure, we create the possibility for taking new Action. And if we don't change our structure, we will find new Action to be impossible. In this sense, learning is literally embodied.

The Connection Between Learning and Interpretations

Many of us begin new Actions, new undertakings with the best intentions. We think about whatever it is — whether it's a new conversation with a difficult employee, or with our spouse, or a presentation in front of a new group, or a big meeting in which we have a new key role — and plan for it and rehearse it over and over in our heads. Two observations:

First, rehearsing something over and over in our heads is not the same as actually practicing it. What's missing? Right — the body, the movement, the physical piece. We simply must put our bodies into it. (Learning = Time & Practice). This is why actually having the conversation with someone ahead of time or going over the presentation out loud, with a listener present, can make a difference. As can going to the new meeting room and familiarizing yourself with the layout, and so forth.

And secondly, how many of us don't practice ahead of time, and then find that our bodies react dramatically during the moment that we're doing the new thing! This shows up as knees knocking, heart pounding, higher pulse rate, sweaty palms, lump in the throat, tightness in the chest, dry mouth... all sorts of physical changes. The next chapter deals directly with the relationship between our language, our moods and emotions and our physical bodies, but for now we can say that they absolutely influence and impact each other. Given this, these bodily reactions should come as no surprise. While our focus may be on having the conversation (language), we cannot avoid the fact that in order to have the conversation, our bodies — the physical side — will have a central role.

It's not a problem, in and of itself, that our bodies do what they do. This is simply the event that occurs. As we've talked about before, it's our explanations that really matter. Here's the key: How do we explain all these physical Actions? As we see it, there are at least two explanations, two primary ways of interpreting our bodily reactions here. Notice how different these interpretations are, as well as the different future Actions (and therefore different future Results) that are likely to arise from them:

- Interpretation 1: My body is doing this because I'm trying to do something I really shouldn't do. This is my body's way of saying run away, this is not for me, it's a bad situation and I made a big mistake by ever wanting to do this... and

- Interpretation 2: My body is doing this because it has little or no practice in this conversation or in this situation. This is my body's way of telling me that I'm a beginner here, and that more practice is needed for me to gain competence and confidence here.

We keep coming back to language, to conversations, to interpretations, to explanations – no matter what. We are the authors of our explanations, and these explanations are directly connected with learning, as they are the springboards for our Actions – or lack thereof.

Connection Between "Learning" and "Knowing"

When you say "I don't know X" or "I don't know Y"... in what sense *do* you know something? In other words, when you say "I don't know trigonometry," what *do* you know? How can these statements about not knowing also contain key elements of knowing?

Many readers will have seen this before, although perhaps not in the particular way we're attempting to frame it. For us, it's important enough to review. When you say or think "I don't know rocket science," what you're really saying or thinking is this:

I <u>know</u> that I don't know rocket science.

That is, you are aware of something out there called rocket science, and you're also aware that you don't know enough about it to teach it or to be a rocket engineer or whatever. You acknowledge the existence of the domain called rocket science, while at the same time acknowledge that you're not competent to take certain Actions and produce certain Results in that domain.

So if it's possible to know that we don't know (let's call this "ignorance"), is it also possible to not know that we don't know? Yes, of course! Let's call this a type of "blindness." We claim that all of us operate in some degree of blindness, all the time. There are many, many things that we don't know that we don't know. Socrates discussed this phenomenon a long time ago, in the context of wisdom. His claim was that he was wiser than another man, even if he and the other man both didn't know X. The distinction he made was that the other man assumed that he knew X when he really didn't (he was "blind") while Socrates assumed that he did not know from the outset.

What are the consequences, then, on learning? Here's a big one: If you don't know that you don't know Leadership Theory X or the latest inventory management technique, how many questions will you ever ask about Leadership Theory X or that particular inventory management technique? Zero. Leadership Theory X and that inventory management technique just never come up for you, do they? No, they don't. Because they're off your radar screen. In these situations, we don't even acknowledge the existence of the domains themselves.

So far, we've said that :

- Ignorance = "I don't know" (but I know that I don't know).
- Blindness = "I don't know that I don't know".

As we mentioned in Chapter 2, when we say, "I don't know," we're not describing anything as much as we're producing something. What do we produce when we say, either to ourselves our out loud, "I don't know"? **We produce an opening for learning where one did not previously exist**. Out of nothing, we declare into being a space for learning, a context in which something (learning) is suddenly very likely and available. This points again to a central theme – the capacity of our language to generate, to create, as well as to describe.

Taking this one step further – it's also possible to be aware of the phenomenon of blindness, or to be unaware of the phenomenon of blindness:

- Being aware of blindness = *I know* that I don't know that I don't know.

- Being unaware of blindness = *I don't know* that I don't know that I don't know.

Without (hopefully) getting too tangled up here, let's now make a few claims:

- Ignorance (declaring "I don't know") is a key first step in learning – regardless of the particular subject matter involved.

- Ignorance is not the opposite of learning, but is the threshold of learning. It is the necessary "jumping off point" from which learning can begin. If we can't get to "I don't know," we're going to have a difficult time learning – no matter what the subject matter.

- Being unaware of our blindnesses is a big barrier to our learning. This shows up, often, as denying the new as impossible. We say things like "it can't be that way," and close ourselves to new possibilities. And in a time of ongoing change, this is not trivial.

- Learning is critical for our organizations, no matter what industry we are in, given the world of change that is the background in which we operate. Because of the impact of learning on our ability to ongoingly adapt, create, innovate, modify, be flexible, improve – we claim that learning how to learn may be the single most important competency for sustainable organizational success.

- Learning occurs "in the body." Learning = time, practice and rigor.

- Learning is strongly connected to language. We "speak into being" for ourselves a context that either supports our learning or makes our learning very unlikely (regardless of the external situation or events).

Friends and Enemies of Learning

Given the importance of learning, especially in a time of ongoing change, let's discuss ways in which our learning can be supported, as well as ways in which our learning is discouraged or not supported. In other words, what helps us learn?

And what seems to keep us from learning, seems to keep us from taking the necessary Actions that equal learning?

Enemies of Learning

- Unwillingness to admit "I don't know"
- When you don't know that you don't know, but you act as if you do
- Being unaware that we live in blindness (arrogance)
- "I should already know"
- "I have to be clear about everything, all the time"
- Forgetting the domain of emotions and its impact on learning
- Distrust
- Confusing "knowing" with having opinions or information
- Addiction to novelty
- Addiction to answers
- Not granting permission to be taught
- Making everything overly significant
- Making everything trivial
- Living in permanent assessments or judgments
- Living in the belief "I cannot learn, given who I am"
- Forgetting the body as a domain of learning

Friends of Learning

- Willingness to declare "I don't know"
- Listening
- Openness
- Respect and admiration
- Willingness to question your questions
- A mood of perplexity and inquiry

This summary, originally developed by Julio Olalla and shared with us by friends at Education for Living and Newfield, contains what we describe as primary supporters (friends) and non-supporters (barriers or enemies) of learning. Notice that many of the barriers to learning are not physical barriers. That is, the barriers to our learning appear to have a great deal to do with that little voice inside (language), as opposed to something physical. Let's take a closer look at several of these.

Unwillingness to admit "I don't know" (= Unwillingness to declare Beginnerhood)

Rest assured, if you are not willing or able to say "I don't know" from time to time in learning situations, not much learning will take place. By declaring "I already know" we are producing (not describing) a context in which learning is simply highly unlikely. For example, how many of us have ever tried to teach someone else something, when the prospective learner thought they already knew it? What's your experience as a teacher in those situations? The single most popular answer to that question is "frustrated." And how much learning took place for the other person? Not much. Big barrier to learning. Not a physical barrier, but a powerful barrier nonetheless.

We see this as being connected to a moodspace of arrogance, with the view that nobody around us could possibly have anything that could be valuable or useful, that it's virtually impossible that others know things that we don't. Moods and emotions have an obvious impact on our ability to learn. In fact, becoming a better Observer of our own moods and of their accompanying internal conversations is a key place to start for those interested in improving their capacity to learn.

"I don't know" can be seen as a declaration of awareness that you're currently unable to perform effectively in a particular domain, based on some standard. That's it – it's not a character flaw. What's missing is your ability to take certain Actions and produce certain Results. And so out of this declaration, you move purposefully and more openly into learning. Without this declaration, the whole context is quite different. Without this declaration, in the end, you're not going to learn very much – regardless of the subject matter.

What you resist, persists. To us, this simple expression says it all. By not acknowledging (in language, of course) the blind spot or the lack of knowledge or lack of competency, no new Actions are seen as needed or valuable. And out of this lack of Action, of course, no new Results are produced.

A quote attributed to Carl Rogers seems perfect here: *The curious paradox is that once I accept myself as I am, then I can change.* Think about it. Here, the power of this declaration is clear, as it opens the door to an entirely new future, an entirely new set of possibilities.

When you don't know that you don't know, but you act as if you do

Clearly, this is a big barrier to learning. It is precisely because we don't know that we don't know that learning is difficult here. We don't acknowledge the blind spot. We are blissfully unaware of the whole range of possibilities that knowing could bring. If we were aware of our not knowing, we may declare ourselves beginners and move into learning... so the first step is to notice. The first step is to become aware. Back to the Big Eye.

Being unaware that we live in blindness

This unawareness also points to a type of arrogance. Here, we don't acknowledge the fact that each of us, each human being, by virtue of how and when we were raised and the life experiences we've had to date, brings to the table perspectives and traditions and capabilities that are uniquely our own. And of course, there's no way that we could possibly know about all of the others and their unique aspects. We've lived our whole lives up to this point totally unaware even of the existence of them!

In some ways the perspectives and capabilities of others differ greatly from our own, and in other ways the differences are more subtle. Our arrogance shows up when we're not able to acknowledge that it's possible and quite likely that new distinctions, new ways of seeing, new concepts and capabilities actually do exist and have existed for a long time. It's just that given our particular history and the particular Observer that we have become, we've not been aware of them.

"I should already know."

This is common for many leaders, especially as we move upward through the ranks of an organization or as we gain experience or age. As we perform and are promoted into jobs or situations with more or different types of responsibilities, we often hear this inside. And if we do this enough, we call it "*should-ing on your-self*" and it doesn't help. We can move through life feeling as if we're "imposters," fearful of being "found out," fearful that others will find out that we really don't know what they think we know (or what we think they think we should know!) We can spend so much energy telling ourselves that we should already know, when it may be more valuable to simply accept that in this moment we do not know, declare ourselves a beginner, and move into learning.

"I have to be clear/perfect about everything, all the time."

Or "All my questions must be answered." "I have to be perfect from the get-go." "I cannot take a chance of making any mistakes or doing anything doat doesn't live up by my standards of perfection…"

These beliefs, that unless every single one of my questions is answered fully and unless I can be absolutely certain that everything will go perfectly right from the start, I can't take the first steps … are barriers to learning because they are barriers to taking Action. Think about the phenomenon of procrastination. For example, with 10 items on your to-do list, you may move very quickly into the 7 for which you already have all the answers. But the 3 items that have some uncertainty, some open-endedness about the outcome or how to go about it… these seem to get bumped to tomorrow's list, then the next day, and so on.

Have you ever noticed, though, that sometimes the answers come once we begin moving, once we've started taking some Action? This is a fairly common phenomenon, that of the answers "coming to us" once we begin moving. But if we never move till we're 100% certain of everything, we may never move, and thus never learn. Then here come all the bad consequences of not learning in a time of change. And in times of relentless change, not being 100% certain of some things may be the rule, rather than the exception.

Forgetting the domain of emotions and its impact on learning

As mentioned earlier, emotions are strongly and directly connected to learning. By not taking them into account, we leave out a key and inter-connected element of the whole picture. Emotional spaces of anger, resentment and cynicism, for example, simply do not provide a context in which learning is at all likely to occur. They provide a context in which punishing and getting even or withdrawing are quite likely, however, given any particular trigger. Make sense? Imagine situations in which you have found yourself angry or resentful or cynical. Were you open to learning then? Was learning even available to you at all in those times? We all have had the experience of emotions influencing what we do and how we do it, in many ways.

It's possible for each of us to become much stronger Observers of our own moods and emotions, and to then become much more active in influencing and designing them. The first step is to acknowledge that we each have moods, we live in them all the time, and they are continually impacting our ability to learn and to be open to new possibilities for adapting and changing. A later chapter will deal more directly with moods and emotions, and will provide some practical tools for more consciously and effectively designing and working with them at work, at home and everywhere in between.

Distrust

Distrust is an enemy of learning, for a number of reasons. Trust and distrust can be seen as moods/emotional spaces, as well as assessments (judgments) about someone or something. Let's explore briefly before moving on with other barriers to learning.

Without trust it's very difficult to imagine a learner finding and keeping a competent teacher or coach. Such a relationship requires trust in order to be successful. Trust is also required in many cases for the learner to begin trying new Actions, even if he/she doesn't fully understand why the new Actions are required. And if the new Actions are not taken (no practice), then no new Results get produced.

The movie *Karate Kid* comes to mind here… the part about "wax on, wax off". The old master had the new student wax his car over and over; the student was frustrated and did not immediately follow the instructions. What the student didn't know was that the repetitive motion of putting wax on and taking wax off was exactly the motion needed to build "muscle memory" which would be extremely useful to him in his further development. Ultimately, trust was required in order for him to take the new Action, build the new competencies. Trust was required in order for him to learn.

As moods or emotional spaces, trust and distrust are the contexts, the backgrounds out of which Actions (or non-Actions) spring. This background is the framework against which all possibilities are considered and decisions made.

Distrust impacts relationships at all levels, and this matters greatly because a great deal of learning occurs socially, with and through others. By limiting or damaging relationships – which is a predictable byproduct of ungrounded distrust over time – we limit our ability to be with people and we limit our opportunities to learn with and from them.

We claim that *I trust you* and *I don't trust you* are declarations that we make, based on four assessments or judgments that we come to. (We'll cover assessments and declarations in more depth in later chapters). These four types of judgments are:

- Our assessment of <u>sincerity</u>; that the other person's external conversations are not being contradicted by their internal conversations; that the other person's Actions are consistent with what they've declared they believe and what they say is important to them

- Our assessment of <u>competency</u>; that the other person is able to do what he or she has proposed or promised to do; that they possess the knowledge, skills, aptitudes, capacity and resources needed in order to accomplish the task at hand

- Our assessment of <u>reliability</u> or <u>credibility</u>; that the other person has kept his or her promises in the past, and will continue to do so in the future

- Our assessment of <u>care</u>; that the other person has our best interests in mind and will make decisions and take Actions that reflect his or her concern about our well-being and what we hold to be important.

If we have negative assessments in any one of these, we then declare that we "don't trust" someone. When we have distrust and we look a little closer, we can usually find that at least one of these is missing. Either I assess that you're not sincere when you say you'll do something, or I assess you're not competent to do what you say you'll do, or I assess that you've broken so many commitments in the past that I can't risk another one this time, or I assess that you don't care enough about me and my concerns to allow me to risk something of value now.

I can trust Dr. Jones to fix my gall bladder, but not my brakes. Here, the issue is competency. Or I can not trust in a situation in which I think the person is sincere and competent to do what they say they'll do, but I've got evidence that in each of the last 3 times we did things together, promises weren't kept and things fell through the cracks. Here, the issue is reliability. And out of these different assessments, we can have different conversations, we can dance in a different way and move in a different direction.

Trust always involves risk, because no matter how well we try to assess, the other person may take new Action which is different and unexpected. The people we extend trust to may let us down. Our assessments of sincerity, competency, reliability or care may prove to be off-target. Risk is involved. The Trust Matrix that follows provides a summary of where we end up, given two variables:

- How competent we are at making grounded assessments in 4 areas: sincerity, competency, reliability and care

- How willing we are to take the risks inherent in trusting.

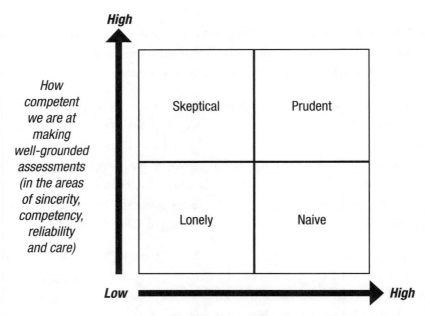

How willing we are to take risks involved in trusting

Not being able to distinguish between "prudence" and "distrust" is absolutely an enemy of learning. Prudence has to do with making grounded assessments (connecting my opinions to facts and having some conscious standards against which to judge, coupled with a willingness to risk in certain situations) while distrust is an unwillingness to risk, unwillingness to coordinate, almost "no matter what." In the end, with enough distrust comes loneliness and involuntary hermithood.

Not trusting, even when there may be evidence that some trust is warranted, is the upper left quadrant – what we've labeled skepticism. Skepticism done well can be healthy and helpful; skepticism done poorly looks and feels more like cynicism and usually doesn't help our relationships or our Results.

Extending trust when there are solid grounds to do so, when some evidence for trusting can be pointed to is trusting with our eyes open, and is considered to be prudent. This is a very powerful orientation, one that lends itself greatly to learning, building relationships and interacting, coordinating with others in a positive way.

However, extending trust without solid grounds, or extending trust when there may even be evidence to suggest that not trusting may be wiser is the same as being taken advantage of. On our chart, this is what we call naïve or gullible. It can also be seen as the "shadow side" of optimism, or "optimism done poorly." Not a great place from which to learn.

We highly recommend Charles Feltman's excellent book, *The Thin Book of Trust*, for those interested in a very practical guide for building and rebuilding trust within organizations.

Confusing "knowing" with having opinions or information

Imagine yourself on an airplane, and the stewardess comes on over the intercom: "Ladies and gentlemen, you'll be pleased to know that our captain today isn't actually a licensed pilot ... (pause) But he <u>does</u> have a lot of opinions about flying!" In this situation, we can readily see the difference between knowing how to fly and having opinions about flying. Knowing how to fly = capacity for performing certain Actions, while "recreational opinions" are an entirely different thing.

Addiction to novelty

Here we see the inability to stick with anything long enough to see it through. Big barrier to learning. It's a constant shifting and changing direction, and it shows up as college students changing majors 9 times during the first 2 years on campus. It shows up as organizations chasing every management or leadership "fad of the month" and implementing in such a way that if dramatic Results aren't seen quickly (and usually without any real change on the part of senior leadership), the effort is abandoned in lieu of yet another. It appears as individuals changing careers or hobbies or projects very frequently, as well as in a number of other ways. Learning = time and practice, and in these situations not enough time and practice are allowed.

Addiction to answers

Have you ever known someone who, no matter what the question, always has an answer? The mailman Cliff Clavin of the old sitcom Cheers comes to mind here. On the show, Cliff appeared to be utterly incapable of saying "I don't know." For Cliff and for the rest of us in real life, this obsession with providing answers is connected to difficulty in learning.

Here's a thought. We have, in our society, whole systems for the purpose of qualifying answers. These systems are integrated throughout our entire educational process. The name we give to this process of qualifying answers is grading. What if, on the other hand, we had a system of qualifying the best questions?

What if we had teachers and leaders who convened sessions in which questions would be listened to and those deemed "best" would be recognized and acted upon? Would this lead to a new opening for learning, to a context in which learning would be likely? We say it would. But we'll never move in that direction as long as we think learning and knowing are only about "having the answers."

Not granting permission to be taught

Not granting permission may be directly connected to distrust. It's unlikely that you'll give someone permission to teach you if you don't trust him or her. The teacher-learner relationship is declared into being only if the learner gives permission for the teacher to teach. It's also possible that not granting permission has more to do with arrogance, with a moodspace and belief that we already know it anyway, so what can this teacher possibly teach us? Regardless, learning is not very likely to occur at all.

Making everything overly significant

This is holding every single part of our past and our histories with a great deal of drama and heaviness and significance. It's as if nobody could have possibly had the things happen to them that have happened to us, and we relate and live these stories with great drama and assign tremendous weight and meaning to them.

The way we hold our experiences (which of course we do in language, not with our hands) has a great deal to do with whether or not we're able to produce the emotional space needed for designing something new.

We would say that some lightness here is very helpful – being able to laugh at ourselves is a big friend of learning. At the same time, it's important to be able to get serious for the purpose of generating the commitment needed to move forward. But seriousness is not the same as significance.

Making everything trivial

The opposite of significance is triviality, being unwilling to ever let the conversation get serious enough to get to the real issues. It shows up when we crack a joke just at the time when something important is about to be revealed, or when we constantly divert or deflect everything using humor.

Living in permanent assessments or judgments

Here, the barrier to learning shows up as an inability to ever update our assessments (opinions) about ourselves, others, and everything else. This is usually consistent with the notion that they aren't opinions anyway – they're the Truth! Another way of describing this is not knowing the difference between "having" opinions and "being" our opinion. It's as if ten years ago we generated certain opinions about X, and from that day forward are not willing to look at any new data or listen to opinions different from our own. Again, in many of these cases we don't even see our opinions as opinions at all, and therefore render ourselves powerless to change them. Big barrier to learning, especially in times of change.

Living in the belief "I cannot learn, given who I am"

Here's an example to illustrate this one. Imagine a doctor delivering a new baby, and the doctor exclaims "Oh, this is a geometry baby... this baby, later on, will have the ability to learn geometry and be an engineer... that's great and wonderful... the future looks great for this baby." Now imagine the doctor delivering another baby and saying "Oh, unfortunately, this is a non-geometry baby... this baby, no matter what, will never be able to learn geometry... there's a built-in organ, right behind the spleen, called the geometry inhibitor, and this baby's got it... this baby is fundamentally, inherently incapable of ever learning geometry... too bad."

But think about it: If you or I have a belief that "I can never learn geometry," it shows up in real life as a profound pre-disposition to take no new Action in the domain of geometry! The belief sets a context in which new Actions on our part will be highly unlikely. Because learning = time and practice, we can predict then that we will produce no new Results in the domain of geometry. This, of course, then allows us to look back and say "See? I told you I could never learn geometry." Well of course not – we didn't <u>do</u> anything!

Which came first, the belief or the Result? We say the belief came first, and this belief lives in language. It's a story, an interpretation, and it impacts our mood. It's a profound barrier to learning because it serves as a pre-disposition to take <u>no</u> Action. No new Action, no new Results – remember Observer – Action – Results. Not magic, all cause and effect.

Another example here is how many older adults may relate to computers and technology. When confronted with a situation in which learning to do something new on a computer, for example, is required, let's imagine we hear the following: "I could never learn that. You young people do all the computer stuff, I'm too old for that." or "You can't teach an old dog new tricks." or "A leopard can't change his spots – I'm low-tech all the way, and that's the way it is."

Let's notice something important here: these interpretations take us away from the one thing that is needed in order to learn to do anything – that of actually practicing, of actually doing something, of actually taking some new Actions. In order to learn how to use computers you have to, at some point or another, "mash the button!" Conversely, because many young people just jump right in and start pushing buttons and tweaking levers (taking some Action... practicing), they seem to learn rather quickly.

This phenomenon is, of course, not limited to math or computers. It has to do with virtually every aspect of our lives. We are constantly encountering situations in which we need to do things we haven't done before, in order to produce some new Results. Our beliefs are incredibly powerful filters through which we see the world. They absolutely impact our orientation toward some possible Actions and away from others. And (back to the Big Eye), many of us are not very aware of this.

These types of beliefs seem to stay hidden from view, and as long as they do, we can do nothing about them. Until we can see them, until we take a look at them, they've got us, we don't have them. In our roles as coaches, much of what we do is connected to supporting people in this way. Being able to see and articulate what have historically been hidden or unseen beliefs is almost always a powerful starting point for designing something different. We touched on the impact of our beliefs in Chapter 4, and will also return to them in a later chapter.

Forgetting the body as a domain of learning

We say that learning occurs in the body more than in the head. Recall one definition of learning, that *Learning = time + practice*. Not practicing is the same as not putting your body into it. No practice, no new Results. We focus so much on "head learning" and memorizing that we forget that learning has to do with building capacity for new Action, which requires that we "do" the thing that's to be learned.

Do you notice any of these "enemies of learning" in your own life? You may find value in listing the barriers to learning which seem to show up for you, those which seem to get in your way. In moving through the rest of the book, you can then make connections back to these as you're considering how to best actually move forward with new Action.

Let's take a look now at some **friends of learning**. We say that these can greatly support us in our learning, regardless of the type of learning we're involved in.

Willingness to declare "I don't know" (= Willingness to declare Beginnerhood)

This is perhaps the most obvious friend of learning – our capacity to declare "I don't know." This is an act of consciously declaring into being a context in which learning is likely and available. As we said earlier, this declaration of ignorance is not the opposite of learning but the threshold of learning. It's the necessary first step for learning to occur.

As adults, and especially as successful adults, many of us find this difficult. One of our favorite expressions here is: *Success is a learning disability*. What is meant by this? How can success be anything but great? We all know people that, by virtue of their success, are utterly closed to learning. They reach a point where they never allow themselves to say "I don't know." They assume they already know whatever it is they need to know. They are supremely confident that what they did in the past that got them where they are in the present will be all they need to take them to where they want to go in the future. Maybe. But probably not, especially in a time of ongoing change.

Listening

Imagine a person who has declared that they want to learn something, while at the same time showing no interest or ability to listen to anybody around them. It's very difficult to imagine such a person learning, isn't it? In a wide variety of situations, whether we listen and the ways that we listen are strongly connected to our ability to learn. As we covered in Chapter 4, we say that listening is far more than passively receiving objective information; rather, listening is active and generative and can serve to strongly orient or pre-dispose us toward learning… or away from it.

Openness

We say we learn more when we're "open to learning" than if we're "closed to learning." These are obviously metaphors, as our heads are not physically open or physically closed. This posture of openness is connected to our awareness that we don't already know everything there is to know! Here, the open and closed refer to our internal conversations, our listening, our mental flexibility, our ability to "get off it" and be receptive to the possibility that another's perspective may provide us with the opportunity to learn something new. *In this way of thinking, finding out more about something isn't automatically equated to agreeing with it.* For the Actions of exploring, of moving into more questions and speculating about more possibilities, this type of openness is needed.

Respect and admiration

Do you learn more from someone you respect or admire than from someone you don't? Most of us say yes, we do. Is it possible, then, to increase the number of people that we "respect"? We say it is, that this attitude or mood or state of mind can be designed on purpose, for the sake of our own learning.

Willingness to question your questions

Have you ever noticed that every single question you ever ask, no matter what the question, is already resting on top of something that you are assuming or presupposing? We claim that this is so – that no matter what, our questions are not "objective" or "valid" in and of themselves; they are always built on top of something we have already presupposed.

A powerful way of exploring this, first learned from Julio Olalla, is: "What is the orbit of the sun as it revolves around the earth?" What are we presupposing here? Here, we are presupposing that the sun does indeed revolve around the earth, and for quite a few years, many people chased that question! The presupposition was wrong. Another question: "What's wrong with Amy?" What are we presupposing here? That something is indeed wrong with Amy. Sometimes the presupposition is meaningless and rather trivial, and sometimes it's not. Sometimes the presupposition is everything.

A big friend of learning is our ability to question our questions, to not take for granted the foundation on which our questions sit, but instead examine those presuppositions on purpose, explicitly and overtly. What is it about me, the Observer I am, that has me produce these questions? Why do you, in the same situation as me, produce different questions? This is interesting. Now we're in a space which is very conducive for learning. It's not a physical space, but it's very real.

Moods of Learning

We've touched on moods a bit already, and will move into them more directly in an upcoming chapter. But for now, would you agree that people have moods? Most people quickly say yes, we all do. Would you say that organizations, departments and families also have moods? Most people say yes, they all do. States, countries, time periods have moods… we can go on and on.

We claim that moods have everything to do with learning, or lack thereof. A mood of optimism, for example, is a far different pre-disposition, a far different "orientation" towards learning and taking Action in the world than is a mood of cynicism. We can say that all moods are not created equal, in that different moods produce very real differences in how we orient ourselves toward Action (or not).

This, in turn, absolutely impacts the Actions we actually take (or don't take) and thus the Results we achieve (or don't achieve). And the key – we often don't even notice that this is happening.

For example, your mood as you're reading this book impacts the way you take in, interpret and orient yourself toward the material, how well you're able to step back and observe yourself and acknowledge situations in which your Actions (or lack of Action) impacted certain outcomes and Results, and so on. Your mood-space directly impacts the degree to which learning may occur. Let's look at a few particular moods and their impact on learning.

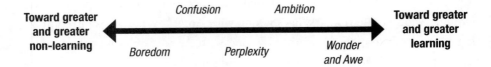

To tee all of these up, let's consider this question: What is our orientation towards "the new?" That is, how do we orient ourselves or relate to anything that is new, novel, unforeseen, unprecedented, possibly also unexpected? What is our stance – and our colleagues' and employees' stance – toward things that are new? Consider this, as well as the predictable Results that are produced, as we touch on a few key moodspaces and their relationship to learning.

Let's take a look – what are the "background conversations" for someone in **Boredom**? These may sound familiar: "There's nothing new for me to learn here, no matter what. There is no possibility that anything here will be of interest or value to me. Whatever this new thing is, I don't care." It's absolutely no coincidence that bored people do not learn very much! The internal dialogue simply is not conducive to learning at all.

Confusion comes with internal conversations similar to: "I don't know what's going on here, and I don't like it. Whatever this new thing is, I don't fully understand it and I don't like that I don't fully understand. It's not okay with me. It shouldn't be this way." In this moodspace, a lot of the energy seems to be around how "wrong" it is that we don't understand and how it should not be this way. And in this moodspace, learning is not very likely.

Please notice that we're not saying "Never be bored or confused" or that it's somehow "wrong" to be bored or confused. Virtually all of us have spent some time in boredom and confusion, at one point or another. The key observation here is that people who spend <u>a lot</u> of time in these moods do not learn very much. The end Result of being in these moods a lot is that learning is not supported very much, learning doesn't occur very much. And without learning to take new Actions, we don't produce new Results (back to Observer – Action – Results). Again, this is no problem if we're steadily producing only the Results that we want. But it becomes important if we're not.

Moving now into moods that support learning, we define **Perplexity** or being perplexed as not knowing everything about the new thing, the given subject or situation, and being okay with not knowing. It represents a shift "up" from Confusion. We still know that we don't know, but here, we're more OK with it. We're not beating ourselves up because we don't know. We simply accept that at this moment, we don't know, and this is the starting point for what's next. We're perplexed, and with this softer stance comes an opening for learning.

Can you feel the difference between this and **Confusion?** This orientation, this moodspace, this internal dialogue, brings with it some openness, some acceptance, and a much greater possibility that learning will occur. Many of us have experienced firsthand the shift from Confusion to Perplexity, though we may not have called it that or used the same words we're using here.

Have you ever been confused or frustrated about something new that you weren't "getting," and reached a point where you just said to yourself "OK, I know I'll get it, let's just relax and see what happens. It'll be all right." You stopped beating yourself up for not knowing, or you stopped blaming someone or something or your background for not preparing you better, or you stopped holding it as so significant that you don't know, or whatever. The shift seems to be one of acceptance, of OK-ness, that it's okay that we don't know. And with this shift in mood – which is absolutely connected to a shift in internal conversation – comes a shift in possibilities for learning.

Moving further up the scale we see **Wonder**. Here, the internal dialogue may be more like "I don't know about this new thing or circumstance or situation, I don't know fully what's going on here, and isn't that neat! I don't fully understand everything, and what excellent opportunities this represents!" Similarly, we say that **Awe** is a moodspace that brings with it this same embrace of possibilities and not knowing, sprinkled with profound joy and big doses of gratitude for just being able to be here.

Two key questions: Given these moodspaces as a framework, where would you say most little kids, most small children, live? What are the predominant, "natural" moods of kids 2, 3, and 4 years old? Most of us would say that little kids live in Wonder and Awe most of the time. Next question: Do little kids learn a lot or a little? Most of us have experiences that lead us to say that little kids are sponges, they learn a lot. And it is absolutely no coincidence.

Levels of Learning and Competence

We offer that our orientation toward learning, what we say learning is and what it isn't, how we understand learning and approach learning can land us in one of two major camps: <u>Suffering</u> (ineffectiveness, ongoing problems, undesired Results) or <u>Effectiveness</u> (success, growth, desired Results). This framework, called Scales of Excellence, was initially shared with us through work at Education for Living. It is a simple yet powerful way of framing our growth and learning, and also for bringing us a measure of satisfaction and fulfillment along the journey.

Suffering / Problems / Poor Results

Bull-in-a-china-shop
Unaware, and unaware that they are unaware. Oblivious to any standards of acceptable practices in the community. No ability to listen for the mistakes being committed. "Innocent." Causes substantial upset and problems around themselves.

Jerk
Pretender; confusion; maximum problems and distress. Knows that he/she is having problems and is ineffective in dealing with the jerkiness. Knows standard practices and does not follow them. Camouflages reality with stories, explanations and excuses. Seeks no authority or respected advice. Creates "breakdowns" all around themselves.

Effectiveness / Learning / Positive Results

Entrance or Beginner - Willing. Declares an honest state of not knowing. Acknowledges that he/she is not competent; no pretense here. Declares a teacher/coach. Grants and respects authority. Produces minimal trust.

Minimal Competence - Produces to certain minimal standards; requires supervision. Takes care of some problems, not yet able to anticipate problems. Emerging capacity. Produces caution and uncertainty.

Competence - Stability; can deliver standard expected performance in the specific area. Standard practices have become "transparent." Is competent, no pretending. Anticipates and deals with problems. Produces trust and earns respect.

Virtuoso - Fully transparent, performance is assessed as excellent, with reliable consistency. Demonstrates style, individuality, imagination, flair. Admired by others. Is gaining public recognition.

Master - Invents new practices; innovates while creating new standards. Produces new students. Has become a public figure. Participates in design of entire discourse.

Let's first take a look at the side of ineffectiveness, of unhappiness, of non-learning, of undesired Results.

Bull-in-a-china-shop

A Merrill Lynch commercial several years back showed a huge longhorn bull, wandering around in a beautiful and well-inventoried china and crystal shop, going aisle to aisle, trotting up and down the store… and not breaking a single thing. We know that in real life, the bull would cause major upset, breaking beautiful, valuable items left and right. And the bull's not doing this on purpose, he's not being mean, he's not really aware of it – he's just being a bull.

Have you ever known a person who, from time to time, seems to operate like the bull? They just don't seem to see what they're doing. This can happen to any of us. For example, is it possible that we could gather a bunch of our friends and colleagues together, fly to a foreign country, and within 10 minutes be offending people all around? Is this possible? Of course! And we find that we really don't have to go as far as another country. We can do this with people from a different state, or a different region within the same state. Regardless of the specifics, this is the bull in Action – causing undesired Results and upset, while being innocent and unaware, sleeping gloriously at night.

Said another way, the bull doesn't know he doesn't know – he's operating in some way in blindness, and producing Results from this blindness.

Jerk

Let's now contrast showing up as a Bull with having the public identity of a Jerk – someone who is causing upset, but in this case he or she knows the standards and chooses to violate them anyway.

For example, let's say you take a new job, first day, and you're told there's a 9:00 staff meeting this and every Monday morning. You attend, but arrive a few minutes late because of some insurance paperwork you were finishing up. At about 9:20 your cell phone goes off and you excuse yourself, trying to be polite and discreet as you back away from the table to take the call.

When you get back you figure you'll get to know your new colleagues, so you tap the guy next to you and introduce yourself (rather quietly, because the meeting is still going on). You may even try to "lighten things up" by telling a joke or two to your neighbor on the left. As the meeting moves into a discussion of some division that seems to have nothing to do with you, you decide you may as well break into that ham and egg biscuit you brought.

Let's also say that, unbeknownst to you, this staff meeting has some definite rules, do's and don'ts... and has had, for years. The main rules which simply must be adhered to are:

- Everyone show up on time – do <u>not</u> be late to this meeting. Actually, a minute or two before 9:00 is preferred.

- Only bring a notepad, calendar and pencil/pen into the meeting. No other materials are to be brought in.

- Coffee is ok; no food is allowed.

- No cell phones, pagers, or other electronic devices.

- And nobody talks until the boss recognizes you.

These were the rules, widely known by everyone – but you! Here, you show up as a bull in a china shop. You're causing upset all around yourself, being totally unaware, and somehow innocent in the whole process.

Let's now say that a colleague pulls you aside and lets you know clearly about the ground rules for this meeting and how important they are... and next Monday morning you still arrive late, though not as late as the first meeting. You have a little side conversation with the guy next to you, then answer a quick cell phone call, as you're finishing the last few bites of your breakfast biscuit. If you do this a time or two, you get to show up as a "jerk." You create for yourself the public identity of "jerk." If you keep doing this, *you begin to achieve full jerkhood in the world!*

Here, you've been made aware of the standards and that you're producing negative Results, and you choose to continue taking the Actions anyway. After a few weeks, when someone asks "Who is (insert your name here)?" the answer that seems to leap from everyone's lips is "Oh, he (or she) is a jerk!" And in many workplace cultures, there's no "space" for others to bring this to your attention; the context hasn't been set for these types of conversations to occur, so you end up being blind to how you're showing up for others, how you're being perceived. And moving forward you may keep wondering why good things aren't happening in your life, why you don't get the promotions you deserve, and so on.

It's important here to be clear that we're not making a claim on who the "real you" is, or what your "core being" is. We are simply pointing out that in this case, your public identity is that of a jerk. That's how you are showing up at work. That's who you "are" to them. And as we've said – the world does not interact with who you think you are. The world interacts with what it sees, with your public identity – and you can either be aware of this or not. It's precisely because of this that being aware of our public identity is so valuable.

Levels of Effectiveness

Let's say you want to move away from the "negative" side – no learning, no new Results, no success or satisfaction – and begin a journey of learning, of increasing your ability and competency in a certain area. How do you begin? For starters, step one is a language step. It is for you to declare, either publicly or internally: "I don't know." This declaration is the catalyst for learning, producing an opening where none existed before. This declaration is the threshold of learning, the starting point from which learning can begin. With this declaration you move over to the Effectiveness side of the chart.

Beginner

This is the first level of ability, the first level of competency. We all know what beginners are like, in any area. They are not very proficient at doing whatever they're doing, and they require assistance and close supervision. They trust and are willing to learn from the teacher.

A beginner is fully aware that he or she is not competent in certain areas (hence you will hear beginners speak "I don't know"). Beginners know that they don't know. It is precisely this awareness of not knowing that moves us into "beginner-hood" in the first place. Learning begins when we "declare ourselves a beginner," and we can all do this, at anytime. A key question for leaders and for all of us: Do you give yourself and others permission to be beginners at anything? Because – like the umpire – we declare beginnerhood into being. We speak it so.

Gaining competency in making and practicing this declaration is central to our ability to learn – regardless of subject matter. And in times of relentless, ongoing change, this is required for us to remain relevant, competent and successful.

Minimally Competent

Here the person has learned to do some, but not all of the new Actions, and still requires a fair amount of supervision. Progress has been made, but the degree of proficiency is not yet where others fully trust this person on his or her own, in this area.

Competent

Here, trust is achieved. The person can perform X or Y without direct supervision and can handle many types of unexpected "breakdowns" or "problems" or "issues" successfully.

Virtuoso

Above competency is the level we call virtuoso. Here, high competency is achieved. People at this level do what they do as if it's "transparent" to them. They appear to not be explicitly focusing on it, and they've done it so long, perhaps, or do it so well that it seems to "flow." They handle many types of significant breakdowns or problems with what appears to be fluid ease.

NASCAR drivers, for example, are virtuosos at driving stock cars. Many aspects of driving appear transparent to them; they don't, for example, consciously consider every shift or brake or turn. With lots of practice, they've learned – their bodies have learned, so to speak, and now many of these Actions occur without conscious consideration. This frees them up for "higher level" things, like race strategy and specific tactics. Virtuosos appear in virtually every domain, of course – not just race car driving.

Master

Above the virtuoso we find what we call the Master. People at this level are already virtuosos in a given field or domain, and they go a step further. They actually invent new standards, invent new practices, new technologies, new processes, new ways of doing things… that others in the field then begin to adopt and use.

Dick Fosbury (Fosbury Flop – the first to go over the high jump bar on his back, rather than the front side), and Michael Jordan or LeBron James (representing professional basketball played at its peak) are considered to be masters in their given domains. There are others, in virtually every industry or field of endeavor, personal and professional.

Our observation is that we can't skip levels. We may not stay in each level for the same period of time, but we simply must move in the direction of less competency to more competency as we learn. And it's critically important to initially get on this side of the page – to get in the "effectiveness" column in the first place!

Let's take a look at some scenarios and questions, considering these levels of learning:

- Do we give ourselves permission to be beginners? In all areas of our lives? In some areas? Which ones? Are you willing to acknowledge that there is some Action you don't yet know how to take and some Result you haven't yet been able to produce (since you haven't yet taken an Action that will produce this Result)? Are you willing to be a learner? Are you willing to give someone permission to teach you or to coach you?

- When we don't, why is it difficult for us to declare ourselves beginners? Why don't we do it more than we do? What story – what interpretation – have we made up about that? Would another story be more helpful and better serve us, given the breakthrough Results we say we want?

- Do we give our employees (and especially our newer employees) permission to say "I don't know" and to be beginners? And do we give others close to us, including family members and significant others, permission to be beginners? How do we treat people who say "I don't know"? What new possible futures open up as a Result of making changes here?

- Who gets to set your standards for competency within the domains of your life (for example, body/nutrition, career/work, money/finance, family/parenting, relationships, social/civic, learning/education, spirituality)? We'll cover standards in greater detail in a later chapter, but for now consider whether or not you set your own standards, and if so, how you go about doing so. Publicly or privately? Involving others or not? And if you don't set your own standards, who does?

- How clear are we about how competent we desire to be (our standards) in these domains? Is it our goal to be a master in some or all of them? If so, how committed are we to do the learning and devote the time and practice that are necessary to achieve that level of competency? Is it our goal to be competent or minimally competent in some other domains? Are we okay being beginners in some domains? Which ones? Our experience is that a great many of us are not clear at all; we don't even acknowledge the existence of some of these domains, and so we certainly haven't consciously set a standard of desired competence or performance within them.

- How clear are we about how competent we currently are in these domains? Are we beginners or competent? Virtuoso? Master? Who gets to assess our competency? Have we given anyone else permission to give us feedback about how we "show up" for them?

- Do you share your standards with anyone else (colleague, significant other, or friend, for example)? Do you enroll others (via conversations) to support you in these areas?

For example, standard-setting in the domain of Career may include these sorts of issues: What does success look like for me? Am I achieving it, and how do I know? What is the contribution I am making or want to make? What is an acceptable balance between my work responsibilities, my compensation and my vacation/family time? Am I achieving this? Am I learning and advancing at acceptable rates? What does my future growth track look like? Can I influence it in a way that's acceptable to me?

Setting your standards in the domain of Body may include these reflections and decisions (declarations): What do I say my body should look like? What does "healthy" mean to me? What is my standard for nutrition? Exercise? Sleep? Posture? Weight? Pulse rate? Cholesterol? What measurements will I use here? Do I want to be a virtuoso or master in the domain of body, like an Olympic athlete or master-level martial arts student? Or will I be peaceful with being minimally competent or competent in this domain? *And this is the key – at what level will I declare "I'm satisfied" for now, and thereby find some peace, some acceptance... some satisfaction or fulfillment?*

Standard-setting in the domain of Education may include these: What level of formal education do I declare to be "necessary"? What learning am I engaged in ongoingly? Do I attend workshops usually? Should I? What types? Do I read certain types of books as a purposeful practice? Again, the same key: What is the level at which I will declare "I'm satisfied, I'm okay with this"?

Many of us have not consciously set standards in these areas. We just do what we do, sometimes seeming to be happy with where we are and sometimes not. If we do have conscious standards, it's likely that we may be, to some degree, blind to the influence of the popular media and our own particular kind of society. Madison Avenue is quite competent in creating demand and shaping preferences. In fact, this is a primary function being performed by the advertising and marketing industries. A quick look at everything from beer commercials to clothing ads tells us that there are a great number of people willing to set your standards for you – and ours for us – if we so allow. But the first step here is to notice, to notice what's going on. Then we can choose something different.

Let's continue – if you don't have a set standard in these areas, and you couple this with an internal conversation of "I'm not good enough or smart enough or assertive enough or whatever enough," we can say *Welcome to Suffering*. Think about it. The good stuff never comes because we have no standard in this area, so we never acknowledge any progress or movement or declare satisfaction, and we continually suffer in our "not-enoughness." It's almost as if we say "I don't know what I'm trying to achieve here, I just know I haven't done it yet." We have no standard so we don't know what Action or Result will allow us to declare satisfaction or peacefulness. We just "know" that we haven't reached it! In these cases, we say welcome to suffering, welcome to unhappiness, welcome to dissatisfaction and unfulfillment.

Additionally, is it possible that just because we don't perform up to our standards in one area, that we "collapse domains" and consider ourselves to be poor (or ineffective or bad or worthless) in all domains? Have you ever known someone who seemed to do this? Have you ever done this? Many of us have. We say that having some rigor here – keeping domains separate and distinct from each other – can allow us room to improve and create in certain areas, while declaring satisfaction (and experiencing fulfillment) in others.

Another Look at Levels of Learning and Competence

Here is another way to look at levels of learning that you may have come across already. These four broad categories are very consistent with how we understand learning, competency and Results. They are also consistent with how we understand the power of language to serve as a catalyst for this learning:

- Unconscious incompetent – we don't even know that we don't know. We are unaware of even the existence of the possibilities represented by the new learning.

- Conscious incompetent – we know that we don't know. We are aware of the new possibilities, and are also aware (and declare) that we aren't competent to perform to certain standards in the new domain.

- Conscious competent – we know that we know. We have moved into some level of competency, others begin to trust us in this domain, and we are able to perform effectively and deal with certain types of problems on our own.

- Unconscious competent – we don't know that we know. We just do it. We perform at a very high level, and our bodies seem to have internalized the learning. We move in transparency, at some level of auto-pilot, and are able to handle even the most difficult situations without breaking stride.

Competence vs. Confidence

In subsequent chapters we will move into moods and emotions, as well as what we claim to be fundamental language acts, and their impact on the Observer that we are, the Actions we take and the Results we produce. For now we will introduce one way of looking at the difference between competence and confidence, and the ways in which our understanding here can influence our ability to learn.

How many of us know people who don't engage in new learning or take new Action? And when asked why, they respond with "I just don't think I can do it... I'm just not a confident person" or "I lack the confidence needed in order to do that..." or some variation of this theme? Many of us do, as this is not an uncommon way of understanding. We offer the following different interpretation:

- By living in the conversation "I'm not confident enough..." we are not describing anything nearly as much as we are creating. What we're creating is a context out of which we take no new Action, we never begin practicing... because we "know already" that we aren't "confident" enough to ever be successful anyway.

- If we never take new Action, we never produce new Results (obviously).

- Even acknowledging the fact that each of us is truly different and that each of us is born with a certain genetic heritage and biological predisposition, we claim that each of us is absolutely also able to learn, to grow, to improve, to gain competency in domains of our own choosing – regardless of our starting point and no matter what.

  Now, we are not saying that each of us will ultimately be able to reach the same levels of competency as others (think world-class opera stars, child prodigy ballet dancers, professional athletes, Broadway actors, superstars in other domains, etc.) but this is not the same as the notion that we are permanently stuck where we presently find ourselves. **Predisposition is not destiny**.

- What if "confidence" isn't a thing that one person was born with 5 pounds of and another person was born with 10 pounds of, and that's the end of it? What if confidence or lack of confidence aren't permanent, objective features of your biological personhood?

  Instead, what if confidence – or lack thereof – are simply assessments (judgments) made by different Observers, out of different standards? And what if these assessments – made by others as well as by ourselves – have everything to do with our behavior and our Actions, and nothing to do with our inherent personhood? What might be available then?

Let's say Ann assesses herself as "not confident" and is also assessed by her peers as "not confident" in month 1. Let's also say that regardless of this, Ann commits herself to learning how to be a better public speaker. She gets a coach, begins practicing night and day, videotapes herself speaking and works with the coach to critique the technique and hone the style, and continues doing this during months 2, 3, 4 and 5.

Let's say that in month 6, others see Ann for the first time since month 1, speaking at an office event and obviously more polished and refined and comfortable in front of the room, embodying the new distinctions and capabilities she's been practicing all these months with her coach. Question: Is she still "not confident?" No! Now she's assessed as "confident" or "excellent" or whatever. What's changed is her competence.

- By focusing directly on improving our levels of competency – by committing ourselves to practicing and getting feedback from those more competent in the domain than we are – we open avenues for new Action and new Results that are utterly closed to those who view confidence (or lack of confidence) as objective, built-in features of who we are or who we aren't.

- Purposefully working on improving our competence – right now, no matter what – is a much more powerful approach than waiting till we are somehow more confident before starting a path of learning or development.

Virtually all of us can look to our past and find examples of when we moved through periods of uncertainty, committed ourselves to new learning and new Results and were successful. And it is through that gain in competence that we gain confidence moving forward. But if we start by searching for more confidence, or simply wait until we somehow find ourselves more confident... we may never get out of the starting blocks. And once again, welcome to no new Results.

We invite you to reflect on your own understandings of competence and confidence as you continue moving through this book, with the aim always being to adopt a way of thinking that is most helpful and most supportive to your ability to achieve the Results you are seeking to achieve.

145

What is the difference between a master and a beginner?

The master has failed more times than the beginner has even tried.

Have you seen this before? It's one of our favorites, as it points to a powerful truth and reinforces the value of perseverance and maintaining the focus on improving competence (vs. searching somewhere in hopes of somehow finding more confidence).

We are also reminded of Albert Einstein's claim here: *Anyone who has never made a mistake has never tried anything new.* Dr. APJ Abdul Kalam, the late former president of India, offered his understanding here which we also find valuable. He said "*F.A.I.L. = first attempt in learning!*" He also said that "*E.N.D. = effort never dies!*"

On a lighter note, we also agree with Will Rogers' wry observations when he said: "*There are three kinds of men: the ones that learn by reading, the few who learn by observation... the rest of them have to touch an electric fence!*"

We invite you to consider how many of us have learned a great deal and have ultimately benefited from our "failures." How many of us would say we are where we are today because of some of these setbacks? And our ability to continue moving forward, into new territory and into new learning, has a great deal to do with the types of internal conversations we are living in and how we interpret these experiences.

The Notion (and the Power) of Distinctions

Let us now close this chapter on learning by moving a bit deeper into the power of "distinctions," initially introduced in Chapter 3. Our focus here will be on how the particular distinctions each of us possess are directly connected to our ability to observe certain things (the Observer that we are) and take certain Actions. Once again, go back to the Observer – Action – Results model and see what connections you can make related to the most important Results you are seeking to produce as an individual, as well as within your broader organization.

With this in place, the remainder of the book will then unfold as we share with you what we feel are some of the most powerful distinctions we've acquired.

This understanding of distinctions was shared with us by Julio Olalla, Rafael Echeverria, and Mike Papania. To us, it represents a very powerful way of under-

146

standing how what we see when we open our eyes has much more to do with what's "in here" than with what's "out there." And what we see matters, because it's from this observation that we take Action, and from those Actions that we produce the Results we produce. Here we can also see, very clearly, another powerful connection between learning and language. Let's continue.

As a starting point, we can view distinctions as *concepts* or *ideas* or *terms,* although distinctions are not seen as mere definitions of things or labels for things. The power of distinctions can be summarized as follows:

- Distinctions in any domain allow us to **see** what others do not see – and what we ourselves did not see before we had the distinctions.

- Upon seeing what others do not see in that domain, we can then **do** what others cannot do in that domain.

- Distinctions in any given domain = **capacity for effective Action** in that domain.

- **No** distinctions = **no** capacity for effective Action.

- **New** distinctions = **new** capacity for Action.

- New Action is required for **new Results** (Observer – Action – Results).

Distinctions in any given domain (like forestry, auto mechanics or leadership) allow us to take Actions and produce Results in that domain that those without the distinctions cannot. With new distinctions comes the capacity for each of us to take truly unprecedented – brand new – Action. Let's take a look at some examples.

In the domain of FORESTRY:

Distinctions	Actions made possible
Pine, oak, maple, callicarpus, calluna, fatsia japonica, various propagation methods, humus, lichen, cinch bug, mealy worm, 2-bladed secateurs	• Effective conical pruning of 2-year old fatsia japonica • Successful propagation of unfertilized calluna through zones 5-7 • Appropriate eradication of first spring mealy worm hatch, without damaging any callicarpus

In the domain of PLUMBING:

Distinctions	Actions made possible
Ballcock, proset flange, flapper, quarter turn angle stops, fernco, no-hub bands, risers, expansion tanks, PRV valve	• Regulate water pressure to individual apartment or condo units • Replace worn proset flange to stop leakage • Properly adjust ballcock to allow appropriate water level • Properly connect PVC pipe together

In the domain of AUTO MECHANICS:

Distinctions	Actions made possible
Electronic transfer case, fuse relay center, torque lock, BTSI, fuel solenoid, injectors, fuse block busbar	• Effectively dampen noise from torque lock • Successfully re-load fuse block busbar • Stabilize electronic transfer case • Check fuel solenoid and refurbish, if necessary

In the domain of LANGUAGE:

Distinctions	Actions made possible
Assessment, assertion, declaration, request, offer, promise, commitment, mood, listening, hearing, context, public identity, Observer, learning, beginner, conversations for Results	• Purposefully design and create a workplace mood or "culture" of accountability, shared understanding, shared commitment and ambition
	• Create mutually-beneficial, productive relationships; sustain healthy relationships that are kept "clean"
	• Resolve problems or conflict in such a way that relationships, mood and future interactions are enhanced
	• Take care of your public identity; proactively design how you "show up" in the world
	• Reach greater clarity about what influences "poor Results" that you may be achieving, as well as what Actions to take to improve
	• Listen to feedback about your Actions without "taking it personally"; create accountability with dignity
	• Purposefully and systematically build trust
	• Make clear and effective requests
	• Take advantage of diverse perspectives while still making decisions and moving forward
	• Reduce stress and sense of "overwhelm"
	• More effectively coach others
	• Achieve a more balanced combination of peacefulness and productivity

Can you begin to see where this is going? By learning and acquiring new distinctions, in these and many others areas, we see what we didn't see before and can do what we couldn't do before. An expression learned from Julio Olalla and Rafael Echeverria that sums up how distinctions impact our capacity to take effective Action is: *"You cannot intervene in a world that you do not see."*

Innovation has everything to do with distinctions. In a time of ongoing change, many of us would agree that innovation is important – for individuals and for organizations. To innovate = to invent new distinctions that allow us to take Action to address recurring breakdowns or situations that we couldn't address before. And once we settle in, using the new distinctions for a time, guess what? New recurring breakdowns or situations present themselves, new distinctions are invented, innovation occurs, and the process begins all over again.

Pick a domain, and we can explore the impact of distinctions. If you were to teach me how to do your job, you would be teaching me distinctions. Virtually any area of learning has to do with the teacher offering the distinctions to the learner and the learner acquiring – and then using – the distinctions.

If someone teaches you new distinctions in the domain of forestry, we claim that your next walk in the woods will be different. The trees and bushes haven't changed or been switched out since your last visit, but what you observe when looking around out there has absolutely changed. Your "world" has changed. Your possibilities have changed. This is the power of distinctions, and how they impact our capacity for Action within given domains.

And so if you also acquire new distinctions in the domains of language and leadership, we claim that your next walk in the world and your next walk through your organization will be different. You'll see what you didn't see before, including ways in which your language serves to:

- orient you and frame situations
- generate sets of options or possibilities
- impact and shape corporate culture
- drive the quality of your execution
- open and close possibilities
- create and sustain and change relationships of all types
- generate commitment to get things done
- improve or diminish accountability
- influence your mood and emotional space, and
- greatly impact your public identity – who you "are" in the world.

You'll also see the extent to which you are the author of all of this, and become aware of new possibilities – new choices – for learning, adapting and designing your organization and your life. This is the power of learning and acquiring new distinctions.

We repeat: We look with our eyes, but we observe with (and through) our distinctions. People with different distinctions live in different worlds. You and your colleague definitely do not see the same things as you walk down the street. You both have eyes, you may share a very similar biology, but what you observe, what you notice when you look out at the world has a great deal to do with your distinctions, and these distinctions live in language.

And as we covered earlier, these new distinctions provide us access to breakthrough Results – literally unprecedented Results. They accomplish this by enabling us to see what we couldn't see before, which then enables us to take Action, to intervene, in ways that were unavailable to us before. This is the key.

Summary of Key Points

Learning is simply required for those of us seeking to produce new Results – <u>any</u> new Results – in our lives. Being able to learn continually, throughout our lives, seems to be directly connected to our effectiveness, productivity and well-being, in a wide variety of situations.

Learning is connected to our language in key ways:

- Being able to say (either to ourselves or out loud) *"I don't know"* is a primary step in creating, in generating an opening for our own learning. It creates a new context, one in which learning is far more likely than it was before.

- A great many barriers to learning are not physical barriers. They are barriers in the form of interpretations and beliefs (language) that paralyze us and take us away from practicing.

- Learning involves acquiring new distinctions in whatever domain is involved. These distinctions live in language.

Learning is connected to our bodies in key ways:

- Learning = time and practice.
- Learning occurs in the body.
- Learning "to do" requires that we put our bodies into it. Learning "about" does not.

Learning is connected to our moods/emotions in key ways:

- All moods do not support learning equally well.
- Moods of perplexity, acceptance and ambition are far more supportive of learning than are moods of boredom, resentment and confusion.

Acquiring new distinctions = acquiring new capacity for effective Action. This book is designed to share with you new distinctions in the domains of effective leadership, personal development and organizational performance.

By simply focusing on improving our <u>competence</u> – right here, right now, through time and practice – we can shift our Way of Being, we can move into learning and we can move closer to the Results we desire. This orientation, as opposed to seeking to find more <u>confidence</u> and viewing the acquisition of more confidence as a pre-requisite to taking new Action – is a far more powerful and far more effective approach to bringing about the Results we are seeking to achieve for ourselves and our organizations.

Application:

For all the items below, keep in mind the 1 or 2 or 3 important Results that you are committed to achieving during the next 12 months, as well as the areas in which you declared you are seeking to learn or learn how to do something differently or better.

1. Identify your most prevalent mindset and your mood, and your top 2 "enemies of learning." Consider professional as well as personal situations.

2. Identify the impact on your future if you don't break down / navigate around your enemies of learning and shift into a more powerful mindset and mood. Then identify ways you can and will break down / navigate around these barriers and make the shift that will better serve you.

3. In order to achieve your most important goals, while keeping in mind your progress and challenges, and your historical "enemies of learning"...

   - What must you learn?

   - Who or what will you learn from?

   - By when will you begin the learning?

   - Then commit and start

4. Share and discuss with your colleagues/direct reports the power of saying "I don't know...I don't understand...I am unclear about..." and explicitly request as well as give them permission to make such statements when needed. In addition, practice making these declarations yourself so as a leader you model the behavior you desire in others. Notice what happens to future conversations, collaboration and Results.

CHAPTER 6

THE YOU THAT YOU ARE

"We see the world not as it is, but as we are."

- Albert Einstein

We have introduced the Observer – Action – Results model, which is our basic framework for understanding the process of achieving breakthrough Results. Now we will take a closer look at the Observer, at each of us as unique human beings, because producing breakthroughs "out there" begins with breakthroughs "in here."

This chapter is an invitation to take a different look at yourself, as well as your colleagues, customers, suppliers, partners, direct reports and employees. It's an invitation to shift your thinking and adopt a deeper understanding regarding who you say you are, what you think is possible and what you think you can accomplish. It's an opportunity to change your way of thinking at a level where doing so can have a very significant and very positive impact, enabling you to produce breakthroughs in any domain, at any time and in any situation.

We Are Each Unique Observers

Let's start with the obvious – no two human beings are exactly the same (even including "identical" twins). Have you noticed? In fact, when you think about it, no two things in nature – no two snowflakes, no two trees, no two rocks, no two rivers, no two eagles, no two grains of sand, no two clouds, no two stars, no two thoughts, no two relationships – are exactly, truly identical.

So we claim that each of us is a unique Observer, looking out at the world and seeing things in ways that are genuinely unique. This is our starting point. No one has "privileged access to The Truth" or "cosmic objectivity." Everyone, by definition, is interpreting. No exceptions, ever.

This is not to say, however, that everyone's seeing and interpreting are equally powerful or equally helpful; that is, equally capable of moving us toward desired

Results. This is not to say that everyone's interpretations are connected to objective facts – actual data – in the same ways. It is simply to say that everyone is doing his or her version of looking out at the world and interpreting it.

The Grand Illusion

In our workshops we invite participants to dispel the Grand Illusion and we invite you to do the same now. What's the Grand Illusion?

That everyone sees things like you do!

They do not and they cannot. When you are running a meeting, do you know who you have in front of you? Human beings who are profoundly and utterly not you... <u>and</u> – like you – they are also valid expressions of what it means to be human. And it's incredible how much they're not you.

Think about the person closest to you in your life, perhaps your spouse or partner. Have you noticed that this person is not a clone of you? (And how many of us are eternally grateful for this?!)

The problem with the Grand Illusion is this – if you operate with this in place, right under the surface, for you, ready to spring out is: *ascribing ill intentions*. If you operate with the Grand Illusion, there will be a built-in tendency, a readiness, to ascribe ill intentions to others. It may show up like this internal conversation, this internal train of thought, when people find themselves at cross-purposes with another:

"Look, Bob, I know you saw what happened at the meeting. You were there, I was there, we both have eyes. You were standing right there, I know you saw it. Now you're saying the priority should be changed... aaahhhh, I know – you must have bad intentions! You're trying to undermine my authority and make me look bad in front of the Board..."

... when in reality, it's far more likely that Bob simply didn't see what you saw, meaning Bob didn't interpret what you interpreted, infer what you inferred, deduce what you deduced, assume what you assumed. All of which happens in language.

So yes, we use visual metaphors: We didn't "see things" the same... He is a different Observer... and that's fine. But let's not let the visual metaphors get in the way of what's actually happening, which is that two people are interpreting differently, making meaning differently, assuming differently, using different standards that lead to different conclusions, creating different explanations and internal narratives. All of which happens in language.

Don Miguel Ruiz, in his book *The Four Agreements*, says it this way:

"We make the assumption that everyone sees life the way that we do. We assume that others think the way we think, feel the way we feel, judge the way we judge. This is the biggest assumption that humans make."

What are the implications of co-workers walking around with the Grand Illusion in place? As you have likely surmised, this can and frequently does lead to unnecessary conflict, breakdowns in trust, disengagement, unwanted turnover and a workplace culture not very conducive to effective teamwork, innovation, creativity... or success. Our experience is that there are certain missing conversations that – when designed and convened – can have a very positive impact here. For example:

- Conversations to surface different standards for X or Y... and to possibly reach a new agreement about the standards moving forward

- Conversations to remove the "assumption of shared meaning" about A or B... and to listen to how different people "made sense" of A or B in different ways... and to possibly help the group or team adopt more powerful shared understandings moving forward

- Conversations to clarify and better understand the actual Actions that don't and do "line up" with declared organizational values... and to make it far more likely that colleagues will begin shifting behaviors toward this alignment

- Conversations to reach shared understanding of how someone else went from Event A to Explanation B in such a different way than you went from same Event A to different Explanation C

You can likely think of many more, given your own organizational circumstances. Can you see how these can be powerful and helpful conversations? And they are all absolutely dependent on the understanding that each of us is a unique Observer.

Larry Bossidy and Ram Charan, in their influential book *Execution*, discuss the importance of leadership (and all) teams being able to engage in *"robust dialogue."* Jim Collins, in *Good to Great*, emphasizes that *"people who achieve greatness engage in dialogue, not debate and not coersion..."*

There is clearly immense value in dispelling the Grand Illusion. It is a pre-requisite for conversations of this nature, as it enables us to consciously and purposefully seek, value and leverage differences. And as the above authors and many others have noted, in a business environment characterized by significant and relentless change, this is not trivial.

Problems, Possibilities, Opportunities, Solutions

Problems, possibilities, opportunities and solutions are all a function of the Observer that we are. Think about it. The world doesn't have any problems, in and of itself. People – individual Observers – have problems. What's a problem to one Observer passes totally unnoticed to another. What's a grave threat to one Observer is a great opportunity or wonderful new possibility to another.

This has to do, of course, with the different concerns of the different Observers, the different distinctions, values, standards and beliefs of the different Observers. This also has to do with differences in biology as well as the predominant moods and emotional patterns of the different Observers.

Different Observers see and interpret differently from the start. From these different initial interpretations, each produces or invents radically different possibilities. And from these possibilities, they produce or invent radically different solutions and ways forward (Actions). This is different than the common view that X or Y exists objectively or independently, pre-given as a problem, and that what's needed is to first see it objectively or rationally, "as it really is," then to solve it. This is different than the notion that possibilities and solutions are "out there" waiting to be discovered. We say instead they are "in here" waiting to be invented – invented by Observers through conversations.

In this way of thinking, we are unique Observers, but we are not detached, indifferent, or "objective" Observers (as in the scientific paradigm). On the contrary, we are concerned Observers. We are extremely invested in the way we observe (although this may be transparent to us). Moving ahead, our intent is to remove a great deal of this transparency, enabling you to see more choices and ways forward in creating the future you desire.

Your Particular Way of Being and Its Influence on How You See Things

We've been focusing quite a bit on language (our thinking, our assumptions, our often-not-shared standards, our often unquestioned and unchallenged beliefs, our concerns, our internal narratives, our interpretations...) but these are only part of the story. These are only part of what constitutes you as the unique Observer you are and others as the unique Observers they are.

To us, the Observer that each of us is can be viewed as a walking, talking bundle of congruency among three separate but strongly inter-twined aspects:

- Our physical body (includes our biology as well as our posture, our breathing and how we move through time and space)

- Our language (includes all of our thinking, our internal conversations as well as our external conversations)

- Our mood/emotional states (we will make some basic distinctions here between moods and emotions)

The graphic below is meant to represent each of us in this way:

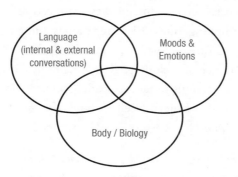

We refer to this particular combination as our Way of Being. And as the Observer – Action – Results model demonstrates – and as you very likely have already experienced – the Actions we see as possible, the Actions we ultimately take, as well as the Results we ultimately produce are strongly and directly related to our "come from", our Way of Being, the Observer that we are. See illustration below:

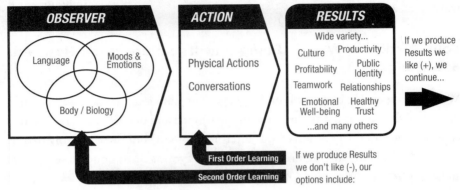

Let's touch on each of these 3 dimensions – language, moods/emotions and body – as well as the connections among them, because we claim that the separation many of us have been taught is an artificial one. We claim that language is not separate from our emotional life and our physical body and physical movements.

Our Way of Being is one in which our language, our moods and emotions, and our body are all linked and are all playing a part. We think and we speak and we listen, but the thinking, speaking and listening are always supported or not supported by the emotions that we have available. Our thinking, speaking and listening are always supported or not supported by our range of physical motions, our capacity to move in one way or another, our physiology.

The following is an excellent example of these connections. It clearly shows the ways in which our thinking, our stories, our moods and emotions and our bodies are consistent with one another and linked together. And in particular, it highlights the importance of including all 3 domains as George – and the rest of us – look for possible Actions to take in leading and moving our lives in different directions. From Alan Seiler's excellent book *Coaching To The Human Soul: Ontological Coaching and Deep Change – Vol. 1*, we read:

> *"George was "shooting himself in the foot" when it came to promotion opportunities, as his performance reviews consistently highlighted the need for improvement*

in his communication with others. Early in the coaching conversation it was clear George was experiencing a major difficulty with delegation. More specifically, he was experiencing a communication breakdown in making clear and effective requests to others.

George reported that he often found himself angry with the people in his unit, and that he was often short and withdrawn in his expression of this anger. When asked what the anger was about he replied that he became angry when he felt that he had to ask people to do things, because they should know what to do and that it was an insult to him to have to ask. Further exploration revealed that this was a pattern of behavior he had learned in his childhood. George grew up in a household where a very strong and clear message is that you offend people if you do not know what to do for them, and that you should not have to be asked. In short, if you cared you would be alert, anticipate what they want and do it for them. Furthermore, a very strong and unstated message he also learned was that if you did not do this, your fundamental worthiness (as a human being) was questionable.

Thus, we could say that George had a very powerful story and associated beliefs in one area of relating to people. His story carried an expectation that not only should he be alert to what others want done without them having to ask, it also carried the unquestioned assumption that others should be as sensitive to him, especially as he was now in a senior position. We might be tempted to say that all he had to do was change the story and he could change his behavior. However, this story (occurring in language) is only one aspect of his Way of Being. His story also had a strong emotional grip on him.

Needless to say, there was a fair bit of tension associated with his story. A lot of emotional energy was required to maintain alertness to the needs of others, and not have to deal with the question of self-worth, as well as deal with the insensitivity of others when they did not spontaneously notice what needed doing. The emotional consequence was that most of the time George lived in a mood of resentment. In other words, anger was almost permanently in the background, easily triggered when he felt he had to ask others.

However, this is still not the complete picture of how George had taken on a Way of Being with respect to delegation in the workplace. His story and his mood were also embodied; that is, he had configured his posture so that he found it hard to ask people and when he did ask, his requests were very ineffectual."

And so everything we cover connected to language (our thinking, our internal and external conversations, our stories, interpretations, judgments, assumptions, narratives and beliefs) is always within this context. It is always recognizing the built-in connections and inherent relationships among our language, our emotional capacity and range, and our physical body and movement.

Even though you may not have started this book consciously aware of the 3-circle model we're discussing, did you start this book already knowing – intuitively – something about these connections and inter-dependencies? Very likely this is the case. Very likely you have personally experienced these connections and interrelationships, in yourself and in others.

What may have been missing, however, from our everyday understanding of these 3 dimensions is the claim that each of them may be used as the starting point, the "lever" for change and for designing a different Way of Being. Each may be used to purposefully impact and influence the other two.

Let us now go deeper into each of the 3 aspects of the Observers that we are. The more distinctions we have in these 3 areas, the better we will be at purposefully designing, shifting and making meaningful changes within each of them. And by doing this, we are able to purposefully design our own Way of Being in ways that enable us to achieve more of the Results that are most important to us.

The topic of the Observer, viewed this way, is a deep one. Fernando Flores, Rafael Echeverria, Julio Olalla, Chris Argyris and others have devoted significant study and made significant contributions in building this powerful way of understanding.

Body and Movement

We begin with statements which are somewhat self-evident, but lay the groundwork for what's to come:

- We can only observe what our biology allows us to observe.
- We can only do what our biology allows us to do.

That is, the starting point for any observation we can make or Action we can take is the biological structure from which we're operating. This is so for each of us.

For example, your eyes only see a certain range of wavelengths of light. Your ears only hear a certain range of wavelengths of sound. Any light waves or sound waves outside of those ranges go totally un-observed, unnoticed by you. We know, of course, that dogs can hear high frequency waves that humans cannot; same with elephants and low frequency sounds. We also know that the light we see is referred to as the "visible" portion of the spectrum. All of us are simply incapable – biologically – of hearing these sounds and seeing the other portion of the spectrum of light. This doesn't mean that these phenomena don't exist, of course. It simply means they are not available to us. We are interpreting no matter what, and we are interpreting from a particular biology.

People with different biological structures observe differently from each other. There are many examples we could point to, from degrees of color sensitivity and hearing acuity, to chemical or hormonal differences to other differences in how our physical bodies are. We claim that in all cases, the Observer is observing from a given biology and that this biology necessarily defines the range of what's possible to observe in the first place.

As an aside, we may consider other creatures such as dogs, cats, snakes, bats, and insects. When we reflect a moment, it becomes quite clear that what a "tree" is to a bat (in its world of echo-location) is different than what a "tree" is to a dragonfly (with its multi-eyes), which is different than what a dog experiences (with its dog eyes and dog nose) and what a snake experiences (with its heat-sensing capabilities) and so on. We can say, very clearly, that what each creature sees has a great deal to do with the biology from which that creature is operating. Said another way, what's "reality" appears to be species-dependent!

Also within what we're calling body is the whole issue of movement and posture. That is, in addition to focusing on the "micro" (our biology, our cells, molecules, genetics, systems), we can also focus on the "macro" (how we physically hold and move our bodies through time and space). Here, we pay attention to and notice how we carry ourselves and how we physically move in the world. This includes:

- How we walk

- How we stand

- How we sit

- How we dance

- <u>If</u> we dance
- How we move, how close we get, our relative body positions – physically – to other people in personal, social and work situations
- Our exercise habits and standards
- The range of physical movements that we're used to, that come easily and are readily available to us.
- The range of physical movements that we're *not* used to and are *not* available to us; that we have virtually no practice in, and have therefore not yet experienced.

For example, some of us exercise in some way, and some don't. Some of us do yoga, and some don't. Same with meditation, walking, and dancing. And there are infinite ways, of course, to meditate, to walk, and to dance! Some of us walk and sit upright, while others are much more slouched over. Some of us talk with others and square up, face-to-face, to have the conversation. Others tend to always be at an angle when interacting with others, assuming a much more sideways position. Some of us stand up in a crowded room to ask a question, and some of us stay glued to the chair. Some of us have a "personal space" that's measured in feet, while others measure theirs in inches. Some of us always look others in the eye, while others avoid eye contact at all costs. Some of us hug others, while others shake hands only. We could go on and on.

We're talking about our bodies and about movement, obviously. But by looking just a bit deeper we can see that we're talking also about much more. And this "much more" shows up precisely in our thinking, in our internal and external conversations, as well as in the range of emotions which are even available to us.

Any conversation about the body domain would not be complete without sharing with you the incredible contribution made by Humberto Maturana, the Chilean neurobiologist mentioned previously. He provides solidly grounded, scientifically rooted evidence that says our commonsense understanding of perception and human capabilities need to be seriously reexamined. Dr. Maturana is truly a pioneer, on the cutting edge of new understandings of living systems – of which we human beings are certainly a part.

Two of his key findings that have direct relevance for us are:

1. Human beings are "closed systems" and are "structurally determined." That is, what we are able to do has everything to do with our physical structure and systems, at a multitude of levels. What we perceive, the Actions we take, and the re Actions we have do not have very much to do with what's "out there." On the contrary, they have everything to do with what's "in here" – with our own individual structure, our own mood/body/language combination. In fact, we cannot and do not have direct access to what's out there. It's biologically, physiologically not available to us. All we have, all we know, is what we know and perceive as we react through our particular structure. What's out there serves more as a trigger, not as a provider or determiner of our experience. What we experience, how we react, and what we do is not primarily a function of the trigger. It's a function of us, of our own structure. (In this sense, a T-shirt in many of us have seen makes perfect sense. The T-shirt reads "It's all about me!")

2. Our structure is not fixed and permanent; instead, it's highly plastic and continuously changing. Our new Actions produce new neural pathways and new physical structures. By learning and taking new Actions – new physical Actions and new conversational Actions – we produce a new structure. This new structure then enables us to take new physical and conversational Action when the next trigger occurs, Action we could not and did not take before. In this sense, our learning is truly embodied.

Language

With language, we can now begin to see big differences in observation among individuals that share a very similar biology. In other words, there are much bigger differences in how people "see things" than can be explained solely on the basis of biological differences! Human beings may have very similar biological structures and at the same time produce wildly different interpretations or explanations of things.

As a leader, you "get paid" to have effective conversations. That is, at its essence, what you do, day in and day out as a leader, is have conversations that produce certain Results, but not others. So as we've said before, learning something about language and these inter-dependencies can be very helpful.

This book rests upon a new interpretation of language – an interpretation in which language is Action, that language is creative and generative. It is in language that our distinctions, our assessments (judgments) and our stories live. We can frame language here by looking at 3 levels, each building on the prior:

- First, we can say that each of us – each Observer – observes the world through a set of distinctions (remember our earlier discussion in which we claimed that we look with our eyes, but we observe through our distinctions). Our distinctions live in language, such that an auto mechanic with distinctions in the domain of automobile engines observes something different than the rest of us when we're all looking at a car motor. Same with the forester looking at trees and the chemist looking through a microscope. Distinctions provide the starting point for observing. They provide the "things" we notice in the first place, when we look around.

- Second, we take a stand on what we see via our assessments – our opinions and judgments. (More to come on these later). We are not purely neutral as to what we see and what we are likely to do. It is here that we orient ourselves one way or another in given situations, positioning ourselves in such a way that certain possibilities are opened and others are closed.

- And third, we tie it all together, we make sense of situations and events, we connect our assessments and opinions together with our narratives or stories. (And we are each the central character of our own story.) Each of us weaves stories around the events and observations of our lives, connecting elements and making sense, making meaning, of what's before us. And this we do in language. We generate these with our language, as we are thinking and as we are talking with others.

And it is through the "filters" or "lenses" of these distinctions, assessments and stories that we "see" the world.

Recall our earlier discussion about events and explanations. A key benefit of this way of understanding is that we can now separate our explanations and stories from the events of our lives. This is a huge benefit, opening the doorway to an entirely new set of options.

Now we can see that the event belongs to itself, while our explanations and stories belong to us. Our explanations and stories have to do with our way of seeing things, our ways of listening and assessing and story-building. *The event just is, while the explanations and stories can be examined in terms of the possibilities for Action that each opens or closes*. This is the key. Our explanations (not the events) have everything to do with what we see as possible, what we actually do, how we actually do it… and the Results we actually achieve.

This way of understanding the Observer also allows us to reinforce the distinction of blindness we introduced earlier. Here, the blindness refers to each of us being necessarily blind to certain possibilities because of our differences in background, experience, distinctions, traditions, learning. In very real ways, we don't know that we don't know these things.

This type of blindness is very widespread and considered quite normal. It's not bad that we have this type of blindness; it's only bad that we don't notice it. We will take different Actions with people – we will form different types of relation-ships with people – if we notice this, than if we don't. We will lead differently, we will interact differently, and we will solve problems differently. Can you see how being aware of this type of blindness sets a different context for leading, relating and being together? Can you see how it sets a different context for achieving de-sired Results? It's a genuinely different starting point.

The world of accounting is not the same as the world of science. Accountants have a very different set of distinctions from which to view the world than do sci-entists. Accountants are very different Observers than are scientists. Accountants have different histories and beliefs. Possibilities which are obvious to an accoun-tant would not be available, not be seen, by the scientists. Or the farmer. Or the neurosurgeon. Or the person from a different region or country. Or the person from a different period in history.

As we've said, what we see when we look out at the world has everything to do with our distinctions and our social histories. We are necessarily blind in areas in which we have limited or no distinctions. We are necessarily blind to the possi-bilities seen by others who come from different life experiences, traditions, beliefs, and practices.

Different Observers are able to see some things clearly, while remaining blind to others. And so we can stop making others wrong simply because they have blindnesses we don't have. We can stop making ourselves wrong because we have our own areas of blindness. We can determine whether or not we're committed to get "un-blind" in an area or domain, and what that learning may involve. We can approach learning more effectively in organizations and schools. We can approach creativity and innovation differently in organizations, communities, and families.

In Peter Senge's *The Fifth Discipline*, the concept of mental models is very similar to what we're describing here. The different sets of distinctions and beliefs that we're discussing all may be seen as mental models or mental maps carried by these people and by all of us. In the book it is summarized this way:

> *"Mental models are the images, assumptions and stories which we carry in our minds of ourselves, other people, institutions and every aspect of the world. Like a pane of glass framing and subtly distorting our vision, mental models determine what we see. Human beings cannot navigate through the complex environments of our world without these 'mental maps'; and all of these mental maps, by definition, are flawed in some way."*

Of course, we would further add that the term "map" or "model" may sometimes take us away from the root of the matter – that being the extent to which these maps and models are really stories, narratives and explanations – all living in language.

Moods and Emotions

Moods and emotions are enormously important to us and have an obvious and dramatic impact on how we think, how we live our lives, how we relate, how we move through the world, and the Results we produce for ourselves. They have a great deal to do with our experience, with the "quality of the journey," as we lead our organizations and do what we do. This section is meant to be a brief introduction to moods and emotions within this context, and will be followed by a more thorough exploration in a later chapter.

In this way of thinking, human beings are emotional beings – meaning that *no matter what, we are always in one mood or emotional state or another.* Apathy is a mood. Calm and collected is a mood. Whatever mood or emotional state you're in – it's not nothing. It's something. We also claim that the mood or emotional state that we are in at any given time influences or pre-disposes us to interpret one way or another.

So at a most basic level, moods and emotions are pre-dispositions for Action. When you're in a mood of resentment, for example, you're simply very pre-dis-posed to get even, undermine, withdraw, or put a negative spin on things… no matter what the event or trigger.   And when you're in a mood of peace or ambi-tion, for example, you're much more likely to embrace or support… again, no matter what the external event or trigger.

Moods and emotions are also very connected to our physical bodies, our biology, and our ability to move one way or another. We've all experienced this firsthand. When we're in the emotion of fear, for example, our bodies are very different (pulse rate, blood pressure, blood flow, muscle tightness, tension, release of cer-tain hormones) than when we're peaceful or playful.

Regardless of what terms we use, let's make a distinction between moods and emotions. Let's start by noticing that one of these is short-term and triggered by external events, and one of these is not. We make the distinction this way:

- Moods are viewed as long-term, lasting weeks, months or years and are very much in the background. They are not triggered by some external event; they come "before" any events. They're already there when we inter-act in the world. They can be viewed as the predominant predispositions to act that we tend to find ourselves in before we actually take one Action or the other.

- Emotions, on the other hand, are viewed as shorter-term, lasting moments to hours or days and are definitely triggered by external events. They are viewed as temporary shifts in our predisposition to act, and they are usu-ally much more visible to ourselves and to others. And after the emotional shift which was triggered fades, we settle back down into whatever our longer-term moods are, our predominant Way of Being… until another trigger has us go to another emotion, and so on.

With these distinctions, then, we can say that being triggered into the emotion (short-term) of anger, for example, is quite different than living my life in a mood (long-term) of anger. Same with resentment, fear, anxiety, ambition, peace, all of them.

169

Have you noticed: we tend to interpret, to judge, to assess, to make up stories, that justify our moods and make them right. Our emotions and moods are obviously not separate from the way we tend to "see things," and we can all point to firsthand examples and experiences in which this connection has played out – in ourselves and in others.

We mentioned this earlier, but it's worth repeating here – Let's go back to the Big Eye, to self-awareness. Many, if not most, of us are very poor Observers of our moods. We don't even see them as moods –we see them as "the way things are." And as we know, if you don't see yourself as having moods, you don't have them. They have you. And they will color your interpretations and you'll never see it.

Moods have a great deal to do with language, with our thinking, interpreting, meaning-making, listening and speaking. And as we know, moods and emotions also have a great deal to do with our physical bodies. In a number of important ways, our moods influence our lives, our Actions and our Results. This is not right or wrong, it just is. So strengthening our ability to notice this can be a powerful starting point for designing something new – should we so choose.

Even if we do notice and want to make a change, we often are operating out of stories that are disempowering, grant the mood or emotion a great deal of weight and authority, grant the mood or emotion qualities that make it difficult or impossible for us to deal with, and ultimately do not take us in the direction of the Actions required for us to produce the Results we say we most want.

Are there any new moods that we need to learn, in order to produce breakthrough Results? And how do language and our physical bodies come into play, should we choose to move in this direction? We will explore these questions and more in a later chapter.

Are You a Human Being or a Human Becoming?

Consider these two questions as we move into this next section:

- Are we human beings fundamentally fixed and permanent when we arrive here on the planet... and therefore our life's journey is or should be all about attempting to "discover" our true self, who we already, objectively, really are?

- Or are we fundamentally growing, learning, evolving and becoming... in which case our life's journey is or should be all about purposefully designing and creating ourselves in each ongoing moment of "now"?

While we like to say that the answers to these questions are "above our pay grade," it appears that while we do obviously arrive with genetic tendencies, personal characteristics, a biological heritage, DNA and a certain amount of "hardwiring", it's also equally clear that we have the capacity to continually learn, adapt, evolve and grow. Given this, (and given what neuroscience is telling us about the plasticity of our brains), we invite you to consider these questions carefully. *Your answers and your thinking here can and do have a significant impact on the Results you are able to produce.*

We've claimed that we are each unique Observers, and that this dramatically impacts possibilities we are each able to see, which impact the actual Actions we take, as well as the subsequent Results we produce – in a wide variety of areas. Always, we return to Observer – Action – Results. Now we can ask a very important related question: *Are you the same Observer that you were when you were 15 years old? Do you see things today the same way you saw things then?*

How many of us would say that we see things pretty much the same way today as we did when we were 15? Most people we've met say that No, they are not the same Observer as when they were 15, that they most assuredly do not see things now the same way they did back then! There are countless examples we could point to, in our professional and personal lives, to reinforce this point. Our perspective, our point of view, the way we see things has indeed changed over the course of our lives. We are indeed different Observers today than we were 25 or 10 or even 1 year ago.

Another question: *When and how did the change occur?* That is, when and how did we go from seeing the world like we did when we were kids or younger adults to seeing it the way we do now? Was it one morning last year, we each woke up and *voila*, the world was different? No – for most of us it was very gradual, moment by moment by moment, day by day. The Observer-that-we-are is constantly changing, gradually (and sometimes not-so-gradually) shifting and evolving and growing.

So perhaps the term "human being" is not as appropriate as "human becoming." Think about it. We are each becoming a new Observer, every moment of every day. This is not an outrageous claim; it's simply an observation reflecting our own experiences. For us, this is a more powerful interpretation. Yes, you're still you, but the "you" that you are today is not the "you" that you were back then. You're not the same Observer you were 5 years ago and you're not the same Observer you'll be 5 years from now.

In fact, it's one of our overt objectives to have you be a slightly different Observer of yourself and your organization after going through this book than you were before you started! In this way of thinking, we are each in a permanent state of becoming. Given a world in which constant change is occurring, we like this interpretation better than Popeye's interpretation.

Do you remember Popeye's slogan? As we recall, the Popeye slogan is: *"I yam what I yam and that's all that I yam!"* Well, we are not who we used to be, and we are not who we will be tomorrow. Human beings have a fantastic capacity for self-transformation, for learning, for growth. Through learning, we have the ability to develop competencies that we did not have in the past, than take Actions we could not take in the past, and produce Results we could not produce in the past.

We can think about our thinking, and choose to think differently. We can talk about our talking, and choose to invent new conversations. While other creatures certainly communicate in some ways, as far as we can tell the communication occurs within the framework of that creature as a given. We've heard it put this way: Dogs and cats communicate, but for dogs and cats, their "dog-hood" and "cat-hood" appear to be firmly established! Humans however, with our language, have the capacity to redesign our person-hood. In a very real way, we create out of what we speak.

Rafael Echeverria shared this perspective with us, and we will share it again with you. To us, it's very powerful and captures in a succinct way what we're speaking about here:

We act according to how we are (and we do). And we also are, according to how we act.

There is a circular influence at work here. We act from our history, no doubt. And we can also act <u>out</u> of our history. We can observe in a different way, we can learn some new distinctions and we can begin to see some different possibilities for new Action. By taking new Actions in the world, we generate a new identity for ourselves. By taking new Actions that are <u>inconsistent</u> with our history, we can produce unprecedented, brand new (for us) Results. We can produce break-through Results. We can literally become different than we were before. We can design anew.

In addition, as the startling conclusions drawn by the neurobiologist Humberto Maturana have shown, the taking of new Action in the world literally creates a new structure within us, which then allows us to take Action and respond in new ways to future events. We are literally – not figuratively – a different person after we take a new Action. We are literally becoming a new Observer (a "human becoming") through the taking of new Actions. We are definitely not Popeye, and it can be proven biologically. Given that as living creatures we are structur-ally determined (everything we do and can do in the world is based on what our structure allows), this has fantastic implications on how we move and create Results in our lives.

Here we highly recommend Amy Cuddy's 2012 TED talk entitled "*Your Body Language Shapes Who You Are.*" In it, she goes far beyond anecdotal evidence to make the powerful and empowering claim relating to our bodies: *It's not fake it till you make it… it's fake it till you become it!*

Purposefully Shifting Into More Powerful Ways of Being

As we've said, all 3 aspects are connected, coherent and congruent with each other. And this coherency is not fixed and permanent. When any one of these aspects changes, the other two aspects are impacted, influenced, altered as they seek to regain their coherence with each other. Therefore, we claim that each of these three – our body, our mood/emotional state, and our language – serves as a domain or territory for learning and shifting and designing a new Way of Being.

That is, we can <u>purposefully</u> invent new conversations, knowing that over time they will have the effect of influencing or designing a new mood. We can <u>pur-posefully</u> do something different with our body (walk differently, sit differently, breathe differently, stand differently, dance, meditate, exercise) knowing that, over time, this will produce different interpretations, different conversations, different available moodspaces. We can listen to music or do something else to purpose-fully change our moods, knowing that this will impact our listening, our interpretations, our language, our posture.

This model has the advantage of explicitly providing three different domains of design, three different causal elements for use in creating new Ways of Being and thus new Results in our lives. And any of these can serve as a starting point for creating the shift desired. Some examples follow:

Have you ever felt better (mood) after exercise (body)? Most of us report that, yes, we have. But what if you waited until you felt better before going to exercise? Many of us would never get off the couch. So you can shift your mood by shifting how you sit, how you hold your chest and shoulders, how you breathe, by purposefully moving your body in different ways, and putting your body in different positions such as in prayer, yoga, meditation and other practices. You can influence your emotions by changing your diet and exercise habits. You can influence your moods and emotions by engaging in some conversations and avoiding others.

When was the last time you danced (body) when you were angry (mood)? Usually those two do not go together. If you're angry and start dancing and keep it up long enough, one of two interesting things will happen. Either 1) you'll stop dancing or 2) you'll stop being angry! (But the reason, of course, that we don't dance when we're angry is that we're *Right* about being angry!) Similarly, it's very hard to duck-walk, quack loudly, and stay resentful. Resentfulness does not stay in the duck-walking body very well!

If people in an organization or department have lots of conversations (language) that can be described as bitching and back-biting conversations... does this have anything to do with the culture (mood) of that organization or department? As we've discussed earlier, we say yes, these conversations have everything to do with that culture or mood. Change those conversations, and change the mood. Or change the mood some other way, and the conversations change. As a Result, people feel better, and they become more energetic, engaged and productive. We all know and have experienced these connections.

Maybe when grandma said "Sit up straight" she was really on to something important. This brings to mind two other claims shared with us by friends and teachers in this work:

- Our bodies are not innocent.
- The way you stand is the way you stand in the world.

(Please note that we are not saying that there's never a time to be angry, or that it's somehow "wrong" to ever be resentful or sad. We are not suggesting that all of us should only walk around in a mood of playfulness and lightness all the time, no matter what's occurring in our lives. That is absolutely not what this is about.

What is important here is being better able to observe ourselves and our moods and emotions, and then make assessments about whether or not these moods (long-term) and emotions (short-term) we live in serve us or not. The purpose of this is to show the connections, the congruency, the linkages that exist among the three primary domains of body, mood/emotions and language. It is our purpose to introduce the possibility of more consciously designing one's moods, one's conversations, one's physical body, and one's Results by taking advantage of the power inherent in these connections).

Embodying New Practices and New Ways of Being

How long does it take to establish a new habit or a new practice? There is now some data on this subject, although the conclusions tend to vary significantly, depending on the particular habit or behavior involved (among other factors). Many studies have come up with an answer that ranges between 21 and 35 days – not a hard and fast number, but a ball-park estimate that is impacted by several variables.

Regardless of the particular habit or the exact length of time required, however, this much we know for sure:

- all 3 of these domains must and will be involved
- you can begin by making a change in any one of the domains; and
- you must keep it up long enough in order for the other two to "come along".

If you do not sustain the new behavior long enough, the old coherency "snaps back" into place and nothing has really changed. If you don't keep it up long enough, the original Way of Being remains as it was, the original coherency remains in place, and nothing has really changed. But if the change is sustained long enough, a new coherency is established and a new Way of Being is the outcome. A new Observer is present.

Think about the implications of this. For those of us interested in producing breakthrough Results... where will you start? Is it, for example, by acquiring and using new distinctions, thinking differently, updating certain beliefs, modifying certain standards, convening new conversations? Or will you start by changing certain physical practices, such as exercise or diet – regardless of what you currently think about this? Or will you start by using certain types of music to predictably and purposefully shift your mood in X or Y situations? Just as importantly, how long will you keep it up? How long will you continue with the new practice?

In a wide range of situations, in order to be successful, you simply must keep up the new practice through an early period in which you see no new Results! Practice, perseverance and feedback are hugely important in actually embodying the new practice and shifting into the new coherency, the new Way of Being. Sustaining the new practices even in the face of no immediately noticeable new Results is the key, if we are seeking this type of learning and these types of shifts.

We can separate language, moods/emotions and body for convenience, to allow us to speak about one and not the other and to create some distinctions that can help us design new Ways of Being and thus new Results for ourselves. But in the end, it is an artificial separation. In the end, we are always dealing with the unique blend, the ever-changing combination, that makes each of us the unique person – the unique Observer – that we are. And there is great power in noticing this, understanding this and leveraging this as we seek to lead more effectively and generate new Results at work, at home and everywhere in between.

Fundamental Conversations, Body Dispositions and Moods for Leaders

Do you think your body language impacts your effectiveness as a leader? Do you have a sense that the way you carry yourself physically has an impact on how you get interpreted and the impact you have on people? Have you sensed that certain types of conversations need to be accompanied by certain ways of carrying your-self physically in order to bring about the Results you're seeking?

As we bring this chapter to a close, we'd like to share with you some powerful distinctions related to the different "body dispositions" and moods of leaders, and how these impact the effectiveness of specific leadership and organizational conversations. Many thanks and much gratitude to Deanne Prymek, Program Director at Newfield Network, for sharing these with us, deepening our under-standing and leading the discussion in the pages ahead.

We have said that leaders are "conversational engines" and that effective leadership involves creating and sustaining desired Results in the 3 broad areas of **relation-ships, culture and execution.**

We previously introduced 5 key clusters of leadership conversations, and claim that they are of fundamental importance for leaders and organizations of all sizes and shapes. Think about the way you and others in your organization currently participate in your version of these conversations, and on the quality of Results that are currently being produced. While these aren't the only important conver-sations leaders design, convene and/or participate in, they have direct impact and influence on relationships, culture and execution and therefore will be our focus here:

- Conversation for Relationship – For the purpose of deepening relation-ships and laying the groundwork for future conversations in which care-frontation and healthy, respectful disagreement may be needed. These include conversations of self-disclosure and sharing, often in areas not di-rectly related to current roles within the organization. These conversations may be viewed as mutual "trust deposits" made among members of a team or organization.

- Conversations for Orientation/Context-Setting – For the purpose of build-ing and sustaining shared understanding of organizational and/or team purpose, values, vision, goals, standards and roles. Include on-boarding processes for new employees, as well as ongoing conversations to sustain high levels of shared understanding throughout the organization. Conver-sations that create organizational context, constructively and consciously shaping the organizational "environment" or culture.

- <u>Conversations for Innovation/Speculation</u> – For the purpose of generating ideas and possibilities in order to address concerns, solve problems or take advantage of opportunities. Include brainstorming and other creative-thinking processes that produce alternatives and take advantage of diverse backgrounds and multiple ways of thinking.

- <u>Conversations for Coordinating Action/Implementation</u> – For the purpose of accomplishing Results with and through others. Of central importance, these may be viewed as the "essence of execution" as they involve the basics of collaborative Action: setting direction, enrolling others, making requests and offers and managing promises and commitments.

- <u>Conversations for Progress/Completion</u> – For the purpose of declaring satisfaction or dissatisfaction, checking in at regular intervals within projects or assignments to analyze and evaluate Results; also repeated at completion. These conversations include giving and receiving feedback, listening to multiple perspectives, and understanding the potential implications on future efforts and related processes. They also include declarations of acknowledgement, recognition and celebration… or conversely, declarations of complaint, requests for change, and possibly even termination.

Each of these conversations is convened and conducted by a unique Observer, someone who is a walking, talking bundle of congruency, expressing him- or herself through a unique combination of language, moods/emotions and physical body.

Below we will cover four body dispositions that leaders may intentionally employ for the sake of achieving desired Results in the above key conversations. We will also make connections to a spectrum of emotional terrains that are congruent with each body disposition, again for the sake of achieving each conversation's desired Result.

We have proposed earlier that language is generative; here we propose that your corporeal (physical) stance is equally generative, having a predisposition for specific types of Action and emotional landscapes. The four stances we'll review here are Stability, Resolution, Flexibility and Openness.

As we move through each of these, see if you can "feel yourself" embodying these physical postures. Consider how your most important conversations may unfold when you are able to purposefully assume certain dispositions within certain conversations.

Stability

The flavor of stability we're referring to here would be a corporeal stance of Sovereignty. One's gaze is towards the infinite, breathing deeply & slowly through the nose to the pelvis, exhaling slowly through the nose, and with a moderate firm muscular tone throughout the body. Energetically you feel firmly rooted to the floor as if you had the weight and power of a sumo wrestler in stillness. The momentum of your energy is moving downward.

When you have embodied the essence of King / Queen/ Ruler, you are concerned about order, fertility and blessings. You provide reason and rational operations, integrity, nurturing, generosity, integration and generative energy. With a calm and reassuring voice the King or Queen gives encouragement, especially in times of chaos and strife. He or she provides clear decisions after careful consideration.

Your predispositions for Action are to: provide order, peace and reliability; postpone gratification; facilitate systematic growth; provide nurturance and approval. These are our CEO's, generals, fathers & mothers, and athletic coaches.

Some of the emotional landscapes accessed here are: calmness, subjective detached, dignified, patience, caring and steadiness.

The **Conversation for Orientation and Context-Setting** draws primarily from the corporeal stance of stability, as it is for the purpose of declaring company intentions, helping others visualize and see the road ahead, setting priorities, creating shared understanding and alignment and answering the question "For the sake of what?"

Resolution

The flavor of the corporeal stance of resolution we are referring to is that of the Warrior. One's gaze is tightly focused on a specific point, breathing is short through the nose to the throat, and firm muscular tone throughout the body.

Energetically you feel as though you're a race car driver with engines roaring as you decisively navigate the course at 200 mph. The momentum of your energy is moving forward.

When you have embodied the essence of the Warrior you are concerned about taking Action, rousing energy and motivation, and moving forward with decisive focus and clarity. Highly alert with clear focus of mind and body, the Warrior adapts quickly, employing his skills as strategist and tactician. He is able to realistically assess capacities and limitations in any given situation or person, including himself, with emotional objectivity. Finally, he organizes himself around a central commitment.

Your predisposition for Action in this stance is: to take decisive Action, to be dutiful, loyal and to succeed. These are our top executives, managers and performers. They are our armed forces, police officers, firemen and professional athletes.

Some of the emotional landscapes accessed here are: ambition, boldness and bravery, alertness, discipline, tenacity, subjective detached, self-denial for the cause, courage, endurance, dutifulness and loyalty.

The **Conversation for Coordinating Action** draws primarily from the corporeal stance of resolution, as it is for the purpose of mobilizing people and resources, moving forward with coordinated Action and committed execution. These conversations bring about the tangible achievement of declared goals and desired Results.

Flexibility

The flavor of the corporeal stance of flexibility we are referring to is that of the Magician. One's gaze is wide, taking in the entire panorama; breathing is a short and quick inhale through the nose with a long extended exhale through the mouth and a medium muscular tone throughout the body. Energetically you feel ready to solve the mysteries of the universe. The momentum of your energy is going up to your brain, to the sky.

When you have embodied the essence of the Magician you are concerned about awareness, illumination, technical skill, and knowledge for the benefit of others. The Magician is one who guides processes of transformation, thinking through issues that are not immediately apparent to others.

Your predisposition for Action is to: observe and monitor the data coming from within and without, and through wisdom, push the right buttons at the right time to channel outcomes. These are our inventors, scientists, doctors, shamans, elders, lawyers and technicians.

Some of the emotional landscapes accessed here are: insight, wisdom, subjective detachment, clear sightedness, thoughtfulness, reflection, and objective perspective.

The **Conversation for Innovation and Speculation** draws primarily from the corporeal stance of flexibility, as it is for the purpose of productively exploring possibilities, alternatives and implications, playing "what if?" and drawing out the unique contributions of all involved.

Openness

The flavor of the corporeal stance of openness we are referring to is that of the Lover. One's gaze is diffused and soft, breathing is through the mouth down to the stomach, and muscular tone is light & supple throughout the body. Energetically your desire is to feel everything and to merge and be one with the universe. The momentum of your energy is moving backward.

When you have embodied the essence of the Lover you are concerned about creating, connectedness through feeling and merging in oneness. It is this stance that keeps the other three humane and energized. It is critically important for the well being of self and others.

Your predispositions for Action range from: satiate primal hungers, socialize, connect, rest and renew, heal, relate, listen, create, play, seek pleasure, be subjective, daydream, be nostalgic, do nothing in particular, seek meaning... and more. These are our artists, fictional writers, composers, innovators, and creators... anyone creating original work through feeling vs. thinking.

Some of the emotional landscapes accessed here are: empathy, intuition, desire, gentleness, enthusiasm, vitality, passion, compassion, longing, sensitivity, sensuality, playfulness, spontaneity, indulgence, addiction, joy, and being romantic about our lives and our goals.

The **Conversation for Relationship** draws primarily from the corporeal stance of openness. Making the effort to learn about and connect with those working for and with you sets the foundation for trust, care, and greater capacity for acceptance when conflict over personality differences, behavior patterns, or work situations arise. Simple moments of "How was your weekend?" or "How did your daughter's soccer game go?" said from the emotion of sincerity in a stance of openness send messages that you notice them beyond their position and care about them as human beings – directly impacting your organization's culture.

Finally, the **Conversations for Progress and Completion** draw from a combination of corporeal stances: from flexibility when analyzing and evaluating Results, from stability when declaring satisfaction or dissatisfaction and from openness when listening to multiple perspectives, receiving feedback or celebrating successes.

Bringing It All Together

While we noted particular professions that embody strong traits of the four corporeal stances, the truth is all four reside in each of us at all times. Each is equally important, as they all serve worthy principles. Our purpose here is to encourage you to notice what corporeal stance(s) you've been leading from and assess if these have been serving you.

As you think about your physical stances and the way you carry yourself through time and space, we invite you to consider and reflect on the following questions:

- Are you habitually leading primarily from one or two most of the time?

- Do you have access to all four, specifically in the moment that it matters?

- What one or two do you assess would serve you to practice and employ more often?

- What new possibilities for Action or new Results might be made possible by incorporating 1-2 new corporeal stances into your repertoire?

- Why is that important to you?

Summary of Key Points

We are each unique Observers. Each of us – necessarily and by definition – "sees things" in ways that are uniquely our own. We are all interpreting, and we're all doing so in our unique way.

The Observer that we each are is composed of three separate, yet tightly interwoven elements: Our language (internal thinking and external conversations); our moods and emotions; and our bodies, biology and physical movements

Dispelling the Grand Illusion – that everyone sees things like you do – is very productive and helpful, for it diminishes the tendency to ascribe ill intentions to people who simply happen to see things differently than you do. It also opens the door for the candid and robust dialogue that's required in order to leverage diversity and innovate effectively.

Language does not occur in a vacuum. We cannot even talk about language without bringing moods and emotions and our bodies/biology into the equation.

These three aspects are dynamic and ever-changing. They are not fixed and permanent. Each of these three impacts the other two. Changes in our mood impact our language and our bodies. Changes in our thinking and our external conversations produce changes in our moods / emotions, as well as changes to our bodies and how we move. Doing different things physically has an impact on how we think, what we say, how we say it… as well as on our emotional state.

To establish a new habit or a new practice, we must persevere and keep it up for a period of time (some studies say between 21 – 35 days). Success requires that we keep practicing and keep doing the new behavior even through initial periods in which no new Results are obtained.

Each of these three – language, moods/emotions and body – can be our starting point for bringing lasting changes to our lives. We can take advantage of the power inherent in these connections. We can purposefully make changes in one area, knowing that if we keep it up long enough, the other two will be influenced as well. In this way, a new Way of Being is brought forth and a new "coherency" is established. If we so choose, we can actively design ourselves.

Four fundamental body dispositions available to leaders (and all of us) are: Stability, Flexibility, Resolution and Openness. By purposefully embodying these dispositions, leaders are able to far more effectively convene certain key leadership conversations. Not all conversations require the same physical and emotional energy in order to be effective. These distinctions in the domain of our physical bodies can serve us in being more purposeful and effective in our most important conversations.

Application

1. Here is one exercise we've done in our workshops to give participants a feel for what we've been talking about here. You can do this now, if you'd like, to give yourself the experience of congruency that we've discussed.

   First, sit in a chair with both feet on the ground, about shoulder width apart. Roll your shoulders forward and slump them over, as you look at the ground between your feet. Your posture should be one of slumped over, head down, looking down. Once you've achieved this position, say the following out loud, with enthusiasm:

   - *I am incredibly enthusiastic about possibilities in my life!*
   - *I am meeting my challenges with tremendous optimism!*
   - *I am achieving great Results fueled by unending ambition!*

   See what you notice regarding the connection between your internal conversation, external conversation, your mood/emotion, and your body's position.

   Next, let's do the opposite. Stand up in a very straight body position, chest out, shoulders back, head up, facing the world this way. Imagine there's a string attached to the top of your head, pulling you straight up. Now smile broadly and say the following, in a loud and confident voice:

   - *Nothing I do makes a difference.*
   - *I have no options or possibilities.*
   - *Things are hopeless, no matter what I or anybody else does.*

   Again, see what you notice.

2. While many of us already know this, and already know at an intuitive level about these connections, most of us haven't taken full advantage of them in designing new Results into our lives. To do this, we need new distinctions, a new framework based on this new understanding of language, coupled with practice over time. For this, consider these exercises:

   - Notice how your particular way of walking, standing, and carrying yourself is compares to that of others. What similarities and/or differences do you notice? How do you describe your own way? Has it changed over time?

- Notice how your predominant ways of walking, standing and carrying yourself are connected to your most-prevalent moodspace. Notice also how they're connected to certain recurring internal conversations. What might happen if you shifted some things here?

- Consider one important conversation that you say you'd like to have, but for whatever reason have been avoiding. What body disposition would best support that conversation? Would it be Stability, Flexibility, Resolution or Openness? Would you be standing tall, looking the person in the eye... or would you be slumped over, looking downward... or would you be sitting down, or what? Where would you be looking? How would your shoulders and chest and breathing be?

- Consider the same conversation as above. What emotion seems to be best for this conversation and most consistent with the body position and body movement you'll need? Similarly, what physical surroundings might be most conducive to having this conversation?

- Identify any physical movements or motions that you avoid (dance, yoga, exercises, massage, sitting meditation, walking, riding a bike)? What internal stories, narratives or beliefs have you created about these? Are these still true for you? Do they work for you today, given the Results you say you want? If not, what new stories might serve you better? What's preventing you from authoring and living out of them?

- Think of the physical activities that you really love and participate in frequently. What is the impact of these on your mood? On your conversations?

- Think of those special places where you can take your body (e.g. beach, mountains, forest, lake) and that produce a positive emotional shift for you. Think of what you can do that will enable you spend more of your time in such places.

CHAPTER 7

THE EXTRAORDINARY LEADER'S BLUEPRINT AND TOOLS

"At a foundational level, your organization can be understood as human beings making and managing promises with each other. Now, you can do this well or you can do this poorly. But you're doing it now, and you can't not do it."

– Chalmers Brothers

The remainder of this book is intended to accomplish three broad objectives:

- To introduce to you a powerful organizational framework for more deeply understanding and more effectively improving your organization;

- To illuminate the relationships and interdependencies which exist among relationships, culture and execution; and

- To share with you a set of proven, practical tools (fundamental Language Acts) that can be employed by you and your employees in order to more effectively produce extraordinary relationships, powerful culture and world-class execution.

A New Organizational Framework

Before moving into specific tools, let's begin with an organizational "blueprint" or framework within which the tools will be used. The claim is this: No matter how simple or complex, centralized or decentralized, large or small your organization may be, it can be understood by the graphic that follows:

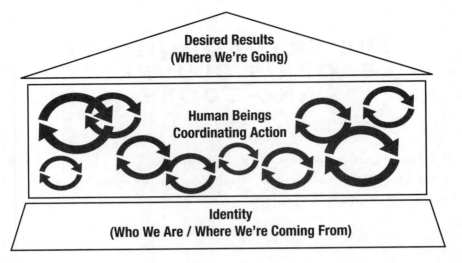

In other words, any and all organizations within any and all industries can be understood as human beings coordinating Action (the middle of the house) for the purpose of achieving some desired Results (the roof). The way the people coordinate Action is shaped and guided by the organization's purpose, values, standards and roles (the foundation).

The roof may be understood as the organizational "go to" – the goals, objectives and future vision – while the foundation may be understood as the organizational "come from." The roof and the foundation may be understood as the organizational context, while the middle of the house can be understood as the organizational content.

The middle of the house – the arena of collaboration or coordinating Action – can be understood as having two equally important aspects:

- Reporting relationships – the "vertical" aspect
- Processes – the "horizontal" aspect

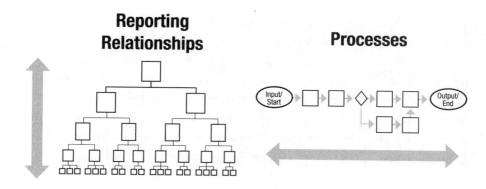

All organizations include both of these dimensions. The reporting relationships involve spheres and boundaries of authority, functional areas, roles, responsibilities and delegation. The processes include the inputs, Action steps, decision points and outputs that comprise the mechanisms by which the organization obtains customers, creates products or services, and ultimately delivers these products or services to the customers.

This "lens" allows us to more clearly see and understand the ways in which leaders, teams and employees collaborate and coordinate Action in order to achieve desired Results. We will move into this more deeply in the chapters that follow, but for now we will state the basic claim: this collaboration and coordination of Action – for all organizations, no matter what – is *accomplished by people making and managing promises with each other*. Seeing and understanding this is hugely different than not seeing and understanding this! These promises are made and managed – ongoingly – both vertically and horizontally. And the way in which this occurs has a dramatic impact on the success of all organizations, including yours.

Leaders are involved, of course, with the roof, the foundation and the middle, although in very different ways. Your ability to produce and sustain desired relationship Results, culture Results and execution Results can be dramatically improved by understanding these 3 dimensions and their relationships to each other.

Here, we make a big promise to you: ***By acquiring new distinctions in these domains, by examining the different types of conversations involved and learning the specific Language Acts included within each, you will dramatically improve your effectiveness as a leader***.

You will more quickly and clearly identify "root causes" of performance issues, as well as more effectively intervene to bring about improvements. You will improve your ability to leverage talent and resources in order to take advantage of opportunities, and you will create environments in which new opportunities are identified sooner in the first place. You will acquire a powerful and empowering set of tools, as well as the ability to share these tools with your colleagues and employees. And in doing so, you will create opportunities to bring about unprecedented possibilities for yourself and your organization. You will open a very real space for creating breakthrough Results.

The Leader's Tool Kit

Every profession has its own set of tools – a carpenter's took kit includes hammers, chisels and saws, while a surgeon's includes scalpels, forceps, refractors and clamps. Used well, these tools enable the users to produce powerful Results.

Similarly, leaders also have their own unique sets of tools. As we covered previously, the work of leaders is fundamentally conversational in nature. Recall: Leaders design and convene conversations that produce desired Results. Leaders at all levels are "conversational engines." Because of this, leaders' tools necessarily fall under the umbrella of what we refer to as Language Acts (also known as Speech Acts). We claim that it is critically important for leaders to gain competency in the use of these "tools." The next few chapters will present and discuss these Language Acts in great detail.

Very early in this book we made a big claim, that our language has to do with Action, with coordination of Action, and with creating and generating. In a very real way, we speak ourselves into the world. This is contrasted with the widely held view that language is first and foremost a passive tool used for labeling, describing and communicating with others about the way things are.

Our active, creative and generative understanding is the broad new interpretation upon which everything else we're sharing with you rests. In the chapters that follow, we go from this broad interpretation of language toward the specific Actions that we say we're involved in with our language. **That is, if language is Action (as we say it is) and if language creates and generates (as we say it does), then *what exactly are the specific, generative Actions leaders take to produce desired Results?***

As indicated below, we will be moving directly into the specific Actions leaders (and team members) take in order to positively shape relationships, culture and execution… and drive breakthrough Results. We will be covering specific types of conversations, and specific Language Acts that are used within these conversations.

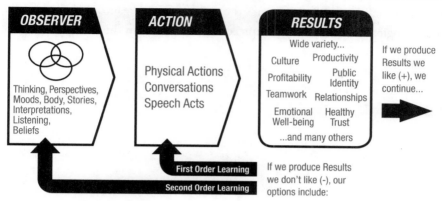

Remember our conversation about the power of distinctions? We are referring now to distinctions in language, which represent new possibilities for taking new Action and producing breakthrough Results. Building directly on the work of John Searle and J. L. Austin, and especially Fernando Flores, we offer that no matter what, when human beings are thinking or speaking, we are always involved with one or more of the following:

1. Assertions

2. Assessments (a special type of Declaration)

3. Declarations

4. Requests

5. Offers

6. Promises

We were initially introduced to these Language Acts – and the incredible possibilities for new Action they represent – through our coursework at Education for Living and the Newfield Network – and especially through the teachings of Julio Olalla. It was here that we were led to more deeply understand the connection to business, leadership and organizational performance – which has formed the basis for how we now share this work.

The above 6 Language Acts are understood as the "universe set" of Actions that we – and everyone – have at our disposal in any and all situations. And how we wield these tools – how we use assertions, assessments, declarations, requests, offers and promises – dramatically impacts the types of relationships we are able to build and sustain, the nature of the workplace culture we are able to establish, as well as the quality of our execution – the ability of our organizations to actually achieve tangible (and sometimes unprecedented) Results in the real world.

So let's begin.

CHAPTER 8

ASSERTIONS AND ASSESSMENTS

"Assertions have to do with what is so.
Assessments have to do with what is possible."

- Julio Olalla

Let's begin this way, with two statements:

I am a man.　　　**I am stupid.**

Our key question is: What's the difference between these 2 statements? (Women usually come up with different responses than men here!) Let's add a few more examples. Please examine all the statements in the **left** column below. What do we traditionally call these sorts of statements? In our everyday speech, what do we call these?

I am a man.	I am stupid.
Tom is the CEO of AA Corp.	Tom is a strong CEO and a good leader.
The book weighs 8 pounds.	The book is heavy.
Anita is 5'11".	Anita is tall.
It's 68 degrees outside, with no clouds.	The weather today is great.

Most of us would say that we usually call the statements in the left column "facts" or something to this effect. We agree, and would like to introduce a new distinction that can be understood as being very close to our traditional understanding of facts. We say that every statement in the left column is an *assertion*. This is one of the new distinctions to be brought forth in this section.

With assertions, the speaker is committed to establishing what is "true" and what is "false" – for him / herself as well as for the community of listeners. Assertions can also be seen as the so-called facts of life. They are where language is most descriptive and least generative. Let's look now at the **right** column below. What do we usually call these types of statements?

I am a man.	**I am stupid.**
Tom is the CEO of AA Corp.	**Tom is a strong CEO and a good leader.**
The book weighs 8 pounds.	**The book is heavy.**
Anita is 5'11".	**Anita is tall.**
It's 68 degrees outside, with no clouds.	**The weather today is great.**

Most of us call the right column statements "opinions" or "judgments" or "subjective" statements. We agree, and offer the distinction of *assessment*. This is the other new distinction that will be brought forth in this section.

We say an assessment is a speech act in which the speaker defines how he or she relates to the world or to a specific event. With assessments, it's "good" or "bad" or "right" or "wrong" or "tall" or "short," etc. Here, the speaker is committed to taking a stand based on what he/she observes, coming to some opinion or choice or judgment about what is being observed.

As a leader, your ability to keep assertions and assessments separate, distinct from each other is absolutely critical – as is your ability to build a team in which all members are able to do this, too. In many ways our language traps us here, because it appears that the statement "John is six feet five inches" is the same sort of statement as "John is tall." In our traditional understanding, it appears that 'six feet five inches' and 'tall' are both properties of John. We say no! But our collapsing together of these very different types of statements has consequences on the Actions we take, the types of relationships we form, and on the Results we produce. Let's explore a bit here. While assertions are close to what we traditionally call "facts," and while assessments are close to what we traditionally call "opinions," there are key differences worth exploring.

Some examples of assertions and assessments: *The room is 65' by 98.'* Assertion or assessment? It's an assertion. It's either true or false that the room is 65 x 98. Any objective third party with a tape measure could prove the true-ness or false-ness of this statement. Let's say in this case that it's a true assertion, that the room indeed is 65 x 98.

How about this statement: *The room is 1,000,000' by 2,000,000.'* Assertion or assessment? In this case, it's still an assertion, but it's false. The objective third party with the tape measure does his thing, and guess what – the room is NOT 1 million feet by 2 million feet.

Assertions can be true or false and can be verified by an objective third party who has the distinctions involved. We already have the distinctions "feet" and "inches," so it's possible for us to prove whether or not the room is indeed 65 by 98.

For example, in order to say whether or not it's true that the computer's combobulator has been degaussed and requires an upgraded fuse pack, the third party would have to already possess the distinctions combobulator, degauss, and fuse pack. Armed with the appropriate distinctions, one could then say whether or not the assertion is true. Without the distinctions, one could not verify the true-ness or false-ness of the statement. As Jeff Spring has said, without the distinctions, all we may be able to do in these sorts of situations is ask, "How does that translate into dollars?"

How about these statements: *The room is spacious.* Or *The room is cramped.* Assertions or assessments? These are assessments. Opinions. Judgments. And what if a colleague also said, "All right, let's get to the truth here. I want the bottom line. Is the room really spacious or is it really cramped? What's the final truth about this?" Some people may respond immediately with, "The room is cramped" while others may just as quickly say, "Well, anybody can see that this room is spacious." And others may say "It depends." This is a key point – we say that the room doesn't have a property, in and of itself, of spaciousness or crampedness. The room just is. All it has are its assertions. Spacious and cramped are not properties of the room. Whether or not the room is spacious or the room is cramped has everything to do with *who's doing the looking!*

So while assertions belong to the thing being observed (in this case, the room), assessments belong to the Observer. This is a fundamental, crucial difference to observe and understand. It makes a huge difference in how we build relationships, work and be together, solve problems, gauge progress and interact, at a multitude of levels.

We could go on and on with examples. "The car is sporty." "The car is boxy." Well, which is it? Is the car really sporty or is it really boxy? We say the car doesn't have a property, in and of itself, of sportiness or boxiness. The car just is. Mr. Johnson says it's sporty, while Mr. Ferrari may say it's boxy. Again, these are assessments. They belong to the Observer, not to the thing being observed.

How many of us know people who act as if their assessments (personal opinions, judgments) are assertions (facts)? Many of us do – this is a common phenomenon. No surprise here, given our traditional understanding and education in this area. Our observation is that many people who live as if their assessments are assertions have difficulty in forming healthy, mutually respectful relationships with the other non-hermits in their lives. They come across as self-righteous, opinionated, stubborn, arrogant and they close off possibilities that alternative assessments may reveal. Said another way, their Actions in language generate this public identity for themselves, and usually this public identity is not what they're trying to create!

Our first key point involving these distinctions is this:

- Assertions belong to the thing being observed and can be true or false. An objective third party can always verify the true-ness or false-ness of the assertion.

- Assessments belong to the Observer, and in many ways reveal more about the Observer than they do about the thing being observed. There is always room for another assessment. No third party can ever "prove" an assessment true or false. They are simply personal judgments made by different Observers out of different standards, beliefs, values and moods.

Let's also notice this – we assess everything! We assess people, plants, buildings, shoes, jobs, weather, movies, traffic, everything. We seem to be assessment-making machines, producing assessments at every turn. This isn't good or bad, it's simply part of living in language. But since we produce such volumes of assessments, our claim is that we can develop some competency here, we can become more capable of making solid assessments and therefore move into the future in a more grounded way, providing us our best chance for producing the future Results we say we want.

This brings us to a second major point about assertions and assessments:

- Assertions are descriptive and "factual" and have to do with the past and the present.

- Assessments have everything to do with the future, and can be viewed as "stepping stones" toward the future.

Influencing How We Interpret Future Events

Let's explore more here, because it's this future impact of assessments that is often unseen and is at the heart of many of our issues. Example: *Wu missed three meetings in a row in October.* This is an assertion, and it can be proven true or false. Let's say in this case it's true. If a camera was in the meeting room, it would not have seen Wu at those three meetings. Can you get a sense that this statement just sits there, that it's a statement of something that already happened and it's describing that situation? It's factual, having to do with the past and it has no particular emotional flavor.

How about this statement: *Wu is unreliable.* This is an assessment, and can you now feel it swing toward a prediction of Wu's future behavior? You are now "orienting" yourself toward Wu in a certain way. For example, if you have the assessment in the present that Wu is unreliable, and in the future he becomes available for selection to your team, guess who you don't select... Wu! Right. But why? Because of your assessment that he's unreliable. Your assessment of him in the present served to influence your behavior towards him (in this case, that of not choosing him) in the future.

Is it possible that Wu could have missed the same three meetings (same assertions) but you could have instead assessed him as reliable? Yes, of course this is possible.

In this case, your assessment of reliable would orient you in such a way that in the future, you may choose Wu for your team. Our key point here is that regardless of whether the assessments may be "positive" or "negative," they all serve to influence our interpretations and Actions and therefore Results in the future. Sometimes the influence is minor and insignificant, and sometimes the influence is huge and is at the heart of everything.

Back to the first assessment of unreliable. Key question – when did Wu go from being "reliable" to "unreliable?" Was it when he missed the first meeting, or was it the 3 in a row that did it? Or was it 2 in a row in a one-month period?

Key question: What are my standards – your standards – our standards – for reliability?

If you miss 1 meeting do we assess you as unreliable? Or is it 3 in a month? Or 6 in a year? What is it? This has to do with what we call *standards*. The reason different people have different assessments about the same event or situation is that different people have different standards. The real problem is not that we have different standards, of course. The problem is that they are often hidden and unspoken. Conversations for the purpose of sharing standards are extremely important and powerful conversations to have, for personal as well as professional relationships. And these are precisely the conversations which are often missing.

What is your standard for "effective?" For "appropriate?" For "efficient?" For being a "good" team member? And have you shared your standards with your team members? With your colleagues? With your direct reports? Can you begin to see that we often make many assessments about many things, influencing our future interpretations all the while, while not having any declared standards and not being aware that this is happening. (Standards live as declarations, a very powerful and generative speech act. We'll cover declarations in our next chapter.)

These standards act as our judge and jury, for we compare everything against our standards. When something is in line with our standards we assess it one way. When it's not, we assess it another way – very often not being conscious at all of what our standards are, and not having had conversations about these standards with people who matter. Another point that you may have come to already: quite often, in the absence of these conversations, we tend to assume that our standards are the "right" or "true" or "natural" or "obviously correct" standards. If you find yourself in recurrent arguments or disagreements with others, we encourage you to bring your standards to the surface. Are others operating with different standards than you are? Discuss and examine your standards and their standards, and seek <u>conscious</u> agreement on a set of <u>shared</u> standards that will be used moving forward.

To continue, if you assess Wu as unreliable, what Actions from him will you readily see in the future? What will you absolutely notice about him? *You'll notice every single time he's late, no matter what the reason.* Make sense? And guess which Actions of his will you miss entirely or write off as an exception or aberration? You guessed it – Wu being on time.

Our personal assessments impact how we see things and interpret them – they influence the Observer that we are (see below) which has an obvious impact on our Actions and Results.

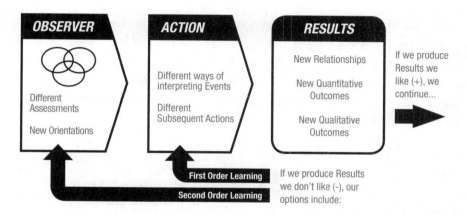

We can also say it this way: If you put me in the "unreliable" box, I often can't get out by myself!

One reason for this may go back to the background conversation of "I'm Right." We each want to be right about our beliefs (in this case, that Wu is unreliable) and so this influences how we interpret things that haven't yet happened. We tend to interpret so as to make ourselves and our beliefs (our assessments) right.

Consider this scenario: Two 3rd grade teachers, Ms. Smith and Ms. Jones, are pulled aside by the principal before the beginning of the school year. The principal says, "Ms. Smith, you've got the most seniority here and have been named

Teacher of the Year. Congratulations – you're getting a special Honors class this semester. We've taken the top 5% of students from the other classes and combined them into our first ever Honors class. Have a great year. I know it'll be exciting, challenging, and fun for you and for these excellent students."

The principal then turns to Ms. Jones and says, "Ms. Jones, on the other hand, you have the least seniority at our school and we've decided to do another pilot. In this case, we've decided to pull out some of the lower-performing and behavior-problem students from the regular student body and combine them in a remedial class. We're tired of this small minority of students disrupting and slowing down the general population, so we've decided to create classes just for them, kind of "out of the way," and see what happens to the other classes without their influence. Now I know you didn't sign up for this, but this is all we've got for you this semester. Do the best you can, and we'll try to get you a regular class next semester."

Get the picture? Now, in reality, both teachers get regular classes. Both are assigned normal, randomly selected groups of 3rd graders, just like always. Make a prediction – what do you think happens, in Ms. Smith's class and Ms. Jones' class, over the course of the semester? You guessed it – Ms. Smith's students *are* the honors kids! Ms. Jones' kids *are* the poor students and behavior problems! And they have evidence to prove it:

In the "honors" class, little Susie's standing on her desk, flapping her arms is viewed as a glorious display of spontaneous creativity... while little Ann's doing the same thing in the "remedial" class is seen as disruptive behavior. In the "honors" class, if a student fails a test, it's "oh, little Johnny failed a test... wait, 3 more kids failed... to have 4 honors students fail may mean that I need to do something different with the pre-requisites or with how this topic is structured in the material..." On the other hand, if little Johnny and 3 other kids fail a test in the "remedial" class it's "Look, I knew you weren't gonna pass it anyway, we've gotta move on, open your books to the next topic."

We claim that it's not the kids' behavior alone that influences the teachers' experience and interpretations. Rather, it's that behavior occurring against the already-held assessments that produces the particular interpretations. For us, this is the mechanism underneath what we commonly call the "self-fulfilling prophecy."

Maybe it's not so much "*I'll believe it when I see it.*" Maybe, in real life, in a wide variety of situations, what is actually more prevalent is "*I'll see it when I believe it.*" And this takes us back to the whole topic of beliefs. The great majority of all our beliefs are assessments, not assertions. They belong to us, as Observers, and do not have so much to do with how things really are.

We say that our assessments say more about the Observer than they do about what's being observed. Consider: One teacher says little Johnny is stupid. The other says little Johnny is rambunctious. You listen, and still don't know very much about little Johnny. However, two teachers have just now revealed themselves to you. You may allow one teacher to teach your child, and the other you will not let near your child. Make sense?

Another example: My (Chalmers') former business partner Mark and I are driving along in middle Tennessee and I look out the window and say "Look at that huge mountain." He looks out and says "Where?" " Right over there" I reply. "I still can't see it… oh, you mean that little hill!" Obviously, what's a huge mountain to me is a hill to Mark, who grew up in east Tennessee. I grew up in south Louisiana, and so to me, anything over the height of an overpass is a mountain! We aren't describing the landscape as much as we are revealing ourselves and our standards (which are often hidden and unspoken).

Here's a prediction: If you are born and raised in New York City and in your early 20's you move to virtually anywhere else in the United States, with the possible exception of Los Angeles, you will find yourself confronted with light traffic! Is this not the case? Is it the traffic, or is it you? It's you. It's you and your standards for what constitutes "heavy" and "light" traffic. This is what's going on.

A woman in a workshop relayed a story to us about her return from a visit to Hong Kong. This woman was about 5'4" tall, and she returned and announced jubilantly to her friends "I'm not short – I'm medium!" What had happened? Had she actually grown during the trip? Of course not. She was with a group of people, over a period of time, who simply had different standards for tallness and shortness. Again, with assessments, we reveal ourselves and our standards more than we describe.

Similar to Facts and Opinions... But With a Very Important Difference

So far it's clear, is it not, that assessments and assertions are very similar to what we have historically understood as facts and opinions? We say yes, but at this point would offer one very important difference: In the traditional teaching of facts and opinions, no one ever taught us that our assessments in the present dramatically impact how we interpret future events! That aspect of the teaching, for virtually all of us, is conspicuously absent from the curriculum – is it not? No one ever taught us that our assessments become part of the Observer that we are, impacting how we observe, see things, interpret, take Action and produce future Results in the world.

And it's precisely this future impact of our present assessments that's crucial to observe and notice about ourselves. It's crucial that our Big Eye is turned on enough to notice this about ourselves, for this is the first step toward being at choice regarding whether or not the assessments that we created serve us, and whether or not we should update them – given the Results we say we want.

Virtually all of our beliefs are assessments, not assertions. And as we have all experienced, our beliefs – in a wide variety of areas – do indeed dramatically impact how we interpret future events and situations related to the belief. And these interpretations, of course, orient us and impact our choices and quality of Actions, which shape our Results. And somehow none of this is taught to us in school.

Jim Collins claims that *"Greatness is not a function of circumstance. Greatness, it turns out, is largely a matter of conscious choice and discipline."* It's precisely because of the future impact of assessments on our choices, Actions and Results that we agree: **One of the most important areas in which we must exercise discipline is in keeping assertions and assessments separate from each other!** It is this very discipline that enables us to more purposefully and effectively produce breakthrough Results – in any given situation and at any given time.

The Social and Historical Nature of Assessments

Our assessments reveal ourselves and our standards, which also points to the social nature or social influence of assessments. When you make an assessment, it's true that you're making it as an individual human being. What's not so obvious is the impact of where, when, and how you were born and raised and live have on the standards and assessments you make. Many of "your" standards are actually the standards of your community, and the same is true for all of us. We simply picked them up as we went, never consciously or actively declaring them ourselves. We personally didn't get to choose these standards. They were part of the history of our community when we arrived, and we simply adopted them as our own. And they continue to influence us today.

Let's also notice that assessments are historical. That is, the standards with which we make assessments change over time. This becomes very apparent in the world of sports, where a 4-minute mile used to be "world-class" or "excellent," (and actually, at one point in time, "impossible") and now runners routinely post times in that range. Or the records in many sprints, pole vaulting, throwing and jumping events. Or what's now considered "very big" or "really strong" for NFL linemen or NBA centers. Consider also fashion, where what's "in" or "pretty" or "trendy" obviously has a great deal to do with when the assessment is made. We could go on and on. The underlying standards change over time, so therefore the assessments that are produced change over time.

Our Assessments About Ourselves

The story about the 2 teachers shows how our assessments of others impact our interpretations and interactions, which strongly influence our relationships and Results. And back to the Big Eye, this often occurs without our noticing that this is happening. We also say that our assessments about ourselves have the same power. Consider the story that follows.

Little Johnny's in the 2nd grade and is restless at school, doodling during math and generally being distracted and not involved in the lesson. His teacher comes up and sees the doodles he's drawn, frowns and says "Little Johnny, how could you do something so stupid? You know we're supposed to be doing our lesson. Go the principal's office." Little Johnny goes to the principal's office and later, goes home that day and wants to play with his big sister. He goes into her room and accidentally knocks off the CD player, which falls to the floor and breaks. She says, "Johnny, look what you did, you can be so stupid. Play somewhere else." He goes downstairs and wants to help his mom so he goes into the kitchen and starts helping her dry the dishes. He drops one on the floor and it breaks. Mom's had a long day and is tired, and she says "Johnny, that is so stupid. Please just go in the other room, I'll finish by myself."

This goes on for a few years, and now Little Johnny's in 10th grade. The teacher puts a problem on the board and says, "Class, this problem is in a new area and is a tough one. Who can try to answer it?" Key question: Does Little Johnny raise his hand? No. Why not? Most people answer with "because he's stupid." More correctly, he sees himself as stupid. He assesses himself as stupid, but doesn't see it as an assessment. He sees it as The Truth, as an assertion, as a fact, as the way things are.

Flash forward to when Johnny's 25 years old and working, and a promotion to supervisor position becomes available. The manager says they're going to promote from within, and anyone wishing to apply should have their application on his desk by Tuesday. Does Johnny apply? No. Why? Because (he tells himself) he's stupid. Again, more accurately, he's holding the assessment – the belief – about himself that he's stupid, and he doesn't see it as an assessment. He sees it as an assertion, as a fact.

This is a clear case of someone living as if an assessment (stupid) is an assertion. We say that there's no such "thing" as stupid. Stupid isn't a thing. It's an assessment. Show me stupid. Where is it? It's not as if right behind my spleen is my stupid. You got 1 pound of it, Bob got 4 pounds, and I'm out of luck because I happened to get 10 pounds of stupid. But Johnny lived as if the assessments others made about him were actually The Truth about him. He lived as if his own assessments about himself were actually The Truth about him. In both cases we claim nothing is further from the truth! Stupid is not a permanent, fixed feature or objective characteristic of Johnny's personhood. Stupid is always an assessment, made first by others and then by himself, about his Actions or lack of Actions in a given domain. Change the Actions, change the standards, and the assessments will change. They're not permanent, fixed, facts or features of anyone's personhood. They're assessments, always open to revision and updating.

Of course, Little Johnny didn't interpret this way when his teacher, sister, and mom said those things to him. His interpretation (declaration) was "I'm stupid." And this is consistent with how a great many children and adults interpret. When I (Chalmers) was first introduced to this, I remember thinking about how important the words we say to our kids are. I still think about this as I'm parenting my own children now.

Moods, Emotions and Assertions and Assessments

Our next big claim about assertions and assessments:

- Assertions are not influenced by moods and emotions
- Assessments are dramatically influenced by our moods and emotions.

You may report that it's 68 degrees, no clouds, and 20 percent humidity no matter what mood you're in.   But you'll never say "it's a great day" unless you're in a good mood!

Recalling our three circles drawing, we see the connection between mood/emotion, body and language. Here we can clearly see the connection between moods and language. This connection shows up strongly, precisely in the assessments we produce. Reflect a moment. It's easy to recall situations when the assessments we came up with about a given event or situation were connected to the mood we happened to be in at that time. We already know this, though sometimes we don't see it so clearly.   If you happen to be in a moodspace of happiness (let's say your daughter just found out she got a perfect score on a difficult test), you will absolutely react to an event – let's say a flat tire – differently than if you were already in a mood of resentment or "overwhelm" when the flat occurred. We will also react to – interpret – conversations differently. We can all point to numerous situations in which this has occurred.

We can also see the connection, starting with observing a person's assessments and working the other way.   For example, imagine you're with a person over a long period of time, and this person consistently produces assessments of "that won't work" or "no, I'm sure that's not going to work out well" or "nothing will make a difference in that."   What mood would you say this person lives in and probably be correct? Most of us would call it pessimism or resignation, certainly not joy or elation. The connection between moods and language shows up very strongly, very clearly, in our assessments.

You want to know something about your mood? Take a look at your assessments. You want to consciously design a different mood? Take a look at your assessments – particularly your competency to ground your assessments (which we'll cover shortly) with true assertions, as well as the way you declare standards for observing that are shared with others. For example, if I'm in a mood of resignation I may have lots of assessments that "this won't work, no matter what." What's possible is to have a conversation with someone in which I share my assessments, as well as the grounds for making the assessment and the standards from which I'm observing. More on this shortly.

Borrowing Others' Assessments

We often "borrow" others' assessments about people that we've never even met. And if we're not careful, these can influence our interpretations without our realizing what's going on. For example, let's say that at work you know Juan but you don't know the newest employee named Bob. One day, Juan may say to you "You know, Bob is a good employee and all that, but he's kinda lazy and seems to be pretty arrogant about how he does his reporting." A few days go by and in the hall you see Juan and another man walking toward me. As you approach, Juan says, "Hi, I'd like to introduce you to our newest employee, Bob." What's the first thing that goes through your mind? "Oh, here's lazy and arrogant Bob." And often, once you get to know Bob, you may have very different assessments of him! He's not lazy or arrogant to you – you may have very different standards than Juan does. Or Juan may not be a competent Observer of Bob. But it doesn't matter – we do it anyway.

We've worked with school systems quite a bit over the last few years, and we see this phenomenon also with kids. Third grade teacher Ms. Smith may say to fourth grade teacher Ms. Jones, "Oh, I see you're gonna get Little Johnny next year. You better buckle up – he's a real troublemaker." Now, to a certain degree we can all understand the reasonableness of sharing information. But the key point to observe here is that it's very possible to do this without being conscious of the influence it has on how we interpret, form beliefs and take Action.

One gentleman at a workshop shared this story with us. He was the incoming manager to an office of about 40 people or so. The outgoing manager offered to take him to lunch to "let him know exactly what he was inheriting." The incoming manager politely declined, saying he'd like to get to know the employees in his own way. In this way everyone would have a "clean slate" to start with.

Who Do You Give Permission To Assess You?

Let's say you're walking down the street in a new city, and someone passes you and says "ugly tie!" and you hurl yourself into the gutter, devastated. This is an example of your granting to the universe the authority to assess you in the domain of your clothes. On the other extreme is giving nobody the authority to assess you, in any domain. This shows up as a profound predisposition to not let anyone else give you their authentic experience of you, to share their assessments about you with you. This, in turn, robs you of information that could be very valuable for you to have, for with it, you could then choose to take different Actions and design a different Result or public identity. Or not. But either way, you'd get to choose. You'd not be blind anymore.

Your spouse may say "I think you were rude to Ms. Jones at the party" and you say "I wasn't rude – she bumped right into me." Or a colleague may say "You know, I think how you steered that meeting wasn't exactly what we were looking for" and you may respond with "Well it certainly wasn't my fault. I stuck to the agenda and everybody else just got distracted." We could go on and on. Here are 2 important questions for all of us:

- Who do you give the authority (permission) to assess you?
- And in what domains?

These are powerful questions to reflect upon, because the answers don't have to have an "all or nothing" flavor. One of our teachers mentioned that one component of wisdom may have to do with who you choose to listen to about specific aspects of your life. We agree with that. And let's be clear – in some organizational settings, others do have the authority to assess you whether or not you like it or think it's fair or right or whatever. Consider the army. The drill sergeant absolutely has the authority to assess the private in the domain of his/her clothing, manner of walking, talking, in a great many areas. But passers-by on the street do not. In many organizations, bosses do have the authority to assess subordinates' performance, and a variety of approaches are in use today (some absolutely more effective than others). But that same boss may not have the authority to assess the subordinate in the domain of his/her hobby, woodworking.

Another example – we give you full permission to assess us in the domain of this book. We're first-time collaborators, relatively inexperienced authors, and we have a great deal yet to learn about writing. So your feedback about the content, context, flow, value, connections from topic to topic, and so on are very valuable to us. We request your assessments here, and we value them. And with all respect, we do not give you the authority to assess us in the domain of our yards. You may drive by our houses, have lots and lots of assessments about our landscaping and lawn, and it's incredible how much we just don't care what those are! And let's be clear – we're not saying that you won't _have_ assessments in this area. You may have them, we just won't care what they are!

We had the pleasure of hearing author Brene Brown speak at a coaching conference in 2014 and she shared with the group something very much related to what we're talking about here. She has a practice of writing, on a 2-inch by 2-inch square of paper, the names of people whose opinions (assessments) of her she really cares about. And this, she keeps in her wallet. What an excellent practice. Think about it – this is not an all-or-nothing situation. But the number of people whose opinions of us really matter should likely be a small number, and likely could be written on a very small piece of paper. One of our teachers said it this way: _As a leader, you will undoubtedly produce negative assessments in others from time to time. Get ready for this, as it simply goes with the territory._ The questions for all of us are:

- Are you clear about <u>whose</u> assessments about you really matter?
- And have you created opportunities for conversations with those people, in which they can share both their "positive" and "negative" assessments with you?

Do you want to know something about yourself? Ask someone else.

This is subtle, but it's important. Do you have anybody in your life who will give you the "straight poop" about your Actions? That is, someone who – with your permission – gives you the benefit of their best thinking. They give you their actual assessments. This means they won't withhold the assessments, even if they predict that you won't like what you hear. We say it's a great thing to have some relationships that include those sorts of conversations (see paragraph above). It's a real blessing to have relationships in which others are truthful with us, though this doesn't mean that they have The Truth about us. This distinction between being truthful and having The Truth is critical to understand, as it can allow us to much more purposefully and effectively design our own public identity – and to do so with dignity.

Nobody wants to be the bull in a china shop, right? That is, none of us wants to be the last person to be aware that some behavior of ours is coming across as particularly damaging or negative, to the extent that it's diminishing opportunities, limiting possibilities and closing doors. Now, what we do with the feedback is another story, and clearly represents a situation in which we get to choose whether to take it on board, how to respond and whether or not to change anything. *But to never get the feedback in the first place means you don't even get to choose.*

For example, let's say that we request that participants in a workshop provide us feedback after the session is completed, and let's say that all 15 people do. Is it possible that everyone is being truthful, and that we may receive 15 different feedbacks? Of course it is – because each is providing us with a different assessment, a different perspective, about our behaviors. One person may have seen us as being assertive, another may have seen us as arrogant, and yet another may have seen us as confident and knowledgeable. One may interpret our discussion in front of the room as being unhealthy disagreement, while another may see that as healthy dialogue. We could go on and on. Each is being truthful, fully honest with him/herself and with us. The key, of course, is that each is coming from his or her own set of standards, beliefs, experiences, moods, and so on.

If 1 person in the workshop reports that we appear rude, that's one thing. However, if 14 out of 15 report this, that's quite another. Or if 1 person on our list shares with us that we're coming across as inappropriate or off-target in a given situation, that's one thing. But if 14 out of the 15 say the same thing, that's a different story.

As related to feedback about how we're showing up, we say this: *Assessments are never The Truth, but they may be useful.*

Does this make sense? In these settings, these assessments are extremely valuable in allowing each of us to create a more powerful public identity, and out of that, healthier and more mutually beneficial relationships. They're valuable because they represent valid information about how we are being perceived, about how we are showing up. They're valuable because they give us information we can then use in making a choice – with both eyes open – about the Actions we will take in the future. They aren't The Truth about our personhood, they aren't permanent and built-in features of our being, but they nevertheless may be very valuable to us, as a non-hermit working and living with other non-hermits.

A Word of Caution

The example above pointed to the usefulness of others' assessments. Without awareness, however, of the notion of permission to assess and assessments in certain domains, we can also see how assessments made by others can trap us and limit our possibilities.

For example, in personal situations we often give those closest to us great permission and latitude in assessing us, even in domains in which they may not be competent to do so. Think about it. Many of us can point to cases in which adults are still driven to the point of unhappiness by the assessments of their parents. Or when parents are extremely triggered and driven by the assessments of their children. Or spouses with each other. We've heard it put this way, describing this tendency to grant those close to us tremendous permission to assess us: *"I love you and I give you permission to define who I am."*

Our claim is that we can all be more conscious here, more deliberate in who we give permission to assess us and in which domains. The reward for doing so, we believe, is more peace and less resentment in our lives.

Assessing Others and Assessing Ourselves

Let's continue with some additional observations about assessments. Have you ever noticed that we tend to assess others based on their behavior, but tend to assess ourselves based on our intentions? We don't have access to your intentions or concerns, all we see are your Actions in the world. And these are what we use as the basis for our assessments.

On the other hand, we know our own intentions and concerns we are trying to address. Even in cases in which our Actions produce upset or negative consequences, we may continue to use these intentions as the basis for assessing ourselves. Others around us, of course, don't have access to these and so they simply assess us based on our Actions. It's possible that we can generate very different assessments out of the same situation. And without sharing our standards and having a conversation, it's also possible that this phenomenon can repeat itself and serve to damage our relationships and our Results.

We've said it this way in our work: *Intention is not the same as impact.* Jim Collins, in his book *How the Mighty Fall: And Why Some Companies Never Give In*, adds: *"Bad decisions made with good intentions are still bad decisions."* As always, back to Results.

Social Commitments Related to Assertions and Assessments

Socially (for us non-hermits), certain expectations also arise when we make assertions and assessments. When we make *assertions*, it is expected that:

1. The assertion is true, and

2. We can and will provide evidence to support what we say, if asked.

Language generates and creates, not just describes. Make a bunch of false assertions and over time, you will absolutely generate a public identity for yourself of "liar." And you'll do so, whether you're aware of this or not and whether you want this to happen or not. Consistently fail to provide evidence to back up the assertions you make, same thing.

Now, when we make *assessments*, the social commitment is:

1. That we have the authority to make the assessment, and

2. That we are making the assessment with conscious standards in place, and that we have some grounds (assertions; facts) to back up the assessment.

So while assertions can be true or false, assessments can be grounded or ungrounded. That is, assessments can be consciously connected to objective facts, observable behaviors and consciously declared standards – or not. When we make assessments (and we make lots of them), it is socially expected that we have some grounds, some basis for making the assessment; that it's not just coming out of thin air.

Consider: how do you assess people who seem to always come up with opinions or judgments that appear to have no basis in fact? (These are what we call ungrounded assessments). Most of us assess these people as "flaky" or "out of it" or "odd," not very powerful public identities to have. And if we find that someone is making lots of public assessments and doesn't have any grounding for them, we begin to think differently and relate differently to that person.

Grounding Your Assessments

So let's talk about grounding our assessments. Whether or not we're able to ground our assessments has an impact on our public identity, as we discussed above, and also on how well we're able to move into the future and produce what we want to produce. Grounding assessments is a very valuable practice to develop, as assessments show up in virtually every area of our lives. And let's repeat – we make tons of assessments and assessments are not bad! We assess and we must assess, in order to navigate and move through the world. Who to marry, who to avoid… when to make the business deal, when to postpone… what to eat and what to purchase… when to cross the street, when to stay put… we are assessment machines.

So given this, and the influence our assessments have on our future, we say that developing some competency in making grounded assessments is very helpful and valuable. Since we're making assessments anyway, and since they're carrying us into the future anyway, let's at least do the best we can to connect our assessments to facts. To make an assessment grounded, follow the following steps:

1. **Clarify for yourself "why" you're making the assessment in the first place.** *For the sake of what* **am I making this assessment?** Usually it's for the sake of some possible future or interaction. If you can't come up with a "why," then the assessment you're making is probably purely "recreational" and can't be grounded. This is not to say that we won't or don't or shouldn't have recreational assessments; only that they're inherently ungroundable!

2. **Clarify for yourself the standards that you're using to assess.** If you say someone is "reliable," then what are your standards of "reliability" against which you're judging this person? What are your standards for "good" or "excellent" or "rightness" or "laziness" or "timeliness" or "high quality" or "supportive" or "risky" or whatever? This step requires that we at least notice whether or not we have consciously set standards in these areas.

3. **Purposefully come up with Actions or events (assertions) that you can point to that support your assessment.** In other words, what are the actual behaviors, Actions or facts that you've observed and compared against

your standards in order to come up with the assessment you've got? Do you have any firsthand information, or are you trusting other Observers' reporting of observable facts? Note – be careful of the tendency to try to use other assessments to ground the first assessment. For example, you can't ground your assessment that Bill is unreliable by then assessing him as sloppy – those are both assessments, not an assertion in sight.

4. **Purposefully try to come up with Actions or events (assertions) that point to the *opposite* assessment.** Even though you may assess a person as "unreliable," are there any situations or behaviors or Actions or events in which he or she has been "reliable?" Is it possible to find observable facts that seem to point in the *opposite* direction of the assessment you've got? If so, what does this mean?

5. **Ground the assessment with other people – share your assessment with others**, especially the way in which you've gone from observation to assessment (from event to explanation). Note – this is not about trying to get others to agree with you. Maintain a mode of openness and inquiry in this conversation, as this can be one way to build trust and lay a foundation for solid relationships. It can also be an excellent source of feedback about the effectiveness and consequences of using our current standards.

Remember what happens when we practice? Practice makes perfect, so be careful what you practice. Well, we claim that we develop habitual ways of making assessments, and over time we get very competent in assessing in that manner. We settle into moods, and these moods influence and shape the types of assessments we make. There's nothing wrong with this, of course. But back to the Big Eye, let's just be aware that this is happening so we can be at choice about the assessments we produce, and the Results that are being influenced out of that.

But just because you and we may come up with the same assessment, and can ground it, that doesn't make it "right" or The Truth. And even if you and we and 1000 others come up with the same grounded assessment, that wouldn't make it "right" or The Truth, either. All we could say in that case is that you and we and the 1000 others are observing from a very similar set of standards. We simply "see things" in the same way. We can only say that in this case, all the Observers are similar to each other. We can't and don't say that our similar or identical assessments mean we have access to The Truth or "the way things really, actually are."

Benefits of Slowing Down the Assessment-Making Machinery

Most of us very quickly assess people when we see them and meet them. We are judging people very quickly, in many situations, personal and business-related. And to navigate successfully in the world, we must assess, to be sure. But even so, awareness – the Big Eye – here is critical. One of our teachers said it this way, and we now share it with you:

If I'm busy judging you all the time, I miss you.

If we're busy judging all the time, we miss the human being. We truly miss what the other has to offer – who the other person is – if we're always busy producing assessment after assessment about him or her. We truly miss what others have to offer if we're constantly and quickly making assessments about them and about everything else. Maybe one benefit of noticing this tendency is to allow us to simply begin to reduce the number of "recreational assessments" that we make. At minimum, we can slow down our assessment-producing mechanisms, and not be so quick in creating judgment after judgment after judgment (especially recreational ones!).

It's been our experience, and the experience of many others, that some measure of peace can be achieved in this way. Should you choose to move in this direction, basic Action steps are:

1. Notice when you "automatically" generate a recreational assessment about someone or something (Big Eye). The recreational assessment will usually be in the form of a spontaneous internal conversation, one that seems to just happen on its own. Many of these also seem to have a "negative" flavor about them.

2. Don't beat yourself up; just notice what's going on.

3. Breathe deeply and slowly, through your nose, down low into your stomach.

4. Let the assessment go. Turn your attention elsewhere. Know that in this moment, you are making a conscious choice to design your own mood.

5. Practice (repeat steps 1, 2, 3 and 4) as necessary!

True Assertions vs. Having The Truth

Distinguishing assessments from assertions in the way that we're doing here also makes it easier for us to take a key step – that of establishing a clear distinction between "true" and "Truth." When we say something is true, we are making an assertion. As such, we are willing to provide evidence to back up our assertion if you ask for it. But when we say something is The Truth, something entirely different is occurring. In this latter case, we make no such offer to provide evidence. In this case, we are claiming to have somehow privileged access to How Things Really Are and are claiming to serve as the conduit through which this Truth flows. We make no offer to provide evidence – instead, in many cases, we make demands for obedience.

Think about it, through history and across time zones, in personal relationships and in relationships among different nations and different cultures. Consider your own experience and your own relationships, at home and at work and everywhere. Whenever people claim to have The Truth, a demand for obedience seems to follow closely behind. This happens in relationships of all sizes and types. And in every case, the impact on relationships and Results, at a variety of levels, is enormous.

Characterizations: Special Types of Assessments

As we move toward the end of this chapter, we'd like to introduce another distinction here, a special type of assessment that we refer to as a Characterization. Jeff Spring's writing and work at Education for Living has been especially helpful and illuminating for us in this area.

Characterizations are assessments that have to do with identities – our own as well as others'. For example, when we're asked to identify someone, one of our automatic responses will be to give characterizations: He or she is intelligent, naïve, funny, arrogant, and so on. With these characterizations, we begin to define who someone is. And we often begin to hold these characterizations as The Truth about the other person, as objective and factual descriptions of their inherent personhood – as opposed to being our own subjective assessments.

You may have noticed that we are also constantly making characterizations about ourselves. We have conversations with ourselves and with other people, in which we identify ourselves by giving our faults and strengths. We do this when we're asked to tell others about ourselves in social and professional situations and we also do it every time we assess blame or heap praise on ourselves. For example, we might observe ourselves saying things like, "I won the contract because I am so smart", "I didn't get the promotion because I am just not good at X, Y or Z", or "I am just not wired to sell."

There are two important distinctions to notice here. First, we continually forget that characterizations live in conversations. We think that identifying someone as intelligent, lazy or smart is identifying some permanent features of his/her person-hood. We forget that these features only exist in conversations, and that they are not objectively real.

Rather, these features we are speaking of are in fact simply sweeping assessments, sweeping generalizations. That is, they collapse many domains into one universal domain. Furthermore, these assessments are implicitly assumed to be temporally infinite, as if they are true for all time and in all domains. For example, because Ann assesses that she is not good in geometry, this is taken to mean she is not good in math. This is then taken to mean that she is not good at studies, and then that she is not good at anything. It's amazing how quickly we tend to generalize and make such broad, sweeping assessments. This is one clear way in which we limit our possibilities through characterizations.

Second, let's notice what characterizations can do if we remember that they are as-sessments and that they occur in conversation. When we make characterizations about ourselves, or when others characterize us, we can use these to locate areas in which we can more effectively deal with breakdowns that happen over and over again (more on breakdowns to come). We can use these to identify opportunities for learning, or for opening new avenues for possible attention and Action.

In other words, when we (or others) describe us with certain "negative" character-izations, they are not pointing to some permanent defect in our character. Rather, even though we and they may not realize this, what we are pointing out are simply certain domains in which we are not currently taking effective Action, and where these ineffective Actions are causing undesired consequences or breakdowns. In this way, negative characterizations do not describe objective, inherent features of our personhood; instead, they identify domains in which we simply need to learn, to practice and to act more effectively.

On the flip side, "positive" characterizations, particularly self-characterizations, can be just as limiting. Think about it. If Alex characterizes himself as "smart" because he has a Ph.D., this means that he has to be smart in all domains. He has to do everything in a smart way all the time, which then comes to mean that he most likely won't try new things where he won't be the "expert", might "look stupid" or might make "dumb" mistakes.

As a Result, he may end up never trying anything new. Or if he does, and makes a mistake, he spends a lot of time and energy hiding and covering up the mistake. As a Result, he never asks for help, never establishes a relationship with a teacher, never declares himself a beginner, never practices and never gets to become more competent in the new domain. This can be a hugely stressful way to live, for we can go through life with an internal conversation of "I'm incompetent, there's something wrong with me" while at the same time, thinking that we have to pretend as if we know it all and can do it all because, after all, we're "smart." There is a name for this: it's called "The Imposter Syndrome".

With characterizations, we can instantly limit our capacity to take Action. And we can also limit our capacity to change our Actions, to become competent in areas in which we find ourselves currently incompetent. If we're not aware, our characterizations can fix our competencies and incompetencies forever, just as they fix the competencies and incompetencies of others around us. And this happens because we forget that characterizations are simply assessments, living in conversations. We produced them in the first place, and we each have the power to change them, if we so choose. With this realization, we can of course update our assessments, our characterizations, and author more powerful ones, ones that can better serve us.

If we are the authors of our own assessments, and if assessments carry us into the future, then why not author ones that serve as bridges – not barricades – to the Results we say we want?

Assessments, Assertions and Organizational Performance

Consider everything we've covered so far regarding assessments and assertions. Now, let's bring our attention to the ways in which our use of them directly impacts organizational performance and our ability to achieve desired organizational Results.

First, recall that all organizations may be understood using the model below:

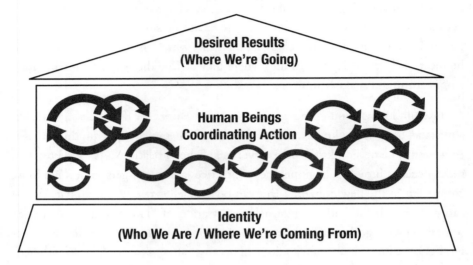

Next, recall that the "middle" of the house is where people collaborate, interact and coordinate Action, and that this interaction may be understood as having both a "vertical" as well as a "horizontal" dimension, as shown below:

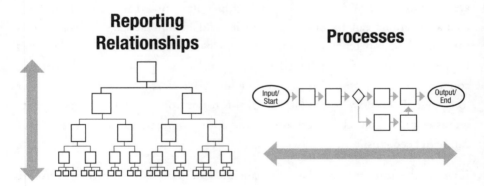

Assertions and Assessments Within "Vertical" Reporting Relationships

Let's start with reporting relationships: Are assessments and assertions involved in conversations and interactions among leaders and their direct reports? Absolutely.

Can you see where all parties operating with these distinctions is drastically different than operating without these distinctions in place?

Can you see where the explicit use of both assessments and assertions can be hugely beneficial within performance management and talent development processes?

We offer that when leaders and their direct reports have these distinctions and are able to openly discuss and agree on standards, as well as go through the process of grounding assessments (both "positive" as well as "negative" assessments) together... that dramatic shifts and improvements become possible. Ambitious people do, indeed, want to hear the negative feedback. But they want to hear it in a context of respect and trust (we'll cover context more directly in the next chapter) and they want to be able to connect the feedback to actual behaviors and actual standards against which the behavior is assessed.

Assertions and grounded assessments can be a foundation for building and re-building trust, as new conversations are now possible in which clear standards are established and clear performance parameters are agreed upon and measured against. We can also reduce the number of recurring conversations in which people disagree about what the same set of underlying "data" means – because all are now operating with the same standards, as well as new awareness of the difference between their assertions and assessments.

And even in cases in which disagreements do occur, we are able to much more effectively and productively move through the disagreement – while at the same time, strengthening the relationships involved. And relationships obviously impact culture. Dramatic improvements in culture are a very real byproduct of a workplace in which assertions and assessments are clearly and widely understood and used within the "vertical" dimension of organizational performance.

But this isn't the only area in which they can be beneficial, as we shall see.

Assertions and Assessments Within "Horizontal" Organizational Processes

Organizations acquire employees and customers, create products and services, manage employee performance and deliver the products and services to customers via processes – obviously. These processes, no matter how simple or complex, automated or manual, all share certain similarities:

- They include inputs/triggers, Action steps, decision points and outputs.
- And they involve people, which means they include conversations.

Are assessments and assertions involved in these processes and these conversations? Absolutely. Would clarity around these fundamental distinctions – these key Speech Acts – be beneficial to the processes and process teams involved? We say yes, in a big way.

As you're thinking about the most important processes within your organization, keep in mind two scenarios: 1) The process team leaders and members have clear distinctions and shared understanding around the use and impact of assertions and assessments; and 2) the process team leaders and members do not have these distinctions, and tend to "blur" their use of facts and opinions. So with these 2 scenarios in mind, please consider:

- On-boarding new employees: performing the process steps; gauging the performance and effectiveness of the process; making adjustments as needed

- On-going performance management / feedback / course-correction / rewards and recognition: performing the process steps; gauging the performance and effectiveness of the process; making adjustments as needed

- Marketing and sales: performing the process steps; gauging the performance and effectiveness of the process: making adjustments as needed

- Operations and administration: performing the process steps; gauging the performance and effectiveness of the process; making adjustments as needed

- Customer service and delivery of products/services: performing the process steps; gauging the performance and effectiveness of the process; making adjustments as needed

Can you see how tremendously different these process conversations can be when all participants are armed with these tools and are operating with these distinctions? The awareness and conscious use of assertions and assessments can dramatically improve leaders' and team members' conversational, relational and emotional competencies. And given the increasingly team-oriented and collaborative nature of more and more workplaces, these competencies matter.

Assertions and Assessments Within Key Leadership Conversations

For another perspective, think about some of the most important conversations that leaders design and convene introduced in Chapter 6. The conversations below take place in the context of both reporting relationships and organizational processes:

- Conversation for Relationship – For the purpose of deepening relationships and laying the groundwork for future conversations in which carefrontation and healthy, respectful disagreement may be needed.

- Conversations for Orientation/Context-Setting – For the purpose of building and sustaining shared understanding of organizational and/or team purpose, values, vision, goals, standards and roles. Include on-boarding processes for new employees, as well as ongoing conversations to sustain high levels of shared understanding throughout the organization.

- Conversations for Innovation/Speculation – For the purpose of generating ideas and possibilities in order to address concerns, solve problems or take advantage of opportunities. Include brainstorming and other creative-thinking processes that produce alternatives and take advantage of diverse backgrounds and multiple ways of thinking.

- Conversations for Coordinating Action/Implementation – For the purpose of executing and accomplishing Results with and through others. Of central importance, these may be viewed as the "essence of execution" as they involve the basics of collaborative Action: setting direction, enrolling others, making requests and offers and managing promises and commitments.

- Conversations for Progress/Completion – For the purpose of declaring satisfaction or dissatisfaction, checking in at regular intervals within projects or assignments to analyze and evaluate Results; also repeated at completion. These conversations include giving and receiving feedback, listening to multiple perspectives, and understanding the potential implications on future efforts and related processes. They also include declarations of acknowledgement, recognition and celebration… or conversely, declarations of complaint, requests for change, and possibly even termination.

Think about everything we've covered in this chapter. With just a little reflection, it becomes apparent that clarity and shared understanding of assertions and assessments can dramatically improve the effectiveness of any and all of these conversations. And this is the key – the ability to convene conversations that more consistently yield desired relationship Results, culture Results and execution Results.

Summary of Key Points

We observe, we take Action and we produce Results in language. Assertions and assessments are two of the six Language Acts which we use to do what we do, get what we get (and ultimately, it seems, be what we be).

Keeping assertions distinct and separate from assessments is critical. They produce very different things and lead to very different Results. This is especially tricky because in our traditional ways of thinking and speaking, we've used them in similar ways. Most of us have grown up without having such a clear distinction drawn between the two.

Assertions are the "facts of life", and are where language is least generative and most descriptive. They can be true or false, and are verifiable by a 3rd party. They belong to the "thing" being observed, and they tend to have a past or present – a very descriptive – orientation. Make a bunch of false assertions and over time, create the public identity of "liar." The assertions we make are not impacted by our mood or emotional space.

Assessments, on the other hand, are extremely generative and creative. These are our highly personal judgments and opinions, serving to orient us toward or away from future Actions and Results. We make a lot of assessments about virtually everything. Assessments are not good or bad, they just are. Assessments have a very strong future orientation, influencing future Actions and ways of seeing. The assessments we produce are very strongly connected to – and consistent with – our mood or emotional space.

Assessments are never "true" or "false." As personal judgments, they can never be "verified" like assertions can. They can be grounded or ungrounded. Grounded assessments are made with conscious awareness of standards and of assertions – that is, specific criteria coupled with observable behavior. Grounded assessments are powerful because they're connected to facts in a stronger way and therefore allow us to more successfully move into the future. We can all learn to make grounded assessments. Make a bunch of ungrounded assessments and over time, create the public identity of "flaky" or "out of it."

Assessments belong to the Observer, not to the thing being observed. They reveal more about the Observer and the Observer's standards, than they describe about anything. In organizational settings, it's often the case that conversations to reach shared understanding of key standards are conspicuously absent. Our assessments about ourselves, about others and about everything have a direct impact on how we feel, how we interpret, how we act and how we interact with others.

Beware of characterizations, positive or negative. These are a special type of assessment concerning identities, our own as well as those of others. If we're not observant, we may end up holding these characterizations as permanent features of who we and others are, and what we and others are able to accomplish. And by doing this, we dramatically limit our possibilities.

The conscious use of assessments and assertions enables dramatic improvements in virtually all of the most important conversations within reporting relationships (the "vertical" dimension of organizations) as well as within key processes (the "horizontal" dimension). These tools enable leaders and team members to much more clearly gauge progress, identify root causes of performance issues, give and receive feedback more effectively, as well as to reach shared agreement of standards.

Application

1. Recall one person who you say clearly does NOT have the distinctions assessment and assertion. What is it like, being with and working with this person, over extended periods of time?

2. Big Eye: Recall a time in which you operated without these distinctions, in situations involving other people. What was the impact of that on you, your relationships, your Actions and the Results you produced?

3. Think of one direct report with whom you sometimes have a difficult time working. List some assessments you have about this individual. For each

one (+ or -), identify how that assessment influences future interpretations, Actions and interactions. For example, out of this assessment what are you more likely to notice, do, think or say? What are you less likely to notice, do, think or say? Then ask yourself, how did you come up with these current assessments? Are they grounded or not? That is, what are the standards and assertions you used in order to come up with the assessments?

4. Enter into a conversation with colleagues in which you share your standards underneath your most important assessments related to organizational performance. What are your standards for "excellent" performance from Team A or Department B or Functional Area C or Process D? What does that look like, in real life? How do you know if you've achieved it, or are moving toward or away from it? What are your standards for all the most important metrics you use to gauge performance and progress? Have conversations in which these are shared, discussed and possibly updated.

5. Ensure that establishing and maintaining shared understanding of key organizational standards is a leadership priority.

CHAPTER 9
DECLARATIONS

"We shall go on to the end, we shall fight in France, we shall fight on the seas and oceans, we shall fight with growing confidence and growing strength in the air, we shall defend our Island, whatever the cost may be, we shall fight on the beaches, we shall fight on the landing grounds, we shall fight in the fields and in the streets, we shall fight in the hills; we shall never surrender..."

- Winston Churchill

If assertions are the speech acts with the least generative or creative capacity, then declarations can be viewed as the most generative, most creative. We contrast them this way: With assertions, first comes the <u>world</u> and then comes the <u>word</u>. We use assertions to describe what is already so. They are dependent upon the existing world.

With declarations however, first comes the <u>word</u> and then the "<u>world</u>" follows. We use declarations to generate new possibilities, new Actions and new Results. These are _not_ dependent on the existing world; instead, they bring a new world of possibilities into existence. In our view, assessments (see previous chapter) are a special type of declaration. As such, as we have seen, they have the creative capacity of all declarations – very different from the descriptive characteristic of assertions.

Here, we make this claim: Through declarations – out of nothingness – the speaker creates a new context, brings forth a new world of possibilities, a new way of seeing things, a new playing field on which to play. Matthew Budd, author of *You Are What You Say*, says it this way: *"A declaration is an utterance in which someone with the authority to do so brings something into being that wasn't there before."* We say that declarations are foundational acts of leadership. We will build on this claim throughout this chapter.

What is the Purpose of Declarations?

Let's start with a brief look at America's most famous declaration – the Declaration of Independence. We say that the primary purpose of the Declaration of In-

225

dependence wasn't to describe anything. What the Declaration of Independence did was create possibilities and shift context. Notice these specific parts of the declaration:

It was declared that *"..these United Colonies **are**, and of Right ought to be Free and Independent States;"* and that *"all political connection between them and the State of Great Britain, **is** and ought to be totally dissolved;"* (our emphasis). This is not describing – this is declaring into being a new situation, a new relationship, a new context. After this declaration, something (a new country) became possible and very likely, and something else (continued colonialization) became very unlikely. Now, after this declaration much work remained in order to fully realize the new possibilities. But notice how it was the declaration that opened the space of possibility and created the new context in the first place.

Again, this new context that was declared into being had the impact of changing how future events were interpreted! Without the declaration, certain colonial and British movements and Actions would have been interpreted one way. With the declaration, these same future Actions are interpreted very differently. Thus, in a very real sense, the United States of America was *declared into being*. For that matter, all countries and organizations that we are aware of are declared into being. Take a brief look at history – Israel also was declared into being, as was India's independence. As were scores of other countries and organizations. And somewhere in each country's or company's archives are charters, original documents upon which those authorized "hereby declared…" and in so doing, brought forth the new country or new organization.

President Kennedy declared that "America will put a man on the moon within this decade," and indeed it happened. Kennedy had the power (authority) to make such a big declaration and have it not be dismissed as wishful thinking or a pipe dream. He declared new possibilities, created a new context for Action, one in which new Actions and new Results occurred. As this declaration shows, to declare has more to do with starting a process and creating something than it does with merely naming a goal or objective.

The team leader who says "No more checking emails during my meetings" is creating a new context with the declaration. Before this declaration, team members could be on their smartphones checking their emails during meetings and nobody raised an eyebrow. But after the declaration, this same behavior shows up as "wrong" or "inappropriate." The reason? The context is different. As we learned earlier, this context isn't physical, but it's real. And it's generated, in language, by our declarations.

Peter Drucker has said: *"The best way to predict the future is to create it."* And this is begun with our declarations.

What is Context?

Before we go further, let's further define and clarify what we mean by "context" and "content." We say that context is very, very important for relationships of all types – personal and professional. Context can be critical for relationships, for individual success, as well as for success for organizations – an obvious leadership priority. Webster's defines context in the following way:

- the parts of a discourse that surround a word or passage and can throw light on its meaning
- the interrelated conditions in which something exists or occurs
- the environment or setting.

Another way of looking at the first part of this definition is to view *con-text* as *with-text*, or as "that which goes with the text." The context "surrounds" the text (goes with the content) and provides the background against which a particular meaning is generated. Change the context, and you change the meaning of the content, of the behavior, of the Action. (Remember Observer > Action > Results).

In our example above, Chu checking her emails can be viewed as the content – the event, the fact, the Action. When the context was changed by the team leader's declaration (no more checking emails during meetings), it had the effect of shifting how that same event gets interpreted. And we claim it is very powerful to notice this and do this consciously.

We can also view context as the background, environment or setting, although in this case we aren't referring to the physical environment or physical setting. While the physical environment can certainly be part of the overall context, we're focusing here on how our declarations create a non-physical environment or background. And we call this the mood or "atmosphere" or "culture" that lives within relationships, families, organizations, communities, even nations.

Context for Individuals, Relationships and Organizations

Think about these situations and declarations, and of the real impact of context on the given individual, relationship or organization:

- Over a period of time, a person regularly declares "There is no way I could ever do that... I am just not cut out for X or Y... that just isn't possible... that will never work out... things never go my way." Let's say that this is the context that is set for him or her, via these declarations, practically on a daily basis. Question: Does this have any impact on how events are interpreted, on the Actions this person takes and the Results this person produces? We say yes, it does. Any of the many different, ordinary events which happen in a normal day will likely be interpreted in a negative way, and be seen as "proof" or "evidence" that things never go his way and that she'll never get ahead. And even seemingly positive events will be interpreted simply as exceptions, aberrations, or the calm before the storm.

- New business partners declare to one another that they want their new professional relationship to be characterized by the following: mutual respect, true partnership and openness in communicating. Does their having this conversation and sharing their commitment and understanding of what Actions constitute mutual respect, true partnership and openness in communicating have anything to do with their ability to actually create these experiences? We say yes, it does, in a big way. By setting such a context, they create from this day forward a background against which their future Actions will be interpreted. They create from this day forward a setting that serves to actively support them in actually bringing about what they have declared for themselves and their partnership.

- An organization's leaders publicly declare a new mission statement and new set of goals and priorities. In addition, over time they continue to participate in and have others initiate conversations at all levels in the organization about the new mission and priorities. In these conversations, people ask questions, engage in dialogue, possibly make changes to the goals and develop a strong, shared understanding of where we are and where we're going. Here, we can say that the leaders have generated a new context, one in which X is now important (where Y used to be) and Z is understood as the most overarching mission. Does this context have anything to do with the Results produced by the organization? We say yes, it does. In fact, we say that the degree to which the context is indeed shared throughout the organization has everything to do with coherency and consistency in decision-making, with trust and empowerment, and with aligning all the organization's resources so that everyone is "on the same page" moving forward.

Leadership and Establishing (Declaring) Organizational Context

In a fundamental way, leaders are responsible for creating and sustaining organizational context. And our organizational blueprint below can be an excellent way to strengthen our understanding of this:

The roof and the foundation can be understood as the organizational context – who we are, where we're going, why we're going there and how we're going to treat each other along the way.

Can you see that the roof and the foundation are literally declared into being? That they are brought forth and manifested and made real by leaders with authority, making declarations? You and/or your designated teams declare the mission, declare the values, declare the goals. You declare the standards, the norms, the vision, the priorities. And if you or those teams have the authority to make those declarations, and you make them – it is so. You speak the roof and the foundation into being. And then you go about the ongoing job of building shared understanding of these declarations.

Leaders are responsible for building and sustaining shared understanding of – and shared commitment to – the declarations that are the organizational "come from" and the organizational "go to." There are many ways to accomplish this, of course, from the initial onboarding processes for new employees to regular performance management conversations, weekly staff meetings, monthly departmental meetings, quarterly retreats, bulletin boards in the break rooms, daily huddles, weekly email blasts, blogs, websites and corporate communications. Shared understanding is the key. How far down does it go? This has everything to do with building and sustaining organizational context.

Context impacts the degree to which organizations are able to have decentralized decision-making with strategic intent – and given the pace and scale of change today, as well as the impact of having those closest to the Action being able to make sound decisions, this is not trivial. It represents a significant competitive advantage.

Let's now take a brief look at this through the lens of the Observer > Action > Results model.

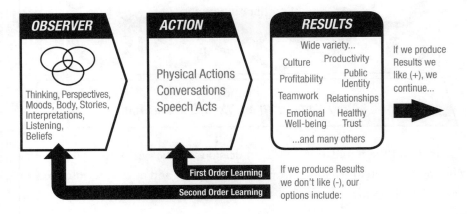

First, the leader – as an Observer with certain organizationally-granted authority – takes the Action of making public key declarations (a Speech Act). These declarations create, bring forth, the Result we call a new organizational context or culture. This context shows up in the organizational "come from" (foundation) and the organizational "go to" (roof).

Then, employees in the organization who are also unique Observers, take Action (middle of the house) within this newly-established context, and produce Results as well. They produce certain quantitative Results, of course. And they also produce qualitative Results – one of which being the way in which their Actions are perceived and interpreted by colleagues and leaders. The meaning of their Actions is dramatically impacted by the context established by the leader. The very same Actions that were assessed as "acceptable" and "appropriate" and "aligned" last month now may be assessed as "unacceptable" and "obviously inappropriate" and "out of alignment." And the reason is that while the Actions themselves may not have changed, the context in which they occur has changed. The meaning of the Actions has changed. And this context was declared into being by leaders and teams with the authority to do so.

Leaders take the ongoing Action of convening conversations that build shared understanding of this new context. And over time, new Results called "high degrees of alignment" and "excellent decentralized decision-making" are brought forth.

So effective leadership – at the organizational as well as the personal level – has a great deal to do with creating and maintaining a certain context. Successful relationships are often built out of conversations in which we share meanings, share views and ultimately come to mutual understanding, make mutual declarations about what we're committed to bring forth – and how we're committed to be – with each other.

Question: Just because you don't purposefully establish a context, does that mean you don't have one? Of course not. You've already got a context anyway, no matter what. It just may or may not be conducive to the Results you say you want. As mentioned previously, purposefully establishing context – both organizationally and personally – is a fundamental leadership competency.

The longer we live, the more we become convinced of the power of context. It's not physical, but it's real. In virtually every setting, every situation, every relationship, context is important for Results. And have you noticed that conversations for the sake of establishing and sharing context are sometimes conspicuously missing in personal and professional situations? Maybe what we need to do is invent and convene some new conversations.

Declarations and Moods

Earlier, we introduced our 3-Circle model representing the unique Observer that each of us is, and we also referred to each of our particular combinations/coherencies here as our unique Way of Being. Here, we will begin to see the obvious connection between our declarations (language) and our moods and emotions.

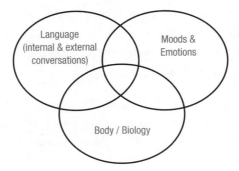

For example, in a mood of ambition we are likely to make very different declarations and set very different standards than we will in a mood of resentment or resignation. This combination has a great deal to do with what we call our *horizon of possibilities*. We like this term because it presents a wonderful visual metaphor, of a sweeping landscape before us. A big, broad horizon, way out there and beckoning us, full of possibilities and choices... as opposed to a narrow, shrunken down view, seemingly closing in from both sides, limiting possibilities and choices. This horizon, used this way, represents the future and the universe set of possible Actions, leading of course to possible Results.

What's important to notice is this: our moods certainly influence the types of declarations we're likely to make. And at the same time, the making of new declarations has the impact of shifting our moods. *Causality is two-way, because language creates.*

Four Primary Actions

We claim that with our declarations, we do four primary things, take four primary Actions in the world:

- We evaluate (with our assessments, a special type of declarations)
- We open and initiate
- We close and conclude

- We resolve

Let's introduce each of these, along with a few examples. As we're going through these, notice the ways in which new or different declarations can be the tools – and are often the starting point – for designing changes into your organization, your relationships and/or your life.

Declarations that evaluate (assess):

- Right
- Wrong
- Good
- Bad
- Arrogant
- Fat
- Skinny
- Tall
- Short
- Shy
- Outgoing
- Timely
- Late
- Pretty
- Ugly
- Effective
- Ineffective
- Efficient
- Inefficient
- Acceptable
- Unacceptable
- (We could go on and on… remember our chapter on assessments).

Declarations that open or initiate:

- "We, the people of the United States of America..." brings into being a new context, and a new possibility for a creating a country.

- "We, the board of directors (or owners), declare..." creates a new organization.

- "Our mission has shifted to include..." sets a new context, a new direction for an organization.

- "Hello, my name is..." opens or initiates a relationship.

- "You're hired" initiates employment.

- "From this day forward, we shall..." opens or initiates a new way of doing things together.

- "Starting tomorrow, I will..." sets a new direction, creates a new context.

- "I love you" sets a context of partnership, mutual legitimacy, care.

- "No more TV after 9:00..." sets a new context at home.

- "I don't know" opens a space, a context, for learning to occur.

- "I'm grateful for..." opens possibility for joy, contentment.

- "This (X) isn't working..." declares a "breakdown" into being, causing a break in the "status quo" or "auto pilot" of doing what we were doing. Generates the possibility for purposefully inventing new Actions to produce new Results; generates the possibility for purposeful, conscious new learning to improve Actions and Results.

Declarations that close or conclude:

- "I'm sorry" closes a chapter with someone (and also opens a new one).

- "I forgive you" concludes an event and closes the resentment that has accompanied it (also opens a new context for the relationship).

- "Thank you" declares that I'm satisfied with your fulfillment of some promise to me; closes a commitment cycle.

- "You're fired" closes employment.

- "The meeting is adjourned" finishes the meeting.

- "Our relationship is over" ends a relationship.
- "We will discontinue this product line as of X" ends an offering.

Declarations that resolve:

- "We the jury, find the defendant..." resolve questions about guilt or innocence (regardless of what *actually* happened).
- Yes and No (every decision is a declaration.)
- In
- Out
- Ball
- Strike

In the above sets of examples, declarations are creating openings or closings, evaluating and resolving. Our declarations serve to open possibilities or avenues for potential new Action. They allow something to begin to happen, as well as to close or reach completion with something that happened in the past. Our declarations serve to resolve issues and enable us to move forward, and they greatly influence the quality of our journey along the way. These opening or closing or resolving or moving are not physical, of course, yet they are very real. They have everything to do with our experiences and with the Actions we take in the world.

Declarations that resolve or evaluate have the impact of orienting us toward certain possibilities and interpretations, and away from others. Once we decide something, we move in one direction and not another, embracing one set of possibilities, and not another. And declarations that evaluate we call assessments, as we discussed earlier. These are like "stepping stones" to the future. They orient us one way or another in our Action, and therefore greatly influence our Results.

For organizations and for individuals, declarations operate like the rudder of a boat. The boat (organization or person) changes directions as a Result of those with authority declaring one thing or another. Declarations are how we identify our priorities and commitments to the future and how we bring certain ways of being into existence (self-worth, well-being and dignity, among others).

Key Declarations

Let's take a look. We say the following are key declarations, having significant impact on our organizations and our lives. In no particular order, we'll explore each one in turn:

- Yes
- No
- I am
- I don't know
- I am sorry, I apologize
- Thank you
- I appreciate you
- I stand for
- This is not working
- I forgive you

Yes and No

We mentioned earlier that the simple act of saying Yes or saying No has a great impact on our lives. You say Yes, and you commit yourself (or your organization) to some Action. You move this way, with these possibilities now open and these others now closed. You say No and you commit yourself (or your organization) to different Action. You move the other way, with a different set of possibilities opened and another set closed. Truly a generative act, saying Yes or No. We say that **every decision is a declaration**. Every decision, every choice moves us and orients us one way or another. Many of us have heard this line before: To not choose is a choice. To not decide is a decision. We agree.

We will return to this in Chapter 10, but let's introduce these questions now:

- What does No mean to you?
- What does No mean to your direct reports and employees?
- Is it OK to say No in your organization?
- What happens to people who say No?

We claim that if you can never say No, Yes doesn't mean very much. Or as is commonly said, if everything is "super-rush hair on fire priority #1" then nothing is. More on this to come.

I Am... (Primary Declarations)

This is the beginning of the declaration of who we say we are in the world – what we can call our identity or "self". We can call this a primary declaration, and it is at the heart of the practice called ontological coaching. In this sense, ontological coaching is defined as coaching people to shift into more a powerful Way of Being, with particular attention to the Observer, language, moods / emotions, and body distinctions. It's the type of coaching done by those who have pioneered this work, as well as by us and others who have followed in their footsteps.

A great deal of suffering and dramatically reduced effectiveness, we claim, comes from human beings operating out of certain primary declarations that do not serve us very well and are not conducive to the Actions and moods that would move us in the directions we say we want in our lives. And often, the "root" or "primary" declaration is not visible to us at all. We don't see it. All we see is that we seem to keep making the same mistakes over and over again and attracting the same type of people and situations to ourselves time and time again.

This is where coaching comes in and where the coach creates a space (in conversation) for the client to begin to see these underlying declarations and interpretations for what they are – declarations and interpretations, not as The Truth. From here the client can see the impact these have on his or her Actions, and can begin to invent and declare and practice new ones. For if all this time we've been operating with one interpretation or primary declaration that we made up about ourselves long ago (which now, we're beginning to see, doesn't serve us very well), why can't we invent a new one now, one that serves us better in going where we say we want to go?

People who make significant changes in their lives usually start with a language step. This step often takes the form of a personal declaration, a new I Am statement about who we say we are. For example, consider the shifts made possible when we declare for ourselves the following:

- "I am an honest, loving, and contributing man."

- "I am a powerful, courageous and ethical leader"

- "I am enough, just as I am."

- "I am a human being, and I matter."

- "I am a powerful teacher.""

- "I am a good friend."

- "I am a worthy and loved woman."

- "I am a forgiven and accepted man."

- "I am an ambitious, passionate woman."

- "I am a courageous, forgiving and authentic man."

Think about what these mean, what these feel like saying out loud, what these feel like saying to yourself, what sort of new context would be in place. Think about how the repeated use of these declarations would impact how you'd be walking, sitting, standing, breathing. Think about keeping this up for 21 or 31 days, while enrolling those close to you in what you're up to. Think about how these declarations would impact your mood and emotional space, how they would impact the coherency that is your Way of Being. Again we see the creative power of declarations.

I (Chalmers) like the expression in Neale Donald Walsch's *Conversations With God* books that points to our ability to choose, to declare and create who we are in the world. He says: *We all have the power to declare and bring about "the grandest version of the greatest vision we ever had about ourselves!"*

With new primary declarations, I'm still Chalmers… but the Chalmers that I am is different. You're still you, but the you that you are is different. And we speak it into being. We speak ourselves into the world. We declare a new context for ourselves and our lives. **We're not human beings, we're human becomings.** This is what primary declarations are all about. What do we choose for ourselves? What do we declare? What will we bring forth? *Because if we're going to do it at all, we're going to do it in language.*

As seen below, here we are seeing the impact of declarations on the Observer portion of the model, as well as the unprecedented possibilities that are opened up through these shifts:

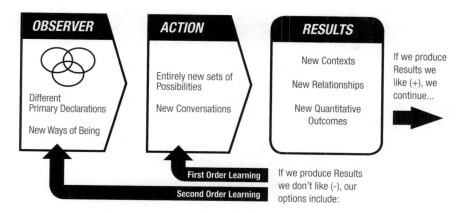

In all of the other "internal" declarations we cover – declarations that we make to ourselves, the ones that don't directly involve conversations with other people – we invite you to keep this in mind. These declarations are profoundly creative, shifting the Observer that we are, shifting how we see ourselves and everything else. It is precisely these shifts "in here" that open the door to new possibilities and breakthrough Results "out there."

In our coaching practices, we often reach a point where we invite the coachee to reflect on and answer two questions, the answers to which are (of course) primary declarations:

- Who are you?

- Who do <u>you</u> say you are?

We invite you to consider these now. What's the difference between these questions? Are they basically the same, only with semantic differences? Or are they fundamentally different questions? What does the first question seem to imply or point to? And what does the second question seem to imply or point to? What difference do your answers make here? And looking back 5 or 10 or 20 years, can you see how your answers today may be different from your answers back then? What's the impact of that on your perspective, your Actions, your Results? Think about those you care about in your life, those closest to you in your life… How would you wish that they would respond to these? And why would you want them to respond one way, and not another?

We intuitively know the power of these types of declarations. The intent of this chapter is to hopefully frame these in such a way as to make them more accessible to more of us.

Consider the declaration "I'm shy". We all know people who, at one point or another in their lives, have characterized themselves in this way. But let's look a bit closer. Where is shy? What is shy? The traditional view says that it's part of our "personality" and that some of us are naturally outgoing and some of us are naturally much more reserved. We certainly do not doubt the influence of our biology and genetic makeup, as it's obvious that our children are truly different from each other and have been different since they arrived.

And at the same time, we all know people who make truly significant changes in their lives, well after their childhood is over. Maybe this has been the case for you. Maybe this is the old nature – nurture debate, in different clothing… we don't know. But our understanding is that in real ways, the jury is truly still out. There appear to be biological influences as well as interpretation-related influences in many, many areas. Given this, we say it's prudent to at least examine different interpretations and their consequences – especially if we want to produce different Results than those we're producing now. So let's explore a bit.

First, we can see that when we say "I'm shy" in the present, that this influences our future. It is a declaration, so it serves as a stepping stone, carrying us into the future as it influences what we're likely to do and how we're likely to do it. Example – William is at a dance, he believes he's shy, and he wants to ask a young lady to dance. Will he do it? Probably not. Why not? Because (he has declared) he's shy and shy people don't dance. Shy people hang out at the edge of the gym, so he guesses that's what he'll do. After all, he's shy. Here we can see a case where our declarations and assessments about ourselves limit our possibilities.

As an exercise, it may be valuable to reflect a moment to see where you may be doing the same thing. Virtually all of us do this to ourselves, to one degree or another. To us, the key in this type of reflection is to have the main focus be on just noticing, and not being so quick to judge and beat ourselves up about what we see.

What if William decides that he is really committed to dancing, and he declares himself a beginner at it. He gets some lessons, he puts his body into it, and he practices… for 21 or 31 days. He watches a lot of music videos and dances by himself in his room, and he ultimately even practices a time or two with his favorite cousin – who is an accomplished dancer and was nice enough to help him. Then at the next dance, even though his body is freaking out, sweating, knees knocking, and feeling terribly uncomfortable… he takes the Action of asking someone to dance, she says yes and they dance. (Or she says no, he asks someone else and this time she says yes, and they dance).

Over some time, learning takes place, and William is much more practiced and in the process becomes more competent at dancing. Let's say at some later date you come into the gym and see him dancing. Question: Is he still shy? No – now he's confident, or outgoing, or whatever. All assessments. All about his Actions or lack of Actions, not about him. None of them are permanent descriptions of his inherent personhood. They are all assessments, judgments, characterizations made by different Observers out of different standards, moods, and beliefs.

If we choose, we can take some Action with this new understanding of shy (or any other limiting primary declaration we may have adopted). We can declare ourselves a beginner at dancing, get a teacher, enter into learning, practice, and develop some competency. Does this mean that all people are equally comfortable and equally competent at dancing? Of course not. *What it does mean is that by holding the assessment 'shy' as only an assessment, we open possibilities for Action that are not available with traditional interpretations. What it does mean is that by consciously harnessing the generative power of declarations, we can orient ourselves today in ways that bring about dramatically different tomorrows.*

With the traditional understanding of shy as some permanent feature of who we are, what are we to do if we want to produce different Results? We can't go to the local supermarket and purchase 50 pounds of un-shy. We do not know The Truth about this matter. A certain amount of this is certainly hardwired as part of our genetic inheritance. But we do know that if we have the interpretation that we are shy (or stupid or not enough or whatever) and if we hold that it's some permanent feature or biological characteristic of who we are, this interpretation limits our possibilities for designing something different. This interpretation – this declaration held as The Truth – can paralyze us. This interpretation usually does not lead to new breakthrough Results, especially if we want tomorrow to be different than yesterday.

It also seems that there's a tendency for many of us, given the infinite number of stories that we could invent, to make up stories that disempower us, limit our possibilities, even paralyze us into non-Action. Do you see this also, sometimes in yourself and sometimes in others? We develop habits of interpreting, we settle into moods, and we may not even notice that this is occurring. We may even get a little self-righteous about our stories, to the point that we don't even see them as <u>our</u> stories anymore. And finally, we may not have conversations with others in which this is talked about and shared. All of this is very much connected to our well-being, our leadership effectiveness and our personal and organizational Results.

I Don't Know

Perhaps no declaration is as important for learning as this one. As we discussed earlier, we say that I Don't Know is a required first step for learning to occur. It creates a space for learning, opens a context for learning, where one was not present before. Remember any experiences when you may have been trying to teach someone to learn, and the learner thought they already knew it? How much learning takes place? Not much! The context is all wrong. No matter what you, the teacher, try to do, it's unlikely that learning will occur. Not in that context.

How important is learning, given that we live in a world characterized by relentless, ongoing change? Obviously, it's immensely important. Another way to look at this is to consider what your future will look like if you don't learn. Learning is directly connected to our ability to produce Results. Therefore anything that has a lot to do with learning has a lot to do with Results. For us, ignorance (I Don't Know – but I Know That I Don't Know) is not the opposite of learning – it's the threshold of learning.

As mentioned earlier, many of us do not have much practice in saying I Don't Know, so we haven't developed a lot of competence here. Also, it appears to be the case that in many organizational, family or relationship situations it may not be okay to say I Don't Know. In these cases, it's likely that I Don't Know is interpreted to mean (by either the one saying it or those listening) "I'm stupid" or "I don't care" or "I don't want to know" or something else, but it is apparently not interpreted to mean "I'm available for learning". What may be missing are conversations about learning, how to bring it about... and to more explicitly grant ourselves and others permission to be beginners at something. We each have the authority to do so.

I Am Sorry (or I Apologize)

This powerful declaration serves to "clean up" broken commitments and acknowledge mistakes. (Again, not to physically clean up anything but to linguistically take care of a relationship). In our work with organizations and individuals, we have repeatedly encountered situations in which promises have been made but not kept, and no apologies have occurred. In others situations, there has been great misunderstanding and uncertainty as to whether or not promises were actually made, as well as whether or not they were fulfilled to everyone's satisfaction.

Imagine a situation in which someone breaks a promise to you, but does not acknowledge it and does not apologize. Does that Action have an impact on your relationship with him or her? For most of us, the answer is yes, it definitely does. Why is this? Well, the answer may vary depending upon the type of promise broken and the context in which this occurs. We say it's because language conveys commitment, and puts in motion events that would not have been put in motion otherwise. Can you see how when someone makes a promise to you, that changes things? You then begin to do something else, confident that the other person will uphold his end of the bargain and do what he said he would do. And if he doesn't, it's likely that your public identity, your financial Results, your other relationships (among other things) may be damaged.

In organizational settings, leaders sometimes make promises and, from the perspective of employees, do not follow through and do not apologize. In our view, this has a big impact on the mood or culture of the organization. It also greatly influences how employees listen to (interpret) anything that is spoken by the leaders from that point forward. Usually it produces resentment and cynicism, two moodspaces not very conducive to the learning, innovation and creativity that's needed for success today. When leaders are made aware of the broken promises, and if they make sincere apologies (and sometimes public apologies), the listening of the employees becomes quite different. And it's the listening – the interpretation – that matters moving forward.

In personal settings, the power of I Apologize is quite evident. Simply reflect on your own experience – on the times in which you have sincerely apologized to someone, and they have accepted your apology, or vice versa.

This declaration is an act of relationship building, of relationship healing, of closing and opening. It acknowledges and allows a chapter to "close," while creating space for a new playing field to open up in front. Conversely, consider the relationships open to someone who never says "I'm sorry" or "I apologize." Consider the way such a person may "dance" in that relationship and how his or her partner or colleague may respond over time. Consider the public identity likely to be generated by such a person. This all has to do with the creative, generative power of a sincere apology.

Who has never made a mistake? The answer is Nobody – we all have. Well then, unless we are planning to live our lives all by ourselves, this declaration can surely serve us.

Thank You

Thank you is an acknowledgement of the contribution or kindness of another. Difficulty in declaring Thank You when someone goes out of his or her way to do something for us tends to have a negative effect on those relationships. We begin to show up as ungrateful and find that many people aren't so interested in being with us anymore. This, of course, isn't an issue for people who never interact with anybody, but it becomes important for the rest of us.

Thank You can also be seen as a declaration of acceptance that brings closure to a transaction, usually a promise or agreement of some sort. For example, when someone brings us the lunch we ordered at a restaurant, we usually respond with Thank You. This brings closure to their part of the promise (to bring you what you ordered), leaving your part of the promise to come (paying for your meal). By responding with Thank You, it's often interpreted by the other person to mean "everything is ok, they've accepted what I delivered."

Thank You is also connected to moods, in a powerful way. **We claim that the moodspace of joy is connected to gratitude**. Think about it. It's hard to imagine someone in a joyful mood who isn't grateful for something. It was taught to us this way: *If you're looking for more joy in your life, begin by declaring gratitude.*

We can declare gratitude to the universe, at any time, for any reason, or for no reason. We can declare gratitude for being alive, for being able to walk or talk or think or hear or see or climb or hug or whatever. At any point in our day, we can simply stop and declare our gratitude to God or a higher power or the universe for the many good things in our lives. In so doing, we can consciously move toward more joy in our lives.

We've also heard statements of gratitude put this way: *Any day being above ground is a good day!* Virtually all of us have something to be grateful for. The only question is whether or not we notice them and acknowledge them.

I Appreciate You (or I Love You)

If we desire Results that include greater engagement and productivity in our organizations, then appreciation is certainly a topic that needs to be somewhere in the mix! Same with the topic of love, if we desire more happiness and intimacy in our most important personal relationships.

Let's start by considering a relationship between two people in which *I appreciate you and your contributions to our team* is never actually spoken out loud. We claim that saying these words – declaring appreciation publicly – is very different from thinking it. Saying it is very different from knowing it. To say I Appreciate You is an act of relationship building and shaping. It is an act of context creation, as it creates a space that was not there before. And it definitely includes our body and emotional domains. Same with the difference between saying I Love You and simply thinking it.

Let's go back to the Big Eye and reflect on your workplace. Notice if there are individuals in your life that you haven't actually said I Appreciate You to in awhile. Think about your personal life and notice if there are individuals whom you love, but you haven't told them that you love them in awhile. Why not? What is the story you have, out of which you don't say I Appreciate You or I Love You? Can you feel little body reactions in yourself simply as you think about the prospect of speaking those words to that person? We may be out of practice in this regard, and we may not have known this step is available as a direct relationship-builder. We may also know at some level that by saying I Appreciate You or I Love You we'll shift the relationship, change the context. And we may or may not want to do that.

One of the most interesting ways of looking at love that we've ever heard is from Humberto Maturana, the pioneering Chilean neurobiologist. His definition of love is: *The radical acceptance of the other as a legitimate other in co-existence with me.* At first we found this extremely odd, but over time it's grown on us, given that the focus is on our declaration of acceptance and of legitimacy. We declare our acceptance of another human being as being "legitimate" in his or her co-existence with us. To us, the words "true and equal partner" come to mind. Think about the implications of such a declaration. Declaring such a context immediately brings about a space of mutual respect and acceptance. It also allows space for us to make requests of each other, and maintain flexibility and openness in designing how we do what we do together.

Eckhart Tolle, in *The Power of Now*, says much the same thing (though in a different way) as he's discussing moving from unhealthy relationships to something better. He says *"The greatest catalyst for change in a relationship is complete acceptance of your partner as he or she is, without needing to judge or change them in any way."* Of course, we're now dealing with our incredible propensity for making assessments, many of them made very automatically, out of habit, as if they just form by themselves. And as we discussed, a great many of our assessments are purely recreational, not able to be grounded, but they influence the future, they influence how we interpret, they influence how we interact, nevertheless. The first step is to notice that this is happening. Then and only then can we begin to choose, and to practice, something different.

One additional point to keep in mind here is that at work, different individuals prefer to be appreciated in different ways. In other words, people may each have different standards as to what constitutes appreciation for them. If we don't understand this, we may end up trying very hard but being extremely ineffective in creating the Result called "Jim feels appreciated."

One rule of thumb that may come in handy for appreciation is the SST Rule: appreciation and acknowledgement should be sincere, specific and timely (as opposed to insincere, vague and well after-the-fact). As we know, the cost/benefit of sincere, specific and timely acknowledgement and appreciation is generally very attractive!

To learn more about the topic of appreciation, we recommend *5 Languages of Appreciation in the Workplace* by Paul White and Gary Chapman.

I Stand For...

Stands are declarations in which we take a position for or opposed to someone or something, and in doing so create a powerful starting point for new Action in a particular direction. In the context of breakthrough Results, stands bring forth a personal commitment to be ready and willing to do whatever it takes (within legal, moral and ethical boundaries, of course), to stay the course and persevere until desired Results are achieved.

There is a clear and steadfast commitment to remain focused and continue working toward the goal, even in cases (and especially in cases) in which new Results are not immediately attained. A long-term mindset and willingness to push through periods of adversity are characteristic of stands. It is our commitment and the power of our stands that can enable us to transform the impossible into the new reality.

Some examples of stands include:

- We take a stand for being a great place to work.
- The treasurer took a stand against the board because of its wasteful spending.
- Roger took a stand for doubling his organization' revenue over the next 2 years.
- Mary stands for repealing mandatory minimums in sentencing.
- We take a stand for sharing this body of learning with a minimum of 1,000,000 people during our lifetime.
- I take a stand for finishing my engineering degree within 3 years.
- We take a stand for our region being the top producer.
- We take a stand for a marriage of fidelity, trust and integrity.

When our stands are made publicly, it is our experience that the level of commitment and enrollment increases exponentially, significantly increasing the likelihood of achieving successful outcomes. As we've discussed: Which goals are more likely to be achieved – private goals or public goals? Public goals, of course. And the energy behind strong stands makes this even more the case.

This Is Not Working

This declaration points to what we call "breakdowns". This distinction, originally developed by Fernando Flores, is very powerful and is truly central to our ability to lead effectively, to respond with agility to unanticipated events and situations, and even to design our own lives.

Simply put, a breakdown is an unexpected "break" in the normal flow of what we were doing, in the normal routine of our day. More specifically, breakdowns (which may be considered "positive" or "negative") are unexpected interruptions in the fulfilling of a commitment, whether that commitment is:

- Meeting this quarter's earnings projections
- Working to become the top producer in my region
- Aiming for zero defects
- Going to pick up a gallon of milk that I said I'd get
- Taking my colleague to meet the new manager
- Getting to meetings on time
- Seeking to produce X new products and solutions that achieve Y
- Doing a great many other activities that, in some way, shape or form, involve others.

Here's a great way to understand whether or not a breakdown has occurred: *If you hear yourself or another suddenly say " Oh, *@%*^%!" rest assured that in almost every case, a breakdown is present!* Not all breakdowns begin with such a salute, but many do. We notice also that breakdowns often happen when we're working to produce breakthrough Results, for in these situations we're operating in new territory. And when viewed and handled well, these **breakdowns can lead to breakthroughs**.

Let's now notice the extent to which virtually everything we do, on a daily basis at home or at work, can be seen as Actions we take in order to fulfill some prior commitments we have made. Now these prior commitments may be explicit or implicit, short-term or long-term, personal or business-related, but they are there. For most of us, we can say that we live in a "web" of commitments.

When a breakdown occurs, we are no longer functioning on "auto-pilot" when taking care of one commitment or another. That is, we are no longer operating in *transparency*. For example, have you ever driven all the way home, and when you arrive home you have no memory whatsoever of the particulars of the drive home? You don't remember the intersection at which you made the wide left turn, you don't remember the stop sign at the corner or whether any other cars were even there... you simply find yourself safe and sound at home. This is an excellent example of what we call transparency, and it seems to show up in our lives whenever we do anything that has even a little repetitiveness involved. Transparency is a fact of life for many of us; it's not bad, it just is.

In this way of thinking, transparency is actually connected to competency. For example, beginning drivers don't have much transparency – everything they do must be done with full conscious awareness. The steering wheel and clutch pedal are very present for them, as are the accelerator and gauges. For experienced and highly competent drivers, however, these seem to recede into the background.

Well, breakdowns are breaks in the transparency. We're now fully conscious, fully aware, fully choosing. What we do in moments of breakdown is absolutely critical to the Results we produce. It's in moments of breakdown that we put our "rudder" into the water on purpose and consciously steer ourselves one way or the other. Here are common examples of breakdowns being declared, at home or at work situations. You can probably think of many others:

- "Something about this is off track"
- "Something's wrong"
- "This is no longer satisfactory"
- "Stop – let's step back and look at what we're doing"
- "This is enough"
- "This is too much"
- "This is not acceptable"
- "This represents a major new opportunity"
- "This represents a major new threat"
- "That's a problem"

- "Things can't keep going like they're going in area X"
- "I need to learn about Y"
- "We need to do something about Z"

Let's explore a few additional points about this distinction that we're calling breakdown, because we all have breakdowns and the way we manage and move through them has a huge impact on our ability to produce breakthrough Results.

- The universe doesn't have breakdowns. People do. Different Observers have different breakdowns. What's a huge breakdown for one Observer (one person) passes totally unnoticed by another. Different Observers come from different concerns, and they observe from different distinctions.

- Breakdowns are not good or bad. They just are.

- Breakdowns may "happen" to us – the external world serves them up for us – or we may proactively declare breakdowns into being.

- We can each declare the status quo to be a breakdown. In organizations, this depends on levels of authority and the type of breakdown being declared. In our personal lives, we have the authority to declare any aspect of it to be a breakdown. Often, this is the first step toward real change, learning or improvement.

- Declaring a breakdown sets a new context for Action – for individuals and for organizations.

- Breakdowns are inevitable and are simply a fact of life. *The point is therefore not to attempt to avoid all breakdowns*; rather, it is to gain competency and ability to deal effectively with the breakdowns that occur, as well as to gain practice in declaring breakdowns proactively as a way of moving ourselves toward the Results we say we want. Jim Collins has said: *What separates people is not the presence or absence of difficulty; but how they deal with the inevitable difficulties of life.* We agree.

- We address our breakdowns through conversations, and *all conversations are not created equal!* Some conversations absolutely move us toward taking care of the breakdown, and some do not.

For example, in many cases right after "*oh (expletive…!)*" we are automatically "thrown" first into a conversation in which everyone shares their own stories, their own personal assessments, of why and how the thing happened and what it means. This isn't necessarily a bad thing at all; in fact, it can be a very useful starting point. But if we stay in this conversation forever we'll never actually move toward resolving the breakdown. At some point we have to take new Action. This requires a new declaration or decision, often followed by new promises, commitments, agreements… not a collection of more assessments and judgments. These new conversations are precisely the Actions that are needed to resolve breakdowns and "move" in the world.

For example, after the initial knee-jerk Conversation of Stories and Personal Assessments, we need to purposefully move into Conversations for Speculation (to surface possibilities) and Conversations for Coordination of Action (to actually make a decision, establish a path forward and enroll others via clear requests, offers and commitments that are the basis for collaborative Action).

How we handle breakdowns impacts us in many areas. A big part of our identity – how we identify who we are – has to do with our Actions in handling the inevitable "breakdowns" or "problems" or "issues" in our lives, and the story we've built around our way of doing this. For example, if we navigate and handle breakdowns successfully and consistently, we seem to make up one type of story about ourselves. And if we are constantly running into trouble, having lots of activity but little new Results, we make up another story about ourselves.

Notice again that how we identify ourselves is always a story we have about ourselves. This story is full of explanations and declarations ("I am…We are…") and personal assessments. And as we've seen, in our own lives and in the lives of others, this story can be very empowering and supportive of our ability to deal effectively in these situations, or it can be disempowering or even paralyzing. Sometimes our story – which we make up as a **Result** of not being effective in handling a type of breakdown, for example – is then turned around and used by us as the **cause** of our not being able to handle the breakdown! Around breakdowns and everywhere else, our ability to observe what we're up to in language can be the difference between successfully producing the Results we say we want – or not.

251

I Forgive You

We will cover forgiveness more deeply in our chapter on moods and emotions, but for now we will introduce it this way: We all make mistakes, do we not? Is it possible that you'll go through your whole life and in doing so, never encounter someone who makes a mistake that involves or impacts you? Probably not. But of all the declarations we'll discuss, perhaps this one has the most direct impact on our mood and on our ability to find some peace in our lives.

Forgiveness is a powerful declaration, one that allows one chapter to close and another one to open. It enables us to "move forward" in a real (but non-physical) way. We "shift" out of something (resentment, for example) and toward something else (such as peace or contentment). The other person may not even know, or need to know, about the Action of forgiveness. In this context, forgiveness is not for the other person. It's for the person doing the forgiving for it this person who is suffering. Thus, when we forgive, it is ourselves that we finally let off the hook. Has this been true for you? In cases in which you have forgiven someone, have you felt this? Many of us have. It's not physical, but it's utterly real.

Forgiveness comes from a Latin word that means "to refuse to hold." And what we refuse to hold is our resentment, our status as a victim, as well as our personal, private promise to somehow, someday, get even. We let go of our willingness to grant the other person so much "rent" in our thoughts.

Like all declarations, I Forgive You is highly generative and creative. Forgiveness may be defined as a declaration in which we say: *What you have done to me caused me harm and damaged my possibilities. I do not condone this, and I do not give you permission to do this again. I choose to forgive you, to let go of these conversations. I now will focus my attention and my awareness in other areas, rather than continuing to live in these conversations about you and about what you did. I choose to move forward with my life. I revoke my promise to somehow, some way, get you back. I choose to move out of this resentment and into peace.*

More on forgiveness to come.

Authority and the Validity of Our Declarations

Let's cover some additional points related to the effectiveness and impact of our declarations. Specifically:

- While assertions can be true or false and assessments can be grounded or ungrounded, declarations can be valid or invalid.

- What makes a declaration valid or invalid has to do with the authority granted by the community to the one making the declaration.

Two people can say the same thing (utter the same words), but the power of the declaration only comes into being if the person declaring has the authority to do so... or the strength (force) to back it up. For example, Doug can stand on the street corner and declare that the new priority for ABC Department Stores in the new millennium will be tires and automotive services. He can declare this until he's blue in the face, and guess what? The world is not different. But what if the CEO of ABC Department Stores, along with their Board chairman, said the same thing? In this case, the world *would* be different, the priorities *would* have shifted, the organizational context *would* be now oriented toward tires and automotive services. The difference has to do with authority; in this case, organizationally-granted authority.

You can pretend you're a preacher, priest, rabbi or judge and say the same words a preacher, priest, rabbi or judge says, and even have two people go through the motions and say exactly what they're supposed to say at a marriage ceremony. And when you say "I now pronounce you husband and wife," they aren't really married. The world isn't really different. But if someone else "with the authority vested in them" says the same words, then the people *are* really married and the world *is* really different.

In many ways, authority is also socially granted. The authority to marry people, judge people (juries), commit resources, go to war, create policies, set boundaries, shift directions and priorities within organizations or governments, set boundaries and standards within the family unit – all can be said to be socially granted by our society, our institutions and our organizations. Notice, however, that the early American colonists did not have the authority to declare independence. At that time, only the British Crown had that authority. In the end, the colonists had the force to make their declaration valid. There certainly was no guarantee that a new country would come to be. What is clear, though, is that *without the initial declaration it certainly would not have happened.*

Are we clear about what we get to declare, in situations involving others? Have we agreed with other members of our leadership teams, our partners, our colleagues on where the boundaries are? In our work, we see a lot of these conversations missing. And in many of these cases, we see recurring breakdowns and problems connected with this un-clarity. It is our observation that difficulty in relationships – both professional and personal – frequently has to do with "fuzziness" or un-clarity about who gets to declare what. In organizations, this lack of shared understanding shows up as recurring arguments or disagreements about roles, responsibilities and spheres of authority.

Outside of work, in our personal lives, the question becomes: Are we clear about what we get to declare for ourselves as individual human beings? Let's take it totally out of the realm of workplace dynamics and stay squarely with each of us as creative, growing and learning human beings. We say that each of us has the authority to declare:

- what public identity we will create for ourselves
- the kind of life we will lead
- who and what we are
- what's important to us
- our own personal standards
- what's acceptable to us and what's unacceptable to us
- how we will be treated in order to remain in personal or professional relationships.
- And so on…

Have you ever known someone who did not believe that they had the authority to declare these things about themselves, and therefore did not declare them? Has this ever been so for you? Does this have anything to do with the quantitative and qualitative Results we achieve? With our well-being, our peace of mind, our effectiveness? We say yes, it does.

Perhaps nothing is more powerful than a person publicly making a new primary declaration about who he or she is, and who he or she is not. Of course, much of the power also comes from the letting go of the old (usually unspoken and unseen) stories and declarations of invalidation, un-acceptance and powerlessness. The new context has a powerful influence on our mood, our interpretations and our movement in the world. This is precisely what ontological coaching is all about, and is the basis for the tremendous, transforming power it represents.

Domains, Standards and Results

We all have the authority to make declarations in the area of our personal standards. Our standards are declared into being, and they greatly influence how we assess situations, ourselves and others. This, in turn, plays a significant role in how we then come to identify a great many things that we "need" to do in our lives. Consider these major "domains" of our lives:

- family / spouse / significant other
- work / career
- social / friends – relationships
- play
- body / health
- spiritual / religious
- mood / attitude
- money / finance
- learning / education
- dignity / self-worth / self-confidence
- world / larger connection.

Our standards (or lack of standards) in each of these areas tend to reveal themselves in the types of assessments we make, and in the Actions we take out of those assessments. Our standards come before the assessments, underneath them, in all the areas listed above. The previous section dealt with assertions and assessments, and we showed how it's very possible (even likely) that different people will produce different assessments about the same thing or event. And this is often precisely because we are operating out of and observing through different standards.

For example, you see horrible traffic, and Atul thinks it's just fine, actually flowing pretty well. You say we need 3 months savings in the bank for emergencies; your partner says you need 1. Alexis says the presentation was excellent while you say it wasn't so hot. We could go on and on. Let's notice that we are each making assessments out of some standard, and our standards are declarations. We declare them into being for ourselves, whether we notice this or not.

We each operate out of our own standards of reliability, tallness, laziness, effectiveness, appropriateness, sportiness... you name it. Then the generative power of declarations kicks in, because from that point forward, the standards are used as the basis for interpreting. And out of those interpretations come the assessments of unreliable, short, not lazy, very appropriate, boxy, and so on.

One reason, as previously discussed, that we focus so much on assessments is because they carry us into the future. Our assessments are how we "take a stand" on things, how we "orient" ourselves toward future interactions with people and events. What are often hidden, often unseen, and seldom spoken about with the very people with whom it could make the most difference... are the standards out of which we generate our assessments. These can be illuminating, trust-building, relationship-building conversations.

In fact, in many cases, our standards are hidden even from our own view. We don't see them clearly and may not remember ever declaring them consciously. But based on the assessments we keep making, we know they must be there. Can you see how this must be so? Here is where the power of coaching comes to the rescue, in the form of conversations that can allow us to 1) take a look at and 2) begin to declare new standards for ourselves. Here's the key: As long as they remain hidden, they've got us – we don't have them.

A key standard that we all have, though we may not see it so clearly at times, has to do with how we allow others to treat us. One expression that points to this is: *We teach people how to treat us.*

In other words, our Actions or inactions with people have the effect of "teaching" them what's okay and what's not okay in being and dealing with us. We allow people to treat us in certain ways, right up until they violate the standards we have set for ourselves related to how we will be treated. This shows up in how we hold people accountable for promises they make to us (more on this to come), as well as in the way we allow people to treat us verbally and physically.

Consider cases in which physical or emotional abuse occurs within a relationship. In this way of thinking, the person being abused may allow the abuse to continue, even over long periods of time, as long as it remains at or below a certain level. This level we may refer to as our threshold standard. It can seen as a story in which a certain amount of abuse is considered to be "deserved." Up to and including that point, no Action is taken. But once that threshold is passed – once that standard is exceeded – new Action is taken by the person being abused. And a new lesson is learned, in our dance together.

Social Commitments, Public Identity and Results

Assertions, assessments and declarations all carry a social commitment with them. You recall that when we make an assertion in the world, we are entering into a social commitment that:

1. The assertion we make is true; and

2. We'll provide evidence if requested.

If we continually make false assertions in the world, and if we continually are unable to provide evidence when requested, we generate a public identity for ourselves as "liar." And, as mentioned earlier, we do this whether we're aware of it or not and whether we like it or not.

Now, when we make assessments, the social commitment is:

1. That we have the authority to make the assessment; and

2. That we have some grounds (assertions; facts; standards) to back up the assessment.

Should we continually make assessments about people or events without any first-hand information and without being able to connect these assessments to any assertions, we begin to generate a public identity as "flaky" or "odd." People begin to think we're off in la-la land, making assessments that seem to be quite different from those of others, and that don't seem to be tied to or connected to anything. And again, this occurs whether we notice it or not. It's social, it's part of what happens when we live life as non-hermits.

And now with declarations, the social commitment is:

1. That the speaker does, indeed, have the authority to make the declaration; and

2. That the speaker will act consistently with his/her declaration.

This authority is socially granted. If we continually make declarations in the world that we are not authorized to make (such as a non-minister or non-priest or non-judge attempting to marry people), we generate a shift in our public identity. We soon begin showing up as a "loose cannon" or "out of it" or "loony" or whatever.

And even if we do have the authority to make the declaration, if we then act in ways that are inconsistent with it, we show up in the world as "hypocrites." Said another way, we generate the public identity of being a hypocrite. And usually, people who show up as hypocrites (especially leaders who show up as hypocrites) have a negative impact on those around them, as well as on the nature of their organizational culture and the quality of their relationships and Results.

There are many instances in relationships, families, organizations and communities in which people make declarations, fail to act consistently with them, and then find that a mood of cynicism or resentment has been produced. (We believe the same thing happens with us, at the individual level. We produce resentment and cynicism for ourselves when we keep our declarations private and then don't act consistently with them). We believe that there are missing conversations which, if they occurred, could help greatly.

For example, leaders could follow their declarations with requests to colleagues to call it to their attention if, in the coming days or months, it appears that the leader is acting inconsistently with his/her new declaration. Something like *"OK, guys, I've just made a public pledge that this product is our highest priority, and that our employees will be treated as full professionals. I know we've all done some things in the past that we're not looking to continue here. I also know that sometimes I'm not a great Observer of myself. Like many of you, I'm a beginner at some of this. What are some specific Actions that we know, right now, we'll need to start doing (or stop doing? (Discuss and identify). I also have a specific request for all of you. I request that should you see me saying something or doing something that seems out of line with this, that you bring it to my attention as quickly as possible. Do you agree to do this? (Get agreement). Thanks. Here's how you can reach me…"*.

Doing this = being very committed to following through, to actually bringing the new declaration into being, to actually making it so. Doing this = enrolling others to support you in your new declaration. Public declarations, especially within organizations, can be far more powerful than private ones. The difference has everything to do with enrollment and support.

Sometimes the Big Eye doesn't work so well for us and we don't see ourselves the same way others do. Sometimes, having these other perspectives can be extremely valuable. Armed with this feedback, now we get to choose whether or not to continue acting as we have been. We get to choose which new Actions we may take, knowing the impact on our public identity and the culture of the organization are at stake. The alternative (not having this information) is not a very powerful alternative. It limits what we see, which limits what we can do.

We can do the same thing in our personal lives. It is much more likely that we will follow through with a personal declaration if we have enrolled others around us to support us in acting in line with it. By keeping these declarations to ourselves and only thinking about them privately (but not speaking them out loud), we limit our effectiveness and our chances for success. What's possible is to let other people know what you're up to!

Invent conversations for the sake of sharing declarations and it seems to up the ante. Now, others knows what we're up to and our identity is at stake. We can ask for support and feedback along the way, and we can have a true team effort in getting there. The alternative (not having these conversations, not sharing what we're up to with those close to us) will absolutely not lead to the same Results. It's not wrong – it's just not as powerful, especially if three of the Results we want are stronger relationships, a more powerful culture and more consistent achievement of our own goals.

Summary of Key Points

Declarations are very powerful, very creative language acts. With our declarations we evaluate, we open and we close. We resolve, shift the context, shift directions and bring into being what was not there before.

The power of a declaration to bring about something new is connected to whether or not the speaker has the authority to make that declaration. In organizations, authority is granted formally. Same with politics, our judicial systems and in many other areas.

An organization's "come from" (purpose, values, mission, standards) and its "go to" (vision, goals, objectives, desired Results) are declared into being by leaders and teams with the authority to do so. These declarations represent the organizational context, orienting the organization one way and not another. These declarations are profoundly important, dramatically impacting how all subsequent employee behavior and Actions are interpreted.

A fundamental job of leadership is to build clarity, shared understanding of and shared commitment to these foundational declarations. This occurs through conversations with new employees (on-boarding) as well as through ongoing conversations, meetings, messages, websites, blogs, posters… all for the sake of sustaining shared understanding.

For individuals, we say we each have the authority to make certain declarations for ourselves, no matter what: who we are and who we're not; what our standards are in a myriad of areas; where we choose to go with our lives; how we choose to live and be; and so on.

Assertions can be true or false. Assessments can be grounded or ungrounded. Declarations can be valid or invalid. Whether or not a declaration is valid or invalid is based on whether or not the person has the authority to make the declaration. Make a bunch of invalid declarations, and produce a public identity of "bozo" or "looney."

Whether we act consistently with our declarations or not has the effect of producing a public identity of either "high integrity" or "hypocrite."

Declarations are very connected to moods and emotions. Like moods, our declarations influence and color our "horizon of possibilities." Out of certain moods, some types of declarations become more likely. And when we make certain declarations, we seem to also influence and produce certain moods. Causality is two-way.

Every decision is a declaration. Every Yes and every No. With these declarations we are not describing how things are; instead, we are moving and taking Action in the world.

The declaration "*I don't know*" creates a new opening for learning. "*I stand for*" establishes and conveys steadfast commitment. "*I forgive you*" dissolves resentment, brings closure and makes peace possible. "*Thank you*" acknowledges generosity, and declaring gratitude makes joy possible. "*I am sorry, I apologize*" takes care of the past and sets a new background, a new context for the relationship. "*This (X) isn't working*" declares a breakdown into being. When we declare something to be a breakdown for ourselves, we have declared acceptance and at the same time have created a new context. This new context serves as the necessary starting point, the key first step, toward taking new Actions and producing new Results.

Application

For all the items below, keep in mind the 1 or 2 or 3 important Results that you are committed to achieving during the next 12 months, as well as the areas in which you declared you are seeking to learn or learn how to do something differently or better.

1.	Convene a conversation with your direct reports using the "house" blueprint as a starting point. Discuss the degree to which your team – as well as the larger organization – is operating with shared understanding about your organizational "come from" and your organizational "go to." Should you identify areas in which shared understanding is not as strong as you'd prefer, initiate and convene conversations for strengthening it.

2.	Big Eye: Identify one person who has done something special for you and whom you have yet not thanked. Send this person a note thanking them for what they did for you and how much you appreciated it. While you're writing, also include one thing you appreciate about this person.

3.	Big Eye: Think of one situation in which, for whatever reason, you fell down on fulfilling a commitment, or where you made a mistake. Reach out to that person to say I am sorry and I apologize.

4.	Big Eye: Identify one person who you believe has "wronged" you and that you have not forgiven. Speculate about what may be holding you back, and about what might need to happen in order for you to move forward and to forgive. Then simply declare forgiveness.

5. Given the breakthrough Results you are aiming to produce, what do you say isn't working (the breakdown) right now? Then identify and convene the necessary conversation(s) that will help you deal with the breakdown and move forward.

6. Reflect and capture your thoughts as you complete these declarations:

- I am_____.

and

- I stand for _____.

Share what you wrote with your Accountability Partner(s).

CHAPTER 10

REQUESTS, OFFERS AND PROMISES

"Strategy is a commodity. Execution is an art."

- Peter Drucker

We've covered assertions, assessments and declarations. Let's now explore the remaining Speech Acts we call requests, offers and promises (or commitments, agreements) and their application and impact in both organizational and personal settings.

We can be alone making assertions, assessments and declarations. But requests, offers and promises are the Speech Acts, the tools, that directly involve other people. Whenever we are utilizing these tools, by definition we are having conversations and coordinating future Action with others.

This point is critical to understand and may be so close we don't notice it: *Human life, for the vast majority of us, is all about coordinating Action with others, in an incredible variety of ways.* We do what we do and produce much of what we produce with and through others. The Results we get in a huge variety of areas have a great deal to do with ways in which we coordinate Action (do things) with others. Requests, offers and promises (or commitments, agreements – we'll use these terms interchangeably) have everything to do with this basic and pervasive connection. These 3 Speech Acts are integral to Results produced out of coordinated Action.

Relationships, Culture and Execution

Recall that we began this book by claiming that leaders are "conversational engines," doing what we do, achieving quantitative and qualitative Results, by virtue of the conversations we design and convene. And three of the most important Results that leaders create and shape are relationships (inside and outside the organization), culture and execution.

Declarations, as we've covered, are closely connected to workplace culture. The organization's purpose, vision, values, standards and goals (the roof and the foundation of the house) are declared into being, and the extent to which leaders are able to then create and sustain shared understanding of these is directly connected to the quality and nature of the culture that gets established. We can understand organizational culture to be the context out of which the organizational content takes place. Culture is the qualitative background within which the quantitative execution takes place. And each, as we shall see, can shape the other.

In this chapter, we move more directly into execution, transactions and organizational content. Here, we bring our attention to the middle of the house, to the actual Actions that drive execution, the mechanisms by which the organization actually achieves quantitative Results. And we'll use our familiar organizational blueprint to get us started:

Here is the fundamental claim on which the remainder of this chapter rests: Any and all organizations, no matter how simple or complex, large or small, may be understood – at a foundational level – as *human beings coordinating Action*. This coordination of Action takes place through certain types of conversations, of course, and it takes place in both the "vertical" dimension of reporting relationships and the "horizontal" dimension of processes, as we've discussed:

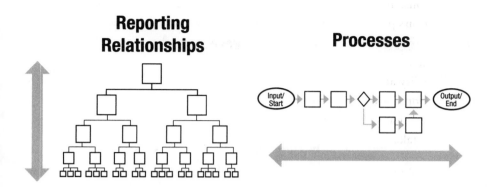

The conversations in the middle of the house – up, down and sideways – that drive execution are those that include *requests, offers and promises*.

So the fundamental claim can be restated: Any and all organizations, no matter how simple or complex, large or small, may be understood – at a foundational level – as *networks of commitments, human beings who are making and managing promises with each other*. It is by understanding and "seeing" your organization – first and foremost – as a network of commitments that you will gain new clarity and open new possibilities for dramatic improvements and breakthrough Results.

Is it possible that something that happens in one department can impact another? Absolutely – because those departments are connected. Not physically connected, of course – but connected via the network of commitments that the organization is. Is it possible that something that happens in a company's office in North America can impact its offices in Europe and Asia? Definitely – for the same reason.

We claim that you can do this well, or you can do this poorly – but you <u>are</u> doing it, if you are in an organization. And the way that you are doing it is the primary driver of your execution, shaping the actual Results your organization achieves and is able to achieve. This chapter is an invitation to view your organization this way, as a network of commitments, as a network of commitment "cycles" that are nested and linked together.

These cycles are the very vehicles by which people make changes, do things differently and do different things. They are the ways in which new goals and new priorities are actualized, manifested, achieved. They are the actual mechanisms that are used in order to reallocate resources, change directions and undertake particular sets of tasks. They are the actual mechanisms that constitute collaborative Action; that is, doing anything in groups of more than one.

Recall these important types of conversations that leaders design and convene:

- Conversation for Relationship
- Conversations for Orientation/Context
- Conversations for Innovation/Speculation
- Conversations for Coordinating Action/Implementation
- Conversations for Progress/Completion

While declarations, assertions and assessments are more central in the other conversations, our focus here will be on **Conversations for Coordinating Action / Implementation.**

Conversations for Coordinating Action – which include requests, offers and promises – are obviously Actions taken by Observers in order to produce certain Results. And these Results involve all of our "big 3" of relationships, culture and execution:

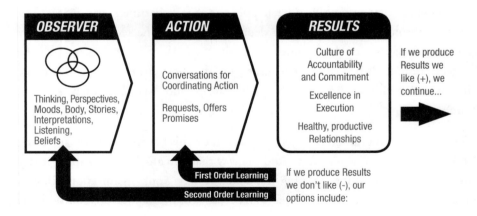

Requests and Results

So organizations can be understood as networks of commitments, people making and managing promises with each other. Doing this well, or doing it poorly. But doing it, and always producing certain Results in the process.

What's the front end of a promise? How do you get there? How do you elicit a promise or an agreement from someone? We do this, of course, by making a request or an offer.

To keep things simple we'll be speaking primarily about requests first. But in virtually every situation, what we say about requests can also be said about offers. The only difference has to do with who is committing him/herself to take some specified Action and who is doing the accepting or declining.

Let's explore, starting with this question: *Do you make requests at work?*

We ask this question in our workshops, and virtually every hand goes up. Many people respond with Yes, of course, they make many requests, every single day. Lots of people say they make frequent requests. The great majority of us make at least some requests. Think about it. Think about the requests you make at work or home, in business or personal situations, even though you may not formally call them requests. We human beings make requests all the time, in a huge variety of organizational and personal situations. So to set this up, we can say that requests are absolutely part of our life.

Second question: *Why do you make requests?* Or *why does anyone ever make any request?* Clearly, people make specific requests for specific reasons. We're looking for a broader answer here. We're inviting you to look at the whole phenomenon of making requests in the first place – what is going on such that anyone would ever make any request? Is it possible to look at the whole category of requests this way?

We say this: *We make requests when we have an assessment that the future is going to unfold in a certain way, and we don't like that. We want the future to unfold in a different way than it seems to be heading by itself, and in order to put things in Action to bring that about, we make a request. Thus, requests are profoundly creative and generative.*

When you make a request (and elicit an agreement) you're not just moving some air. You're putting in motion very real events and very real circumstances that would not be put in motion had you not spoken. There are countless examples we could explore. You may believe, for instance, that if left to its own devices, the future will unfold in such a way that your company will continue doing Process A or Procedure B the same way. You don't like this, as you see opportunities to do things better. You request that the appropriate people get together to discuss possibilities and develop alternatives. You may offer to lead or coordinate the conversation. A new possible future has just been initiated.

This is not the only way to view requests, of course. But seeing requests in this manner enables us to more clearly and consciously exercise some power and influence in creating a different future than the one that appears to be heading our way – if left to its own devices. We can shape the future and put in motion events that lead to more of the Results we are seeking.

For Men (Mostly)

Next: What do the Hollywood characters portrayed by the Lone Ranger, John Wayne, Clint Eastwood, Sylvester Stallone, Steven Seagall and Chuck Norris (and others) have in common? We also ask this question in workshops and many people respond with things like "They're all heroes" or "They're tough" or "They take care of business" … you can probably think of similar other responses, and they'd all be OK.

One additional observation we'd like to make, is this: "They never make requests!"

Think about it – these guys don't make requests. They just do what they do, often silent and almost always alone – because they can. This observation is more for men than for women, but it may apply to many of us: *What Hollywood will teach us, if we don't watch it, is that to request is weak.*

Question: Who is more powerful – power being defined as capacity for effective Action in a given domain: Someone who has and leverages a large network of help, or someone who does everything by him/herself? Obviously, the person who has and leverages a large network of help – which is done by making requests and entering into agreements. And this is the key: to never make requests is the same operationally as not having a network of help!

So if you have inadvertently latched onto the "To request is weak" interpretation, we invite you to loosen your grip on it for the remainder of this chapter, as we introduce some new tools that we believe can be very helpful. We are also reminded here of an African proverb that some of you may be familiar with: *To go fast, go alone. To go far, go together.*

268

Getting to Yes and Getting to Shared Understanding

What would it be like for any of us to make requests, and always be turned down? We're talking 100% here. How would you characterize a situation in which someone gets No for an answer in every single request that's made? Well, most of us would say it would be pretty lonely, very ineffective, not very good at all. In such a case, the person would do everything by him/herself. He'd go to the store by himself, she'd do her job by herself, he'd go fishing by himself, she'd do it all, by herself. In these situations, welcome to involuntary hermithood. For most of us, welcome to unhappiness, dissatisfaction, non-productivity and ineffectiveness.

We can say that when we make requests in the world, we do so because we want to invent a new future and to do that we've got to get a few Yes-es. It is important to us that we get positive responses to our requests. Without Yes, we don't have a promise or commitment to do anything different. Without Yes, we don't have anybody supporting us or helping us or collaborating with us. Without Yes, we are greatly limited in what we can do in our organizations and in the world. So one question becomes: *How can we make requests in such a way that people say Yes?*

This is not about manipulation, or in any way hiding or not sharing information so that the other person is damaged or misled. This is about having distinctions that allow us to more clearly see some "underneath" aspects of the interactions. And once we see some new things, we can do some new things, take some new and different Actions.

A second question becomes: *How can we make requests that provide a solid foundation of shared understanding that is the basis for highly effective collaboration, highly effective execution?*

Here's the claim: ***Not all requests are created equal.***

Some requests are more effective than others. Some requests, by virtue of how they're made and what they include, have the effect of ultimately producing the Results we say we want... and others do not. So let's take a look – what do we mean when we say *effective request?*

To set this up, you may want to do this little exercise. Think about a non-trivial request that you have been avoiding, that you say you'd like to make but for whatever reason haven't made. Or think about a non-trivial request that you have made in the past, but for whatever reason, it didn't lead to the Result you wanted. Think about the people involved, the situations, what's happened in the past, what you'd like to have happen in the future. **Bring the request clearly to mind.**

If you'd like, write your request down so you'll be able to take a look at it as we move through the pages ahead. Once you've done this, you can check your request to see which, if any, of the elements below may be worth investigating further. We say that these six key elements can help make our requests be most effective.

Elements of Effective Requests (or Offers)

1. Committed Speaker

2. Committed Listener

3. Future Action and Conditions of Satisfaction

4. Timeframe

5. Context

6. Mood

Let's explore each one, and notice how different our conversations – as well as our Results – could be.

Element 1 – Committed Speaker

First of all, someone needs to make the request. Most people don't respond very well to anonymous requests (words written on a wall, for example) that can't be attributed to anyone. And if I'm making a request of you, there are some Actions I can take to generate the needed commitment.

For example, instead of throwing your request over your shoulder as you pass Bob in the hall, you can ask Bob to stop and you can look directly at each other, face to face. You can say "Bob, whenever you've got a minute can we talk about the ABC? It won't take long, but we'll need to have a little time to think through some things because there's a request I want to make..." Then you and Bob can either move to the edge of the hallway right then, or set up a time in which you can have the conversation. A committed speaker does not throw a non-trivial request over the shoulder as he or she is leaving the room.

A committed speaker does not make a non-trivial request of you, as she is sticking her head around your office door, while you're jotting down notes and eating pizza at the same time.   Instead, she can say "Ann, I've got a request I'd like to discuss with you – is it possible for you to stop what you're doing for a moment?" A committed speaker puts his or her body into the request.

We like to frame it this way: You can't call yourself a committed speaker unless you take the Action required to elicit a committed listener.

Referring back to the exercise and your own request: In the request situation you've identified, were you a committed speaker? If not, what can you do differently in the future in order to become one?

Element 2 – Committed Listener

What are some clues that you may have a committed listener in front of you? Here are several:

- He or she makes and maintains eye contact
- Everything you know about body language is a clue
- He or she may be taking notes and asking relevant questions
- He or she is not texting someone else… not talking on the phone with someone else… not typing… not watching TV… possibly not eating

A committed listener is one who is present and aware, and is not actively engaged in something else. It's your job as a committed speaker – if you're making a non-trivial request – to get such a person in front of you.

One caveat: Is it possible that the person you want to talk to cannot be present with you at this moment? Possibly because he or she is distraught, as something bad has just happened? Of course, this is possible. So in some cases postponing the request, for an hour or for a day, may be the wisest course of Action. Remember: *The right conversation in the wrong mood is the wrong conversation.*

Consider also this example: A person sends an email to a group and ends the message with "Someone please take care of this." Obviously not an effective way to coordinate Action, as virtually everyone on the distribution list is thinking "That's for someone else" or some variation thereof. There is no committed listener in sight.

Can you think of times in which you've made requests to less-than-committed listeners? What were the outcomes of these? Now, refer back to your own request: Did you have a committed listener? How will you produce one next time?

Element 3 – Future Action and Conditions of Satisfaction

Here, we share what we want the listener to do (future Action) and something about the standards we want him or her to apply while doing it (conditions of satisfaction).

For example, you may say "Son, I want you to cut the grass. I want you to cut <u>our</u> grass, and I want you to cut <u>all</u> of our grass, and I want you to use our lawn mower while doing so. Also, I want you to edge our lawn using our edger, and I want you to edge 100% of the perimeter of the yard. When complete, please rinse off the mower and the edger in our driveway using our hose, and after the sun dries the mower and edger, put them back in their respective spots in the garage and close the garage door. Lastly, put the hose back on the rack on the wall and turn off the water."

Here we can see the future Action and conditions of satisfaction, clearly and explicitly articulated.

Or you can say "Son, I want you to cut the grass." Here's the key – *if you're getting the Results you want by making vague requests, by all means continue making vague requests!* Honestly! That's the bottom line, isn't it? In these situations, a big chunk of meaning is successfully being transmitted with a few tiny words. If you have this going on, don't mess it up!

But let's now play with a scenario in which you did <u>not</u> go into great detail in a previous request with Jonathan, and you did <u>not</u> get the Results you wanted. And let's say now you have Jonathan in front of you again, for something different, and you're going to make another request of him. And at this point, your little voice inside goes something like this: "All right, if I always do what I always did, I'm always going to get what I always got! And that was not acceptable, not OK... last time, we absolutely did not have shared understanding and absolutely did not coordinate well... " Even with this thought, when you think about going into the level of detail we included in the lawn-mowing story, you find yourself hesitating. This is the case for many of us, especially if we're working with adults, not kids.

Question: For many of us, why the hesitation? Why do we hesitate when thinking of the possibility of going into so much detail in our requests?

We ask this question in workshops, and many people respond with:

- Not wanting to insult his or her intelligence
- Not wanting to micro-manage
- Not wanting to come across as patronizing
- Concerned about demeaning the other person

We agree. These are indeed very common thoughts we have in these situations. But here it is: You have enough history with a person to conclude that "no details" obviously did not work in the past. You clearly did not achieve shared understanding then. And you find yourself hesitating now at the thought of "more details." These are situations in which *speaking into your concerns* and *declaring yourself a beginner* can come to the rescue.

Speaking into your concerns and declaring yourself a beginner, as we discussed earlier in the book, are powerful conversational competencies. They have the power to create and shift context, and context is directly connected to the ability to achieve shared meaning, shared understanding. It may sound something like this:

> *"Jonathan, I'm not entirely sure how to proceed here so let me just share with you what's going on with me. I want to be specific in requesting your involvement in X, but I have a concern that the way I'm going to ask it may come out wrong, it may insult your intelligence, and I promise you, that's not my intent. I respect your work and I need you on this team.*
>
> *But if you remember, last time, we did not go into detail and we got sideways pretty quickly, and neither of us was happy with that. So I'd like to try something different, something we've never done before… because I really need us to be on the same page with this.*
>
> *So are you okay this time with me being pretty specific here, even in areas where it may seem obvious, so that we can make doubly sure we're understanding this in the same way? As uncomfortable as it may be, I think it'll end up giving us a lot better starting point for moving forward and avoiding misunderstandings later on. OK?"*

What exactly changes when you speak into your concerns and declare yourself a beginner? As we now know, the context changes. A new context is now present, one in which a new listening on the part of the other person is much more available. Think for a moment, and it's quite likely you can come up with a variety of situations in which such a context can be helpful – at work or in personal situations.

Let's be clear – we are not saying that in order for a request to be effective, it must look like the rather facetious lawn mowing request, containing all of that detail right up front. Sometimes, a very collaborative and open-ended beginning to the request is completely appropriate, as there may be cases in which we don't really know exactly what we want. It may look like this:

> *"Riley, let me share with you what's going on. I really don't know what I want to ask you, so perhaps you can help me think it through and then we'll see where we are. I think I want the Vector team to take a more active role in preliminary systems design, but I'm not sure exactly who on the team should lead it, and what some of the unintended consequences might be. I also think I'd like you to have a support role, especially if Shaun isn't the lead person, but I haven't figured out how much of your time that would entail..."*

Now, ultimately you and Riley would agree one some specific future Action, conditions of satisfaction and timeframes… but you don't have to start there. And if you and Riley end up being vague in these areas, you are <u>consciously</u> vague. This impacts, of course, how you follow-up and interact moving forward.

One additional point – How many of us have resisted making a request, or have resisted going into the type of explicit detail we've been covering here, because we have this internal conversation: ***"I shouldn't have to ask you that…!"*** This comes up in workplace and personal situations. We observe something we'd like to change, but we don't make the request because we think the other person should already know or the other person should just do the new behavior on their own, out of "common sense" or something like that. Does this sound familiar?

This is a wonderful example of a key choice that we all have: ***Do we want to be right or do we want to be happy?*** Which actually means: Do we want to be right or do we want to be effective? Do we want to be right or do we want to actually increase the possibility of getting what we want?

We can be so right, so incredibly right, about how we shouldn't have to ask the other person. And we can even poll 10 of our colleagues and ask them if we should have to ask the other person and they may all agree with us, saying: "Yes, you're absolutely right. I agree with you. Given his position, you definitely shouldn't have to ask him. You're right."

And out of this position of "right-ness," we don't make the request and so don't bring about what we want to bring about. Usually we then simmer in silent resentment, continue to find evidence that supports how right we are and how wrong the other person is, and still nothing is in place to bring about a new Result.

Or we can choose to make an effective request, produce the Result we want to produce, and achieve some degree of satisfaction. In other words, we can ask for what we want. We can take responsibility for what <u>we</u> can do, and operate more out of the works / doesn't work orientation and less out of the right / wrong orientation. The choice is ours.

Can you think of times in which you could have improved the effectiveness of your requests by being more specific and more explicit with what you're requesting? Now, refer back to your own request: Did you have shared understanding regarding future Action and conditions of satisfaction? If not, how will you obtain this next time?

Element 4 – Timeframe

Let's say you get back from a trip and you look at the yard, which obviously hasn't been cut. You say to your son, "Son, what's going on with the grass? I thought we talked about this – you were going to cut it." And he responds with "I'm getting around to it."

What was missing in your request? Right – the timeframe. <u>When</u> do you want it done?

Now, please make a note of this because it's important: Element #3 and Element #4 – the Future Action / Conditions of Satisfaction and the Timeframe – are dramatically impacted by what we call the ***Background of Obviousness***. The implication is that every single request you ever make will land on top of some already-existing background. And this already-existing background impacts the interpretation and degree of understanding that's achieved.

Is it possible that what's obvious to you is not obvious to your listener? Of course. And this impacts the effectiveness of the request.

For example, is it possible that you do not need an overt, explicit timeframe in a workplace request and you will still achieve shared understanding? Of course it is. And is it also possible that you won't? Absolutely. Sometimes the background of obviousness may fill in the timeframe clearly and successfully. And sometimes it doesn't. Again, back to Results. If you're getting the Results you want by not including an explicit timeframe, then certainly continue not including it in your requests.

Here are some interesting ways in which we bring timeframe to our requests in less-than-effective ways:

- "….and I'd like it *as soon as possible.*"
- "… and that's needed *as soon as you get a chance.*"
- "… make sure that's done *in a timely fashion.*"
- "… to be done *promptly.*"

Do these sound familiar? We say this: if you really don't care when someone fulfills your request, ask them to do it as soon as possible! If you want something by 2pm ET tomorrow, why not ask for it to be completed by 2pm ET tomorrow? In this way, we now have a much clearer shared understanding of what's being requested.

The background of obviousness also impacts the future Action and conditions of satisfaction elements of our requests. Consider these requests:

- "My request is that you be more supportive of Amy."
- "I'd like you to be more creative and open in your approach."
- "Please clean up the room."
- "I'd like you to have this area squared away."

It's clear that what support looks like to you may look like micro-management to Amy. And that there are a whole lot of ways to interpret "creative," "open," "clean up" and "square away." What do you want the other person to do? What do you want them to design, develop, procure, provide, deliver, produce?

Whether your background of obviousness with a person is "thick" or "thin" has a direct impact on the level of explicitness that your requests of this person need in order to achieve shared understanding. We suggest that at the beginning of relationships, and especially in cases where a lot is at risk, that we all assume a fairly weak, fairly thin background of obviousness. Then as our relationship grows and we develop more of a track record together, we can make adjustments.

It's wonderful to be able to say very little (or sometimes, nothing at all) and have the other person consistently understand a big amount of meaning in our requests. This is usually reserved for those in long-term relationships and is developed over time and with lots of practice. And even here, the invitation is to always be open to the possibility that you could inadvertently be interpreted in a way differently than that which you intended.

Can you think of times in which you could have improved the effectiveness of your requests by being more specific and more explicit the timeframe? Now, refer back to your own request: Did you have shared understanding regarding timeframe? If not, how will you obtain this next time?

Element 5 – Context

We've touched on context already, as we've talked about how speaking into your concerns creates a different context for your requests. Certainly, if you have enough of a track record with a person to feel that you need to go into a lot of detail in order to achieve shared understanding... and if you also have a concern that by doing so, you may insult his or her intelligence... then speaking into your concerns is the conversational competency that's needed. It's a proven way to shift the context and open a different space for listening.

There's another, broader way in which context is important, and we already know this. How many of us like to know "why" we're being asked to do something? Virtually all of us. What's the bigger picture in which the request is being made? What's in the background? How does the request fit in or connect to other things that have already happened, are happening now or are anticipated to happen? The context of your request is how you provide this to your listener. It may look like this:

"Alicia, I've got some things I'd like to talk with you about and a request or two I'd like to make of you, but before that, I'd like to give you a bit of background. For the last 3 years, Ace Molding has been our largest and best customer. About 35% of our revenues come from Ace, and almost 40% of our profits. Well, Jim's been the account rep since October and some issues have come up that neither he nor I anticipated. We're seeing a sharp decline in orders and an unusual spike in returns and refunds. Here's where we may need your help, but it's important that you're aware of what Jim's already done, what we're thinking may be next and why we're thinking this way..."

or

"Carlos, you know our relationship is very important to me. We've worked together almost 14 years now, and we've had a lot of ups and downs business-wise during that time. You've been a big part of our success, and we've made a good team. It's because I value our relationship so much that I'd like to talk with you about some things I'm noticing that I think you're not, and that if are allowed to continue, may jeopardize some of the good things we've accomplished..."

With our context we inform the listener of where we're coming from, what else is going on in the background or what else has occurred in the past, in order to give the listener a broader or more adequate perspective on what the request means and how it fits into the bigger picture. Again, many people do this without really thinking about it. Others consciously make it happen. We say that no matter how it happens, it's an integral part of an effective request.

Question: Just because you don't purposefully set the context, does that mean you don't have a context? No, of course not. As we've discussed earlier, you've always and already got a context, no matter what. That context just may or not be conducive to the Result you say you want. In this case, the Result includes shared understanding and shared commitment. The cost/benefit of purposefully setting context – in cases involving non-trivial requests – is usually a very attractive cost/benefit.

A simple graphic may help to identify one or two "layers" we may include in the context of our requests. Some requests are so straightforward, so cut-and-dried, that you may not need to spend very much time on context at all. The background of obviousness may be so thick, so strong, that all you need to do is focus on content – simply make the request, get a valid response (more on these to come) and you're done. You know that a high degree of shared understanding is achieved, so you and the other person head on down the road. This type of request is represented by the middle circle below – simply focus on and provide content, and you're done.

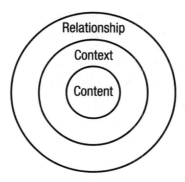

In other requests, however, you may need to self-disclose, explicitly focus on and create a certain context (the middle level) in order to achieve shared understanding. And in others still, due to the nature of the request, the risks that may be involved, the history of the people involved and a number of other factors, you may be well served by having your self-disclosure start at the level of the relationship. From here, you work your way "in" as you continue shaping context and ultimately providing content – the future Action, conditions of satisfaction and timeframe of your request.

Can you think of times in which you could have improved the effectiveness of your requests by creating a more powerful, a more helpful context? Now, refer back to your own request: Did you create a context most conducive to achieving shared understanding? If not, how will you create one next time?

Element 6 - Mood

When we say "mood of the request" we refer to the emotional space or "mood-space" of both the speaker and the listener. Obviously, as we learned earlier in this book, the way the listener interprets and responds is not separate from the mood he or she happens to be in at the time. And, as speakers, it's easy to see how our moods will absolutely impact *how we get listened* in the request situation. Many of us know this already – how we say what we say is often more important than the words we choose. To repeat: *The right conversation in the wrong mood is the wrong conversation.*

Being able to flex the Big Eye muscle and observe when we (ourselves) happen to be in one mood or another can definitely serve us. We can take steps to design a mood that's more conducive to what we want to accomplish, or we can simply take time out and wait till "the time is right" to make the request.

On the other hand, being a better Observer of others' moods can also serve us. If we see that the other person is in a mood of anger or sadness, for example, we can speak into it. We can ask if something is wrong, and if later would be a better time to have this conversation. Again, many of us do this already and without consciously thinking about it. And some of us do not, pushing forward anyway, asking the request in the same way that we would've had the person been in a mood of joy. And in the latter case, probably not producing the desired Results.

Can you think of times in which you could have improved the effectiveness of your requests by paying more attention to both your mood and the mood of the other person? Now, refer back to your own request: Was your mood conducive the Results you were seeking with your Request? Was the other person's ? If not, what will you do differently next time?

The Front End of Making a Workplace Commitment

What we've just covered is shining a light, bringing some rigor, some standards and a new shared vocabulary to requests, to the "front end" of making a workplace commitment.

And our claim is this: If you are seeking a sustainable culture of accountability and sustained excellence in execution, the front end of the commitment is not enough. The "back end" is also important. That is, the elements of an effective request are necessary but not sufficient – they are only half of the story. It's also important to pay attention to the back end, which includes how you respond to requests and how you allow other people to respond to requests.

So our complementary claim is this: In order to sustain a culture of accountability, as well as drive excellence in execution, there are four and only four valid ways to respond to workplace requests.

The Back End – Valid Responses

We're not saying that these are one-word responses that are blurted out in a vacuum; no, we talk, we engage, we explore. But when all the conversation is over, when we ultimately do leave the table, we say that one of these four needs to be in place:

- Yes
- No
- Commit-to-commit
- Counter-offer

Yes – One possibility is that after we talk, the other person ends up saying Yes. In this case, you now have a commitment. Future Action, conditions of satisfaction, timeframe… all that is in place.

No – Another possibility is that after we talk, the other person ends up saying No. In this case, no commitment is in place. You may have had an informative and interesting conversation, you both may have learned something, but no commitment is in place.

Commit-to-commit – Here, the other person may not have enough information in order to say Yes or No in the moment. She may need access to another calendar, for example, in which she may have recorded some prior commitments that impact her ability to respond definitively here. The response here may be: "Vinay, I understand your request but I can't even answer you at the moment. I need my other calendar, because I think I've already booked a travel date for that segment but I'm not 100% sure. When I get back to the office this afternoon, I'll check. I will have a Yes or a No by 8am tomorrow morning." Commit-to-commit is committing to a specific time by which you will have an answer. It is not "I'll get back to you later." No, it always includes a specific time by which the response will be provided.

Counter-offer – Here, the dialogue may unfold like this: "Bree, I understand you want 5 sites up and running by July 1. I can't promise 5 by that date, but I can commit to 4. Or 5 by August 17. Will either of those work?" Here, the responder declines the initial request and initial conditions, and couples that with an offer to accept if certain conditions are changed.

As different as these responses are, how are they similar? What do they have in common? They are definitive. They are clear, they are not fuzzy. They represent a much more "clean" interaction, so that all parties better understand what's going to happen and when it's going to happen. They provide a much more solid foundation for working together and coordinating Action together.

What responses are conspicuously absent from our little list? We ask this question in workshops and the responses include:

- Maybe
- I'll try
- We'll see
- Perhaps
- I'll do my best
- Possibly
- I'll get back to you later
- Let's circle back around in a couple of weeks
- Silence
- Many others

These don't make the list. They don't lead to the Results we're looking for.

Effective Requests, Valid Responses, Culture and Execution

So given that all organizations are, at their foundation, networks of commitments (the middle of the house) we can now begin to see how these Speech Acts may be of value to leaders and team members of all types.

Let's connect effective requests and valid responses to organizational Results by asking two basic questions:

- If you build the middle of your house with a bunch of commitment cycles that are allowed to be "<u>opened</u>" with requests that contain unclear conditions of satisfaction, nebulous or assumed timeframes, uncommitted listeners, weak or nonexistent contexts... and multiply this across all the human interactions in your organizational web of commitments – the face-to-face interactions, the email interactions, the phone interactions, the sticky-note interactions – what will happen? **Make a prediction about Results: What do you predict?**

- If you build the middle of your house with a bunch of commitment cycles that are allowed to be "<u>closed</u>" with "Maybe...", "I'll try...", "We'll see...", "I'll get back to you later..." and multiply this across all the human interactions in your organizational web of commitments – the face-to-face interactions, the email interactions, the phone interactions, the sticky-note interactions – what will happen? **Make a prediction about Results: What do you predict?**

The Results are all bad. You will sub-optimize at best, and you will train wreck at worst. For instance: Sam will request something from Les "as soon as possible"... Les interprets (listens) that as "October" but Sam didn't mean October, he meant by Friday at 4pm ET... but he didn't say Friday at 4pm ET... and now Les has hung Sam out to dry because what he didn't know was that Sam needed his output as his input, because both of them don't operate in a vacuum, they operate interdependently, as parts of the web of commitments that is the engine of the organization's productivity.

We make a big claim now: The elements of effective requests and valid responses we've shared here are the **"nuts and bolts" of execution**. We can go down no further than this. This is where the rubber hits the road with Collaborative Action. These are the fundamentals of coordinating Action, the actual tools that human beings use in order to accomplish anything in groups of more than one.

Armed with these tools – these Speech Acts and these distinctions – in both the vertical and horizontal dimensions of organizational life, leaders and employees can and do dramatically improve execution.

One of our desired outcomes from your reading this book – and especially this chapter – is that from this point forward, you will notice these elements of effective requests every single time you make a request, as well as every single time someone makes a request of you. And you will notice whether or not you're getting a valid response when you're making a request of another, as well as when you are (or aren't) providing a valid response to someone else's request of you. You will notice these elements in conversations you overhear, and what you will often notice is that many people are very sloppy in this regard! And you will notice these elements every time you or your team is involved in any type of action planning following brainstorming or speculation conversations.

It is our desire that the Observer that you are has shifted a bit, to the point where you are now a slightly different Observer of yourself and others in the domain of collaborative Action, in the domain of execution. And because what you now see is different, what you're able to do – and able to be – is different. This is the key.

Two-Way Causality: Execution and Culture

It is demonstrably true, is it not, that your organization's culture impacts how your people work together? Definitely, this is so. We claim that it's also true that by improving how people coordinate Action, you can shape the culture. Causality is two-way, because language creates. By taking tangible Action with specific tools, you and your colleagues are able to shape something very intangible. By bringing some rigor, shared understanding, new standards and a new shared vocabulary to the mechanics of collaborative Action, you are able to purposefully shape and sustain a culture of accountability. And this is not trivial.

Promises, Commitments and Agreements Are Everywhere

Think about it – so far, this chapter has covered the making and managing of promises inside the organization. This chapter is built around a foundational claim: that all organizations are networks of commitments, and that by more fully understanding the elements by which these commitments are established, dramatic improvements in both culture and execution may be achieved.

What's very interesting to notice is that all these internal interactions are for one basic purpose. The network of commitments that includes all this collaborative Action inside the organization is for one overriding purpose:

To satisfy the external promises the organization has made to its customers!

Promises are pervasive. They are everywhere. What do we call promises between companies? Contracts. What does it say on the bottom of a credit card slip, usually right by the X where you sign and usually in very small print? Something to the order of "I agree to pay... according to the cardholder agreement..." One of the terms for a dollar bill is a promissory note. Employees are employees because they've agreed to do X work for Y pay under Z conditions. Somebody promised to turn on the cable between 10 and 2, somebody promised to take input A and perform Action B on it before sending it as output C to the next department; we could go on and on.

Promises, agreements and commitments are the essence of non-hermithood. They undergird everything we do with others. The entire systems of global and local commerce and industry are built around them. And once we see them clearly, a whole new world of opportunities opens up for us.

The Cycle of the Promise

Fernando Flores' pioneering work in this body of learning includes a powerful yet simple way to "tie together" what we've been covering here. All of the commitment cycles within the middle of the house may be explored and understood via the following graphic:

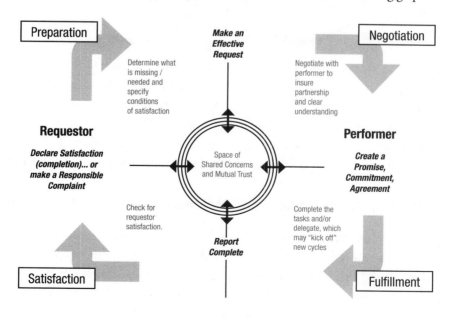

Source: Dr. Fernando Flores,
Business Design Associates

285

We invite you to share your version of the Speech Acts you've learned here, the House Drawing, the Cycle of the Promise and all these other distinctions with your direct reports and colleagues. The conversations and new agreements that will ensue are the first steps toward purposefully creating your own version of a culture of commitment and accountability.

Accountability and Commitment (Not Time) Management

Let's focus now a bit more squarely on accountability. First question: Is it easy or hard to hold someone accountable who responded to our request with "I'll try"? It's hard. It's like nailing jello to the wall! So these elements of effective requests and valid responses can serve virtually all of us, because virtually all of us are concerned about accountability in our spheres of influence.

Next we claim: There's no such thing as time management. You never had it, you never will.

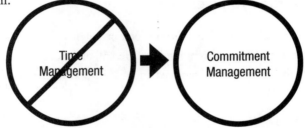

We understand the term, of course, but would like to invite you to reframe it slightly. How many of us – right now – are walking around with invisible backpacks on our backs, and in those invisible backpacks are 47 different promises in different stages of completion? This is the modern human. This is us. We are managing commitments, not time. We invite you to adopt this slight shift in emphasis, this slight shift in focus, as you think about yourself, your team and your organization.

Managing Commitments and Making Responsible Complaints

It is not required that you or your people keep 100% of your promises in order to establish and sustain a culture of accountability. This is not the standard, this is not required. This is actually impossible, is it not? Life occasionally does throw us a curve. But it is required that you and they manage 100% of your commitments, no exceptions. Commitment management is the standard, not commitment keeping. Let's explore – what does this mean?

It means that every time Sue makes a promise to Samir, both Sue and Samir know that if at any time during the promise's timeframe Sue even gets a sniff that it may not be possible for her to keep the promise as originally intended, that it's <u>her</u> responsibility to let Samir know – absolutely as soon as possible. This is publicly known, by Sue and Samir and everyone else at the table. They even agree on <u>how</u> she is to let him know – whether it's an in-person conversation, an email or a phone call. This is above board, publicly known by everyone. Commitment management is the key.

The cardinal sin, for organizations seeking to maintain a culture of accountability, is this: A promise is made, it's not kept, the deadline comes and goes, and nobody does anything.

Pay attention to any trends that may emerge related to managing or having to renegotiate commitments. While we say managing 100% of commitments is the key and is required, at the same time, if one individual is continually having to renegotiate commitments in a particular area, this may be a valuable conversation to open up.

Managing commitments is also an act of relationship building. If we don't care about our relationship with you, we let our promise to you go unfulfilled without talking to you. That Action will have the predictable effect, on your end, of you not wanting to deal with us in the future. We begin avoiding you anyway, the next time we see you coming, and so we both are moving in the direction of no future relationship with each other. In organizations, obviously, this is not tenable. The main reason we do actively manage our commitments is because we do care about the relationships and the Results – both of which are at stake within our organizations.

If you are a parent, you are likely very aware of these next two claims:

- You get what you tolerate.
- We teach people how to treat us.

Is this not the case with our children? Now, our colleagues and employees are not kids, but in the domain of accountability at work, the truth of these two claims is demonstrably and glaringly obvious. If we make a promise to you, and we do not keep it, and you do nothing, what have you taught us? That we don't have to keep our promises to you. Everything we do, as we know, is a teaching. We are always teaching people what's OK and what's not OK in order to be in relationship with us. You absolutely get what you tolerate, and in the domain of accountability this is incredibly clear.

Key question: *What has become the norm in your organization when people do not keep commitments?*

This is a culture question, is it not? If the norm has become "recreational character assassination" (rampant gossiping and complaining to others), then you have a certain type of culture. If the norm instead is that people simmer in silent resentment – playing "take-away" and acting in a passive/aggressive way – then you have another type of culture. Many of us have experienced this, and it shows up as people being compliant but not committed… and definitely not enthusiastic. If the norm has become people blowing up, loudly and publicly in fits of anger in the hallways, then you clearly have yet another type of culture.

If, on the other hand, the norm has become people making **responsible complaints** to each other, you are well on your way to sustaining a powerful culture of accountability and commitment.

Experience has taught us this: Even if you and your people are fairly good at making effective requests and using valid responses, without the responsible complaint in the toolkit, something is missing. Some version of responsible complaints is required, in our view, in order to sustain a culture of accountability and support excellence in execution.

A responsible complaint is a conversational competency, which means it can be learned and practiced. It is a tool, a move to make if you are seeking to minimize resentment, keep relationships "clean" and sustain collaborative Action at a high level. We've talked a lot about context, and it applies here as well.

Consider: *The most powerful and effective context for making responsible complaints is the ability to refer back to a previous conversation in which we agreed to start using responsible complaints!*

One approach for using responsible complaints would be for you to simply start using them, right now, even if you've never used them before and even if you've never discussed using them with your team. We don't recommend this approach, as it's likely to cause unnecessary surprise, upset, concerns, uncertainty. Instead, we invite you to set the stage for <u>using</u> responsible complaints next week by having conversations <u>about</u> responsible complaints this week.

For example, in these conversations you and your team (the people who will be using responsible complaints with each other) discuss and define them, talk about how they differ from complaining or "bitching," why you want to start using them, the benefits to culture and execution that they can bring, as well as anything else that comes up that may impact them. In these conversations, you may even discuss previous situations in which you did – or didn't – make responsible complaints and what those outcomes were. You may discuss your commitment to strengthening accountability within your culture, and how responsible complaints are directly in support of this Result.

It's also suggested that you and everyone else declare yourselves beginners at making responsible complaints, if you don't have a robust history of already using them, and give each other permission to not be experts at this right out of the gate. Learning requires time and practice.

How to Make a Responsible Complaint

Below is one suggested approach to making responsible complaints. Notice the use of other Speech Acts within this conversation.

1. Set the context. Remind yourself of the value of carefrontation. Remind the other person of past conversations in which you agreed to use responsible complaints in situations in which it appears that someone didn't keep or didn't manage a commitment. Remind the other person that the use of responsible complaints is to support the team in sustaining a culture of accountability, as well as ensuring that things that need to get done actually get done. Check your mood. View this a type of learning. Breathe.

2. Start with the facts – make some assertions. Did we – or did we not – have a commitment in place in which you committed to do X by Y? Is it – or is it not – complete?

3. If indeed a promise was made and not fulfilled or managed, share your assessments. Failing to manage this commitment caused this problem... had this negative impact...

4. Make additional effective requests, leading to a new commitment and timeframe. Or revoke the initial agreement.

5. Discuss: Is this an event or is it a trend? How can we keep this from happening again?

By doing this, among other things, we're "teaching" those around us about the dance we do around promises or commitments. Depending on the given situation, of course, there may be very different types of consequences for *continually* falling down on commitments: legal consequences, financial consequences, social and relationship consequences, consequences related to public identity and career, consequences related to the prevailing mood or atmosphere, and so on.

Responsible complaints are powerful language moves, powerful conversational competencies, having a direct impact on:

- Our ability to achieve the Results we want to achieve, with and through other people
- Our ability to be effective leaders and managers in organizations
- Our ability to be "assertive" and "stand up" for ourselves
- Our ability to create mutually respectful relationships
- Our ability to create and sustain a workplace atmosphere characterized by trust, accountability, personal responsibility and effectiveness
- Our dignity, our happiness.

By setting the context – and with practice – we can bring the responsible complaint into our own repertoire in both personal and workplace situations.

Promises Broken vs. Expectations Unmet

Responsible complaints are only used in situations where a promise – a commitment – was not managed or fulfilled. This is an entirely different situation than one in which someone doesn't fulfill someone else's (usually unspoken!) expectation. Make sense? This is a critical distinction to have: ***Promises broken are NOT the same things as silent expectations unmet.***

We learned it this way: Expectations are free. You can have all the expectations you want. And what's amazing to notice is this: The world does not care about your expectations. Or mine.

There's nothing wrong with having certain expectations, of course. We all have some. The problem is when they start to become more than expectations for us, when we don't see them as our own personal and private expectations anymore. The problems start when we begin treating our expectations as if they were promises that other people have made to us. These problems almost always include negative impacts on our relationships, our moodspace, our public identity and our Results.

Expectations live in language, as internal conversations and narratives. We often do what we do without really seeing them, without really being aware of them (Big Eye). And whether we call them expectations or assumptions, they can have a powerful – and often negative – impact on us. Don Miguel Ruiz, in his book *The Four Agreements*, says it this way:

> *We have the tendency to make assumptions about everything. The problem with making assumptions is that we believe they are the truth. Whenever we make assumptions, we're asking for problems. We make an assumption, we misunderstand, we take it personally, and we end up creating a whole big drama for nothing. It is always better to ask questions than to make an assumption, because assumptions set us up for suffering.*

For promises unkept, a responsible complaint is a very powerful move to make. For unspoken expectations unmet, different story. In these cases, nobody violated anything; nobody fell down on any agreement. They simply didn't spontaneously take the Action we expected them to take. What's possible here, of course, is a conversation in which some actual requests may be made, and actual promises may be entered into.

Additional Key Points: Requests

As we move toward the end of this chapter and our coverage of Speech Acts, let's cover some additional points about requests, offers and promises.

Requests also carry with them social commitments, just as declarations, assessments and assertions do. For requests, these are:

- That we are sincere in asking for what we're asking for; and
- That we will declare satisfaction if what we ask for is delivered.

Our sincerity shows up in how we follow up (or don't follow up) with those making promises to us, and what we do with what we're given. And should we consistently not declare satisfaction – even when others do fulfill their promises to us – we can expect problems and relationship difficulties to quickly arise.

Next: Have you ever found yourself wanting to make a request, but for some reason not doing so? Many of us have. There are many ways to understand this, of course, but we invite you to consider that sometimes we don't ask for what we really want because we don't want to be declined. We're fearful that if we ask for what we really want, the other person will say No. To avoid this (which we probably interpret as "rejecting me") we make really fuzzy and nebulous requests, allowing lots of room for misinterpretation and misunderstanding, ultimately, not leading to the Result we really want. Does this sound familiar?

It's also possible that we have an interpretation that we really don't deserve to be requesting, that we really don't have permission or authority to make such a request. Out of this interpretation, it's easy to see how we could tend to be vague in requesting, leading to all the things that happen when one person thinks we agreed on one thing, and the other thinks something entirely different.

A very positive and helpful type of request is a request that others support us in keeping prior commitments or in acting consistently with prior declarations. We claim there is great power here. In the last chapter, dealing with declarations, we had examples of this. After the declaration comes the request for support in acting consistently with the declaration. None of us want to show up as hypocrites, and feedback from others in these cases is invaluable.

Practicing these types of conversations – requesting support and then listening to others give us their assessments and perspective of our Actions – has the impact of making us more competent, over time, to have them. They become less and less scary, difficult and awkward. They become much more ingrained into "how we do things," becoming part of the norm in how we operate in an organization or a relationship.

Requests, Public Identity and the Nature of Our Relationships

Consider this. Have you ever been in a situation in which you wanted to make a request, but didn't? Something stopped you, either fear or worry or whatever, but you didn't do it. Now bring to mind a similar situation in which you did make the request. It may have been hard, but you somehow did it. Notice how different those situations were, for you and for others. Our claim is that when you make a request, you're not just making a request. You are shifting who you "are" in the world. Whereas before you may have been a person who lets something like that pass without saying anything, now you're a person who stands up, takes a stand and makes a request. You are seen differently by others. You are different to them. You are different.

Also: Consider the differences in these 2 relationships:

- In relationship A, one person does what he or she does, and this is not what the partner was looking for. It bothers the partner. But the partner never makes a request to discuss it in any way. The behavior simply goes on and on.

- In relationship B, one person does what he or she does, and again this is not what the partner was looking for. It bothers the partner. In this case, however, the partner makes a request to have a conversation to talk about it.

That conversation, in turn, may include a request that the person begin doing X or stop doing Y in a certain way. If the request is answered with a Yes, a commitment is made and the first step is taken toward inventing a new future.

Question: Which of the relationships above do you believe will be more successful? More fulfilling? More mutually beneficial?

We can talk about balance in the relationship, we can talk about the context of the relationship, we can talk about dignity in the relationship, we can talk about the Results of the relationship. All of these come up as we reflect on these two relationships, one of which includes requests and one of which does not.

Offers

Much of what we've discussed applies equally to requests and offers. Certainly the 6 elements of effective requests can be seen as the 6 elements of effective offers. Just as we make requests in order to get a Yes, leading to a commitment (promise or agreement) that leads to our coordinating future Action, we make offers for the same purpose.

However, there's another aspect of offers that's also important, and in some ways sets offers apart from requests. Offers are connected with career and with business in ways that requests are not. For example, one way to look at a career or a business is as a set of coherent offerings, made to the public ongoingly. Limo services offer to carry passengers from one location to another for set fares. Tax preparation services offer to provide assistance, for a fee, in the areas of personal and business finance. Oil companies offer petroleum products to the market for set prices. Car makers offer vehicles and services. Consulting firms offer professional services. We could go on and on.

When you become associated with a coherent, related set of offerings, we can say that you've built a career, a business. Change the offers you make to the world, you change your career or business. For people looking for a job or a life change, perhaps this way of looking at offers can be helpful.

Maybe one way to think about what we'd like to do, is to think about what we'd like to offer. And this way of thinking takes us to the notion of concerns. Offers are made to address concerns. Broadly speaking, this is the function of business – to offer goods and services that address the concerns of people. This is also the function of non-profit and other organizations. They make different offers, because they're committed to addressing different concerns.

So we may ask ourselves: What concerns that are "out there" in the world already would I like to address with my offers? or What concerns are not out there yet, but I believe soon will be? and What specific offers would I like to make to address these new concerns? This has everything to do, of course, with what we call innovation. Listening is also clearly important here, as we seek to learn and understand these different types of emerging concerns that may not have yet reached "critical mass" and thus not be obvious yet to many people. Also, we can ask ourselves "Where are the boundaries of my competency to be able to offer this or that? What new learning on my part – or the part of my organization – is needed in order to become competent enough to do this or that?" And so on.

Making offers publicly – and keeping commitments consistently – have a very positive impact on our public identity. We begin to build this identity and become associated with our ability to address these concerns. Individually, this identity may be connected with our careers or our personal relationships. Organizationally, this identity may be connected with our business success or failure. And in both cases, we're directly dealing with our productivity, our fulfillment and our ability to achieve the Results we say we want.

More on Promises

As we've shown, promises (or commitments, agreements) are at the heart of execution within organizations. They are also obviously important in our personal lives, as virtually all of us have experienced.

Whether we consistently keep or break our commitments has immediate and direct impact on four important dimensions within our lives:

- Trust
- Relationships
- Success
- Self-Esteem

Consistently making clear promises and keeping them has predictable positive impacts on all of these. It's a win-win proposition. And this, of course, is not new. For ages people have talked about whether or not people are "as good as their word."

This has to do with integrity, and with our ability to build solid relationships. Many of us have seen this quote from Aristotle before, and there are many instances in which it is valuable to think about: *We are what we repeatedly do. Excellence, then, is not an act, but a habit.* And a great deal of what we "repeatedly do" is actually brought forth out of what we "repeatedly say".

And when we do not keep our commitments – even occasionally – we may expect predictable negative impacts on trust, relationships, success and self-esteem. If we're not careful, once we start failing to keep commitments, we can tend to go "unconscious" here. We drift along, not paying attention to the times we say Yes, not realizing that every Yes establishes a commitment, and because we haven't been paying attention we end up not keeping some or even many of the commitments we've made. And one day we look around and what used to be strong relationships are much more precarious. Our public identity is significantly damaged. Doors seem to not be opened for us. No one wants to play with us.

Unconsciously making and breaking commitments is a no-win situation. On the other hand, consciously making and keeping commitments is a proven path to improvements in trust, relationships, success and self-esteem. Consciously making and keeping commitments is how we can actually design who we are and expand what's possible for us in the world.

Now consider this: Let's say someone breaks a promise to you, and then you don't see the person for a year or two. Then, as you're walking down the street, you see this person walking straight toward you. Question: What's one of the first things that goes through your head? For many of us, it's remembering that the person broke a promise to us! And we don't plan to do this, we don't try to do this. We just do. We human beings apparently do not deal well with incompletions. And a broken, un-cleaned up promise is a giant incompletion.

Let's turn the tables. What do many of us want to do if _we_ have broken a promise to someone, and then soon afterward, we see that person walking right toward us in a hallway or on the street? Many of us want to hide, to duck into a room or closet; some of us even cross the street! All to avoid the person to whom we've broken a promise.

Think of it this way – if you break enough promises to enough people, and then begin to avoid all these people, welcome to being by yourself quite a lot. Those people will also tend to avoid you, and will certainly avoid doing things – coordinating Action – with you. Break enough promises, and we end up doing whatever we do, by ourselves. It's a fairly sure and well-proven path to involuntary hermithood.

Speaking of this, consider self-esteem. Who is it that we often break the most promises to? We say it's to ourselves. Anyone who's ever had self-esteem issues knows this is true. Even though we make up many stories and rationalize and have great excuses for why we didn't keep the private promises we've made to ourselves, our bodies know. The broken promises "live" in our bones and our bodies, and over time this impacts our mood, our Actions and our Results. Remember our 3-circle Way of Being. Our moods and our bodies and our language are definitely connected.

If you have a choice, will you work with or be with or play with people who break promises to you? Probably not. We know this very well – our making and keeping or making and breaking promises has a giant effect on our public identity, who we "are" in the world. And it is our responsibility to take care of our public identity.

Many of us are not aware that this is happening, as many of us are sloppy in our making of promises. We say Yes casually to others' vague requests, or we make promises that we have a sense we aren't going to keep, but in that moment it seems like the most expedient thing to do. We say:

- "Sure, I'll be home at 6:00" and then something comes up and we don't make it till 7:30.

- "I'll take you to the game this Saturday, Bobby" and then something else happens, likely connected to work, and we end up not going.

- "I'll take care of that, Joe" without fully understanding what we just agreed to. We're in a hurry and we don't clarify our understanding, and maybe we don't focus on it well enough to ever write it down. It never makes our to-do list and so it doesn't get done.

In each of these cases, we can point to how trust, relationship, success and self-esteem are all diminished – for both the one making the promises as well as for the person on the other end. And if we do this over time, we can predict the (usually unspoken) responses of people to whom we've broken promises. In these cases, our public identity is already such that other people listen (interpret) insincerity even as we're making the promise itself. Their internal responses to the three promises above include something akin to:

- "That's BS. You won't be home then."

- "That's BS, Dad. Something always comes up. We won't be going."

- "That's BS. He's not gonna do it. I better make other plans to handle this."

One way we cover this topic in our workshops is to share a simple analogy. We say that for all of us, an angle exists. This angle (see below) represents the difference between what we say we're going to do and what we actually do:

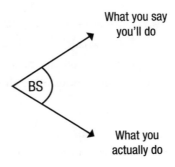

We call the angle between the two the angle of inauthenticity, or in layman's terms, the angle of BS. We can reframe our question, in light of this angle, in this way: *How much BS are you producing?* This matters. Because, whether or not we know it, other people "smell" it! As we mentioned earlier, most of us have pretty good BS-detectors. And in some cases, we've also gotten a lot of practice using them.

Strong, Shallow and Criminal Promises

Let's take a look at three types of promises and how they show up in our lives and in the world:

- Strong promises: Promises that I am absolutely committed to keeping. You can count on me, no matter what. Put it in the bank.

- Shallow promises: These look like a strong promise, but what I don't say out loud is "unless X or Y happens." For example, I may say "Yes, I'll be at the gathering on Saturday" but what I don't say out loud is "unless it rains." Or "unless I have other work to do." Here, we reserve a private "out" for ourselves, but we don't let the other person know.

- Criminal promises: These are promises that at the moment of making, we know we have no intention of keeping. We may think it's just the most expedient thing to do to say Yes in the moment, in order to get out of the conversation. Or we make a promise because we think someone else wants us to, but we know in our hearts that we are not committed to what we just said Yes to.

As related to these types of promises, an interesting exercise for many of us is to take a look at the major domains of our lives:

- family / spouse
- work / career
- social / friends – relationships
- play
- body / health
- spiritual / religious
- mood / attitude
- money / finance
- learning / education
- dignity
- world / larger connection

and see if any patterns emerge related to the types of promises we make. Take a look at the types of promises you make to yourself, your significant other, your family members, your friends, your co-workers, your direct reports, your customers, your suppliers, your partners, your boss... and see what shows up. Flex the Big Eye here, and what do you notice?

Our experience is that many of us find that we make criminal promises to ourselves. Or that we tend to make shallow promises with family members and that we somehow take them for granted, thinking that they'll be there for us no matter what. Others have different patterns. But in our experience, our way of making and keeping promises is tightly connected to our public identities, our relationships, our well-being and our Results. What's possible here is to clean up relationships containing broken promises; but of course this is *not* possible without first noticing and then accepting what we've been up to. From here, we can declare the current situation to be a "breakdown" for us – to be "not working" for us – and move into new Action.

Stress, Overwhelm and Saying No

Next we will explore the phenomenon of overwhelm, which we see as a fairly prevalent moodspace for many leaders and non-leaders alike. We see a great number of time management books and seminars and systems out in the marketplace, some of which are undoubtedly more effective than others. Many people have shared with us their experience of achieving some short-term gains out of selected time management programs, but for whatever reason not keeping those improvements over the longer term.

Let's return to the example of the invisible backpack we're each wearing, containing the 47 other promises we've made that are in different stages of completion. And now we say Yes to your request of us.

You're not aware of these other promises we made. All you know is that we said Yes to your request, and so we have a promise. Here we are, all covered up with these commitments. This is the situation. And here's the kicker – out of this, we get to be resentful when you innocently ask us how things are progressing a few days later! What we forget is that we're the one who made the promise. We're the one who said Yes in the first place! Back to the Big Eye.

Have you ever found yourself "stressed out?" In our workshops, when asked this question, the vast majority of hands immediately go up. We call it being over-committed or living in overwhelm, and it seems to be everywhere.

Not being able to say No translates into this way of living. So learning how to say No can serve us. It is a powerful declaration that enables us to manage our commitments. Without it, managing commitments is virtually impossible and we very quickly realize that others are running our lives. Recently, we've begun to practice declining, and we're slowly getting better at it. It's all time and practice.

But do you know anyone – maybe yourself – who has difficulty occasionally saying No? Many of us have experienced this, and for some it's not occasionally. Not being able to say No translates into more than simply not being able to utter a word or two. We say that this is connected to personal power, and ultimately to our dignity. Here, we again claim that not being able to <u>say</u> a certain thing (in this case, "No") = not being able to <u>be</u> a certain way (in this case, assertive, designing our lives, with dignity).

Try to imagine a person of dignity who also happens to be unable to say No to any request made of him or her. It's difficult, isn't it? (In the practice of ontological coaching, the underlying internal conversations and interpretations which are behind the Action of not saying No are explored and shown to the client. Armed with this new insight and awareness, the client then gets to be at choice about inventing and practicing new, more powerful interpretations and internal conversations that more enable him or her to say No).

Speaking of interpretations, what does No mean to you? Our experience is that many of us tend to equate No to "rejection." In other words, we think that by saying No to someone, we're rejecting them. Or we think that when others say No to us, they are rejecting us. We say something different. We say that *No isn't rejection of a person. It is simply a decline of a request.* The person and the request are separate. When we say No, we're simply declining your request, we're not rejecting you.

Have you also noticed that the traditional understanding of "No = rejection" is very widespread and pervasive, even though no one actually sat us down and taught us that on purpose? What's available is to adopt a different interpretation of No, one that can serve us and support us in designing the Results we say we want. Also, just as others have the right to decline our requests (in a great many situations), we all (in a great many situations) have the right to decline others' requests of us.

Like anything, learning to say No takes time and practice. There is no substitute. We do not want to imply that this is easy, especially if we have years and years of acting in different ways. We have a lot of practice doing it differently, so we're very competent at not saying No in many situations. And in many situations, those around us may have gotten used to our not saying No and have grown accustomed to it. But the payoff is worth it.

Being able to say No also means being able to design your life, to designate priorities and take Actions that support you in going toward the goals you've declared to be important. Being able to say No means being able to be a person of dignity, being able to "stand up" in some way for your own life. Being able to say No means being able to be a full partner in a relationship, be it personal or professional. This is a wonderful example of the power of our language and our conversations. So we repeat: *As human beings, we each have the right to decline others' requests of us.*

Let's now turn for a moment to saying No and managing commitments within organizations. Many participants in our programs have shared with us situations at work in which they legitimately cannot say No. Certain workplace requests, for example, are really demands or workplace requirements of the position. In some ways, by agreeing to be an employee in a certain organization means that we agree to say Yes to certain requests made of us by appropriate people, and agree to perform accordingly. What is possible, however, is to have conversations to clarify where the boundary is between these "requirements" and those which are really requests.

Our experience, and the experience of many of our colleagues, is that these conversations can be truly revealing for everyone involved. It's often the case that the person making certain requests has viewed them as requests (which by definition may be declined or counter-offered), while the person responding has historically viewed them as demands or commands, with no leeway for declining or renegotiation. Such conversations can lead to redefining work roles, as well as building more healthy and productive employee relationships.

Extraordinary Leaders and Extraordinary Companies Say No

One of Apple's core value statements is: *"We believe in saying No to thousands of projects so that we can really focus on the few that are truly important and meaningful to us."*

Patrick Lencioni, in his wonderful book *The Advantage*, discusses the importance of *"brutal intolerance around the company's core values."* What this means is that not every behavior is OK. Some behaviors are decidedly not OK, and they elicit a clear and unequivocal "No" when they occur. The predictable Result, over time, of this ability to say No is what he calls "organizational health" – a clear advantage for any and all organizations.

Jim Collins talks about the importance of *"the relentless discipline to say No to opportunities that fail the hedgehog test…"* which means that the answer to all the following three questions must be a strong Yes:

- Are we deeply passionate about this?
- Can we be the best in the world in this area?
- Will it drive or positively contribute to our economic engine?

Marissa Mayer, CEO of Yahoo, has famously said: *"You have to ruthlessly prioritize."*

Marshall Goldsmith says: *"We spend a lot of time helping leaders learn what to do. We do not spend enough time teaching leaders what to stop. Half of the leaders I have met don't need to learn what to do. They need to learn what to stop."*

And of course, saying No becomes quite difficult without one other important condition. Stephen Covey reminds us that *"You have to decide what your highest priorities are and have the courage – pleasantly, smilingly, nonapologetically, to say No to other things. And the way you do that is by having a bigger Yes burning inside."*

Creating a Culture of Accountability and Driving Excellence in Execution

Within every organization, right now, requests are being made and promises are being entered into and managed. Leaders are delegating to direct reports, processes are being built and are functioning, Actions are being coordinated and taken for the purpose of achieving some desired Result – the successful fulfillment of whatever was promised externally to the customers.

The cumulative effect of this collaborative Action directly shapes the culture of your organization – just as your culture shapes these interactions. These interactions, as we have shown, are the actual drivers of excellence in execution within your organization.

Improving in this way includes an assumption that everyone is always at least partially responsible for things being like they are, and moving away from the "blame game." Organizational improvement here focuses directly on the underlying interactions out of which everything else flows – the way in which the people coordinate Action with each other. It's all about bringing some awareness and purposefulness to the ways that leaders and employees ongoingly make, keep and manage commitments.

Viewed this way, the goal for organizations is "impeccable" coordination of Action. This doesn't mean, as we've discussed, that every person will always keep 100% of the commitments he/she makes, but it does mean that every person will actively manage his or her commitments. It means that relationships will always be kept "clean." Actively managing commitments includes the ways in which we communicate with each other (and the ways that we don't), the types of discussions we have (and don't have) when it becomes apparent commitments will not be kept as originally planned. It includes the way we handle situations when commitments are not kept, and whether or not we make responsible complaints. It includes how clear we are when we make commitments. It also includes how much of our internal dialogue about this we share with others and in what manner the sharing occurs.

We invite you to consider the following steps in order to improve execution and sustain your version of a culture of accountability and commitment within your organization:

1. Assume the role of CCO (Chief Conversations Officer). Convene conversations that help others see and understand that at its most basic level, **your organization is a network of commitments**. Share and discuss the "house" drawing.

2. With your leadership team, **publicly declare** your twin goals of 1) creating and maintaining a Culture of Accountability and 2) driving and sustaining excellence in execution. View the way people coordinate Action as shapers, drivers, of these qualitative and quantitative Results.

3. Given these desired Results, convene conversations to discuss and identify which conversations should be **prohibited** and which conversations should be **required** in order to get there. Include discussions to identify any conversations which may have historically been **missing**, and take steps to begin building these into key processes.

4. Begin building a **shared vocabulary and introducing new distinctions**: Introduce your version of Elements of Effective Requests and Valid Responses.

5. Introduce the difference between **Responsible Complaints and "complaining"** and give explicit permission for everyone to make Responsible Complaints.

6. Introduce the difference between **promises broken and silent expectations unfulfilled**.

7. Request assessments and **feedback from those you trust** related to your own history of managing and keeping commitments.

8. Introduce **Sincere Apologies** and gain commitment to use when commitments are not fulfilled and not managed. Model its use – apologize if you fall down on keeping your commitments.

9. Ongoing – Pay attention to body language and the tone or "mood" of conversations in your organization. **Resentment and cynicism** virtually always accompany an environment with "un-cleaned up" broken commitments.

10. Ongoing – If you are ever the third party in a problem-solving or conflict-resolution situation, **launch this as your opening salvo across the bow... the very first thing you say as you start the session: "Are we here today because of a broken commitment or the perception of a broken commitment?"** Our experience is this: If you start here, you will cut through 15 minutes of non-productive conversation and get "legs" to stand on very quickly. You may find that the timeframe was unclear, and Person A thought the deadline was Monday and Person B thought it was Tuesday. In this case, a conversation about elements of an effective request can be very helpful, as well a a discussion that the background of obviousness (obviously) isn't thick enough to support implicit timeframes within important requests.

It's also possible that you may find that the conditions of satisfaction weren't clear enough – in which case, a similar review and conversation about how to improve moving forward is warranted.

You may also find out that while Person A made the request, Person B didn't actually say Yes. It was assumed, but none of the 4 valid responses was actually obtained. In this case, the conversation focuses on the need to make sure that one of these is always obtained before the conversations is closed.

You may also find that you're in the room because someone simply didn't fulfill someone else's unspoken expectation. In this case, a teaching moment is still available. You can help the people involved see that while everyone does have some degree of shared corporate understanding by virtue of the fact that they all work together, we're still not able to read each others' minds! You can emphasize that moving forward, in cases of non-trivial situations, let's be sure to make actual requests and not operate with unspoken assumptions or expectations.

Finally, you may find out that you're dealing with a case in which Person A not only did not <u>keep</u> a commitment; they didn't <u>manage</u> it. In this case, you can ask one of our very favorite questions (that we hope may also become one of yours, if it isn't already): **Is this an event, or is it a trend?**

If it's an event, a one-off, then the conversation goes a certain way. Everyone makes mistakes now and then, of course. But if it's a trend, you may need to have an entirely different conversation. This trend of not managing commitments does not occur in a vacuum – it occurs in the web of commitments that is the engine of your organization's productivity. It has significant and negative impacts on the quality of execution as well as the culture.

Jim Collins echoes this point when he says: *"Letting the wrong people hang around is unfair to all the right people, as they inevitably find themselves compensating for the inadequacies of the wrong people. Worse, it can drive away the best people. Strong performers are intrinsically motivated by performance, and when they see their efforts impeded by carrying extra weight, they eventually become frustrated."*

We've also heard it put this way: Sometimes it's easier to change people... than it is to change people!

11. Frame **all of this as a type of learning**, a **set of competencies**. It's a process. Keep practicing, keep working, keep improving.

Summary of Key Points

All organizations, at their core, may be understood as networks of commitments – people making and managing promises with each other. Seeing and understanding this opens new avenues for improving execution (quantitative Results), culture and relationships (qualitative Results) within organizations.

Requests and offers are language Actions, speech acts, in which other people are necessarily involved in our bringing about some new Action and producing some new Results. Making requests (or offers) is seen as a very creative act, in a number of ways. First, it puts in motion new Actions and new commitments, which are the basis for doing things – *any* things – with other people. Second, a person who makes a request or offer that he or she historically has not made is a different person. In these cases, we show up differently to others around us, and we ourselves are different Observers than we were before. Choosing to make different requests or offers than we used to make is choosing to be different than we were before. To never make any requests or offers is to not participate in actively guiding or designing our own lives.

As non-hermits, we all make many requests at home and at work and everywhere. The only reason we make any requests at all is because we think the future – if left to its own devices – will unfold in a certain way, and we don't want it to. Requests and offers, if accepted, generate a new today and a new tomorrow. Requests are the front end of creating a commitment or promise on the part of another; offers are the front end of creating a commitment or promise on our part. And how we make and manage promises, commitments, agreements has a huge impact on our productivity, our peacefulness and our Results.

All requests are not created equal. Some requests are more effective than others. That is, some requests are more likely to be accepted than others. Some requests lead to a clearer and more solid understanding than others. Some requests are the starting point for working and doing things well together, while others are the starting point for misunderstanding, resentment and poor Results. Elements of what we call Effective Requests and Offers include:

- Committed speaker
- Committed listener
- Future Action and conditions of satisfaction
- Timeframe
- Context
- Mood

Paying attention to these 6 elements can greatly serve us in making effective requests and bringing about the Results we want in our organizations and our lives.

Sloppiness here is often a big part of the problem in situations involving misunderstandings and claims such as "so-and-so didn't do what he or she promised" or "so-and-so never listens," among others.

Some degree of a "background of obviousness" always exists between the speaker and the listener. That is, some things may be obvious to <u>both</u> the speaker and listener, in which case solid mutual understanding is reached without certain specifics, details and descriptions. However, in many other cases what's obvious to one person isn't obvious to the other. In these cases, paying particular attention to the future Action, conditions of satisfaction and timeframe can be very beneficial.

Shared commitment only comes after shared understanding. Shared understanding is produced in conversation, and is at the heart of why we pay so much attention to our requests and offers, and how they can be made to be more effective.

Promises (or commitments, agreements) are created when a request or an offer is followed by a declaration of Yes. They are seen as the primary "move" that we make in language, in order to do anything and everything we do with others. Understanding promises is central to understanding our relationships, our public identity (how others "see" us) and our Results, for us as individuals as well as for our organizations.

The whole social fabric around us is seen as being constructed, at a very basic level, of people (and the organizations they comprise) making promises with each other. We then go about the ongoing business of managing and fulfilling these commitments, as well as entering into new ones, in a wide variety of ways.

It's not possible for us to <u>keep</u> 100% of the promises that we make, as originally promised. But it is possible for us to actively <u>manage</u> 100% of the promises we make. This is the key – do we or do we not operate with conscious awareness of the promises we enter into? Do we or do we not pay specific attention to what we say we'll do and when we say we'll do it… and then follow up actively should something happen that may prevent us from doing so?

When people break commitments to us, we have effective options available to us. Not dealing with broken commitments almost always leads to resentment and a lessening of the relationship, as well as to a drop-off in productivity and effectiveness in accomplishing anything together. A powerful language move to make here is the responsible complaint.

Other tools for managing our commitments, improving execution and building a culture of accountability include gaining more ability to say No and using four "valid" responses when answering requests: Yes, No, Commit-to-Commit, and Counter-Offer.

Many of us are not very good Observers of ourselves and how we make requests and offers and how we manage the web of commitments that we each live in. Because of this, we often don't see the negative Results we may be producing for ourselves by failing to make clear and effective requests and offers and taking care of our commitments and the relationships that are at stake through them. Whenever an unclear request is made, or a promise is made but then broken, we say that something is diminished in the relationship. Something is less than it was before. In many cases, not doing this well has a negative, downward effect on:

- Trust
- The relationship
- The success of whatever is involved
- The self-esteem – the emotional space – of those involved.

Time management is a misnomer. What we really have is commitment management. It is here and with our declarations that we drive execution, design our lives and bring about our own futures.

Application

For all the items below, keep in mind the 1 or 2 or 3 important Results that you are committed to achieving during the next 12 months, as well as the areas in which you declared you are seeking to learn or learn how to do something differently or better.

1. How would you characterize the way in which your organization coordinates Action? Consider convening conversations with direct reports and others in which the following questions are posed and discussed publicly:

   - Consider how requests and promises are made; internally and externally; formally and informally; email and in person; at meetings and in the hallways. How effective are our requests? How effective are our responses?

- Are commitments ever misunderstood? Often? Never? In some areas more than others? Consider what happens to productivity and operational Results when parties have not reached shared understanding of what is to be done. Consider what happens to the "mood" or "morale" or culture also, particularly if these misunderstandings happen over time.

- To what extent are people personally responsible for actively managing their commitments? How does this play out in their Actions?

- What has become the "standard" or the "norm" within the company regarding keeping and managing commitments? Are commitments broken frequently, infrequently, never? Consider what – if anything – happens when commitments are not kept; all levels.

- What percentage of people make responsible complaints when confronted with a promise not managed or not kept (positive impact)? What percentage of people gossip and complain to others (negative impact)?

- Are there some missing conversations here? What new conversations and new agreements are needed in order to begin improving?

2. Have a conversation with others about the importance of promises and the importance of managing them and keeping them. Share views about how promises impact success, productivity, the relationships involved, the emotional space, the Results which are achieved. Discuss responsible complaints and their value, as well as ways in which our agreements with one another can be made clearly and understandably.

3. Make new agreements about how promises will be managed and relationships will be taken care of. Put into place a context such that you and others have permission to make responsible complaints, to decline requests, to make counter-offers and to commit-to-commit. Put into place a context of learning, of improving, of getting better with time and practice.

4. Big Eye: Are there situations you can think of in which you fell down on managing your commitments? If so, what steps have you taken to clean up those situations and take care of those relationships? And what additional steps will you take moving forward?

CHAPTER 11

MOODS, EMOTIONS AND RESULTS

"Dispirited, unmotivated, unappreciated workers cannot compete in a highly competitive world."

- Frances Hesselbein

We've touched on moods and emotions in previous chapters. Here, they are the central focus and we begin with some basic questions:

- Do moods and emotions have anything to do with leadership effectiveness and organizational performance?

- Do moods and emotions have anything to do with relationships, culture, execution and breakthrough Results?

- Are moods and emotions connected with our capacity to create a life of balance, meaning, fulfillment and contribution – however we may define and understand these terms?

We say yes, on all fronts. So learning about moods and emotions is absolutely critical for leaders at all levels… and yet very few of us have spent any real time at all in <u>purposeful</u> learning in these areas. Whatever most of us have acquired here has largely been as a by-product of simply living our lives. That is, the main learning most of us have done in this area has been through trial-and-error, our unique versions of on the job training. We've done the best we can, without any real guidance or structure, in an area of immense – and growing – importance.

This chapter will serve to build on the groundwork laid in earlier chapters, and go further. We hope to share some distinctions that will strengthen your ability to see, understand and strengthen three inter-related key competencies that are simply critical for leadership effectiveness and organizational success today:

- Conversational
- Relational
- Emotional

Most of us – especially those in STEM (science, technology, engineering and math) related organizations – are already highly competent functionally and/or technically. In cases where we need improvement here, functional or technical training is usually readily available. However, structured and practical learning to strengthen the emotional, conversational and relational competencies is typically conspicuously absent from the standard training curriculum.

Yet these are the very competencies that are essential for leadership and managerial effectiveness. These are the very competencies that separate the good from the great, from those who are able to shape culture and drive execution from those who are not. This is especially true in many of today's organizations, in which accomplishing critical business Results through cross-functional teams, collaborative organizational structures and multi-cultural workforces has become the norm rather than the exception.

This chapter provides a framework and set of tools to help you expand your ability to understand yourself and others, in ways that will support you in leveraging your talent in order to produce breakthrough Results. It is intended to improve your ability to lead more effectively, as well as to create and maintain a more solid balance of productivity and peacefulness in your personal life.

Setting the Stage for Learning about Moods and Emotions

Before moving into specific new distinctions and offering new tools, it's important to share with you the context in which we see this type of learning.

Learning that includes the emotional domain is relatively new in organizational settings, as many readers well know. In our view, two important books opened the door to the ability to include this type of learning or training within contemporary organizations: *The 7 Habits of Highly Effective People* by Stephen Covey (1989) and *Emotional Intelligence* by Daniel Goleman (2005). Prior to these publications, conversations about moods and emotions may have occurred in psychologists' or therapists' offices, in medical clinics, or in religious or perhaps family settings... but not in organizations. And certainly not in the executive boardroom!

These books demonstrated clearly the impact of moods and emotions in virtually all settings that involve human beings and collaborative Action. They identified particular ways in which dramatically new and better bottom-line Results could be achieved once new understandings were acquired and new practices were implemented. And this demonstration of positive impact on the bottom line was the key.

The ensuing 25 years have seen remarkable progress and growth in the acceptance of what had historically been undervalued and misunderstood as "charm school", "soft skills", "psycho-babble", "not relevant for bottom-line-oriented companies" or "merely subjective." This type of learning is now widely understood as a critical complement to more traditional workplace skill sets, as it has demonstrated its value in supporting and driving hard business Results. In fact, in many settings, the functional and technical skills have become somewhat "commoditized," the threshold for acceptance into the organization, the price of entry. The conversational and interpersonal skills – and the ability to effectively shift and leverage one's moods and emotions – are increasingly emerging as the real impact differentiators among leaders, managers and employees of all types.

A *Fortune* magazine article from August, 2015 entitled *"Humans are Underrated"* by Geoff Colvin reinforces the extent to which the business community now fully understands the value and impact of these competencies. He says *"As technology advances, the economy increasingly values the most deeply human interpersonal abilities: empathy, social sensitivity, collaboration, storytelling, leading and relationship-building."* Oracle group vice-president Meg Bear goes as far as to say *"Empathy is the critical 21st-century skill."*

The article goes on to state that the Oxford Economics research firm asked employers which skills they'll need most in the next 5-10 years, and the answers that came back did not include business acumen, analysis or P&L management. Instead, employers' top priorities include relationship-building, teaming, co-creativity, brainstorming, cultural sensitivity and ability to manage diverse employees – the "right brain" skills of social interaction.

A Different Type of Learning is Required

Next, it's important to understand that this type of learning is different from the learning many of us are already very familiar with. We say this up front so that readers may recognize this, in themselves and in others, and thus be able to anticipate and deal with any possible obstacles to learning that may arise. In a nutshell, here is our claim: Many of us equate learning with gathering data, facts or information… and for some topic areas, this type of "learning about" may indeed suffice.

But learning trust, empathy, and gratitude for example, do not involve information and data analysis in the same ways that learning products, strategies and markets do. The same goes for learning how to inspire commitment or improve important relationships; how to promote innovation, alignment, and more effective collaboration; how to resolve conflict while strengthening the relationships involved; and how to create a space where acknowledging mistakes is valued as an opportunity for learning, growing and adapting… so the company can avoid making the same mistakes in the future. The entire realm of moods and emotions is central to the new understandings that are required here. Yet our ways of approaching learning in these areas are often utterly inadequate for the task. In fact, in many instances, this entire emotional domain is completely ignored.

Learning to live in longer timeframes, learning to move through difficult events and situations, learning to listen – and listen deeply – to the concerns and perspectives of those who may be quite different from ourselves… these are all growing, not diminishing, in importance. And they don't lend themselves at all to the long-established information-gathering approach to learning.

Moods and emotions are critical for those of us learning to update beliefs which may have served us in the past but no longer serve us today, as well as learning to take responsibility for them as our beliefs in the first place (as opposed to "the way things are" or "attributes of Reality"). Moods and emotions are obviously connected to our ability to learn to let go of simplistic either/or, this/that, black/white ways of understanding our complex world. These are all profoundly important and are also not at all well suited to the traditional, quantitatively oriented approach to learning. A quote attributed to Albert Einstein: *"Not everything that can be counted, counts… and not everything that counts can be counted."* comes to mind here.

Learning to see and hold new possibilities, learning to design and create a work-place culture of commitment, adaptability and trust, learning to create a space where each individual employee can grow, develop and contribute as fully as pos-sible, learning to facilitate creative conflict or carefrontation that yields both su-perior decision-making as well as strengthened relationships... all are incredibly important and point to our need to somehow un-learn or re-learn a great deal of what we have been taught about our organizations, our employees and ourselves.

The fundamental goals of this body of learning involve improving our ability to create a balance of productivity (objective Results) and peacefulness (subjective Results) – both personally and professionally. Given this, we agree with Julio Olalla, founder of the Newfield Network, when he says:

"Some of the most important types of learning, for today and tomorrow, must include and transcend this historical focus on information gathering for the sake of effective Action... with a new concentration on developing self-awareness, self-responsibility and wisdom for the sake of effective living."

Julio Olalla's teachings around learning, learning how to learn, and the types of learning that include moods and emotions, self-awareness and understanding, empathy and compassion, meaning and purpose, trust- and relationship-build-ing... are the central underpinnings from which this chapter is built. From the basic distinctions to the challenge and invitation for all of us to expand how we think about and understand learning, growing, relating to each other, as well as the entire emotional realm – in all these areas we are grateful to be sharing with you what we have been taught.

Learning in the emotional realm and learning of the types we are describing do not occur by command or by memorization or data analysis. These types of learn-ing occur by immersion, by example, by choice. They occur by acquiring some new distinctions and then <u>practicing</u> the distinctions with others, in a community where feedback is obtained and discussed and progress toward desired Results is evaluated. These types of learning occur through self-assessments and reflection, the enrolling of networks of support and accountability and an ongoing process of choosing, observing, learning/adjusting and choosing again. Here, we can see clearly that learning "about" is not the same at all as learning "to do" or learning "to be."

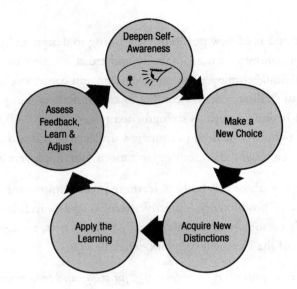

Given the types of issues we are now facing, and the types of goals we are seeking to achieve, we simply must expand and broaden our understanding and practices in this area. We must bring balance to it by including all aspects of the human experience, including our moods, emotions and "subjectivity." And here we must include the Observer as part of what is observed. We must include ourselves and our very ways of relating to and experiencing the world and everything in it – and this obviously moves us into a very different type of learning.

Moods, Emotions and Organizational Results

Many organizations today have adopted their own version of what has come to be known as a "triple-bottom-line" or "PPP" focus; that is, an overt desire to include Profitability (of course), People and the Planet in their approach to doing business.

In other words, in addition to the obvious need for organizations to be profitable enough to sustain themselves and achieve company objectives (think "no margin, no mission"), many leaders clearly see a connection between this and the way they treat their employees – at all levels. Many also have embraced the value of being "responsible corporate citizens" in their approach to the use and disposal of resources, as well as their overall orientation to the communities in which they operate. For these leaders and these organizations, moods and emotions are clearly connected to their ability to achieve desired Results.

But even in more traditional organizations, where profitability may still be the only publicly declared priority, we claim that moods and emotions are critical influencers and drivers of performance. Consider the influence and impact of moods and emotions on the effectiveness of:

- Strategic planning and goal-setting
- Creating and sustaining a powerful and healthy corporate culture
- Building shared understanding and shared commitment to key goals
- Individual and team sales efforts
- Developing and implementing marketing campaigns
- Delivering customer service
- Teamwork and internal communications
- Innovation and new product/service development
- Acknowledging and recovering from mistakes
- Solving problems
- Supervising subordinates
- Managing / improving performance
- Developing talent and retaining quality employees

Consider also the entire realm of leadership and management, and the role and influence of corporate culture (which both impacts and is impacted by moods and emotions) on organizational effectiveness.

With just a little reflection, it becomes clear that the Results of virtually every significant business function, aspect or process are at stake. This is because, of course, people – human beings – are central to the effectiveness of each and every one of these functions and processes. And as we've covered earlier, every single one of us – in addition to being a physical being and a linguistic being – is also an emotional being.

We simply cannot escape the fact that everything we do, at work as well as at home, involves our own way of "seeing things" as well as the ways in which we relate to, understand and interact with those around us. In these areas, moods and emotions play a critical role, whether we're aware of this or not. In the end, a great many of the Results that we say are important to us – at work as well as in our personal lives – are produced directly out of these interactions. As always, we remember Observer – Action – Results.

Basic Distinctions: How We Understand Moods and Emotions

Webster defines emotions as: "… a conscious mental reaction subjectively experienced as strong feeling usually directed toward a specific object and typically accompanied by physiological and behavioral changes in the body…" Moods are defined as "… a conscious state of mind or predominant emotion…"

While we have no disagreement with these, we offer that in a fundamental way, moods and emotions can both be understood to be **predispositions for Action**. We find this understanding to be a more powerful, more useful, more actionable, and more helpful representation of what is actually going on here. The distinction we make between moods and emotions is this:

- Moods are understood as <u>long-term</u> predispositions for Action, lasting months to years (to lifetimes), and are "<u>already there</u>" when events occur. They are not triggered by external events; rather, they are already present when events occur. They have a huge impact on how events are interpreted, of course, and serve to "orient" us one way or another toward different possible Actions, and therefore different possible Results. Moods are often hidden or unseen, difficult for us to see… especially in ourselves.

- Emotions, on the other hand, are understood as <u>short-term</u> predispositions for Action, lasting moments to hours to possibly days. They are triggered by some external event, and are much more visible to us and to others. We can say that emotions are more often worn "on our sleeve." Once they are triggered, in the short term, they also have an impact on what we are likely to do, and how we are likely to do it.

In this way of thinking, it's clear that an emotion of fear (such as that caused by turning a corner and almost stepping on a poisonous snake) is quite different from living our lives fearfully. It's clear that an emotion of anger, when triggered by someone attempting to harm our children, is quite different from living our lives as angry men or angry women. An emotion of happiness, initiated by a child's excellent report card, is different than living one's life with an ongoing sense of contentment, satisfaction or fulfillment. So to repeat: moods and emotions are <u>both</u> predispositions for Action, but moods are <u>long-term</u> and not triggered by some external event... while emotions are <u>short-term</u> and triggered by some event or situation.

An analogy may also be helpful here: Moods can be understood as the current of a river, deep and unseen, but strong and having a great impact on where the river goes. The current is constant, continuing, lasting a long, long time... but it's not always very visible. Emotions, on the other hand, can be understood as the surface of the river, such as waves pushed by the wind or ripples caused by a thrown stone. When the wind dies down, the waves cease. When the rock is not thrown, or after some time passes after throwing it, the ripples end. Emotions are quite visible, but once the trigger or initiating event is over, the emotional state reverts back to what it was before, to whatever the "baseline" mood is.

Again from Webster, we learn that the word emotion has both French and Latin origins. From the French, it comes from emouvoir, to "stir up." And from Latin, it comes from emovere, which means to remove, to displace, to move. Interesting... given that we see moods and emotions are pre-dispositions for Action, we can also say it this way:

E-motion = that which puts us in motion! Or that which moves us into Action, which of course leads to the Results we do or don't achieve.

Moods, Emotions and Each of Us

As we've said in previous chapters, each of us may be understood as a walking, talking bundle of congruency among three separate but highly inter-dependent aspects, as shown below:

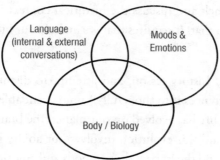

By the time we've reached adulthood, by virtue of how we've lived our lives so far, we say that our unique congruency or combination of these three fundamental aspects is our particular Way of Being. And this Way of Being has a huge impact on how we see things, how we interpret things, how we orient ourselves toward certain Actions and away from others, how (and whether) we end up taking certain Actions and not others, and how we ultimately end up producing certain Results and not others. This is depicted by our familiar graphic below:

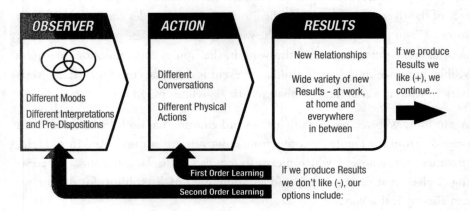

Everything in this chapter is in support of stronger awareness and more purposeful design of our moods and emotions. We believe this focus is warranted, given the tremendously important part they play in our ability to be, do and have what we say is most important for us to be, do and have – at work, at home and everywhere in between.

The History and Biology of Moods and Emotions

The way we would like to consider and understand moods and emotions requires that we take a step back and discuss the historical context in which moods and emotions exist. To do that, it requires that we include our biology and even more specifically, our brains.

Let's take a very brief history lesson, and attempt to distill incredibly complex physiology and occurrences into (hopefully!) understandable concepts. Over the millions of years that life has evolved on our planet, the brains of living creatures have also evolved... and this evolution involves our ability to experience certain moods and emotions and the impact those moods and emotions have on our lives.

Neuroscientist Paul MacLean, as well as many others, use the term "triune brain" to indicate three fundamental aspects or elements or structures within the human brain. The "reptile brain" is found in all reptiles, amphibians, fish... as well as all mammals and humans. It is understood to have developed very early in evolutionary history, and it handles instinctive responses, respiration, circulation, reproduction, etc. It is relatively small and is located directly at the top of the spinal column.

Millions of years later, the "limbic brain" apparently first appeared with the appearance of mammals on earth. So all mammals – in addition to having a reptile brain – also are equipped with this newer biological structure. This increased biological complexity brought with it new motivations and emotions involved in feeding, reproductive behavior, parental behavior and care/nurturing of their young. In other words: it's not just that reptiles and fish <u>don't</u> show emotion the same way mammals do... biologically speaking, it appears that they <u>can't</u> show emotions the way that mammals do!

We observed this in a very real way several years ago when my (Chalmers') kids had a terrarium with pet-store turtles and an aquarium with fish. A new, smaller turtle was brought home to join two slightly larger turtles that had already been with us for a few months. You can probably guess what happened... overnight, the little turtle was eaten by the larger ones! And no guilt! About that same time, we noticed one of the aquarium fish was giving birth, and all the other fish in the tank were gathered around the mother fish. What were they doing? Of course, they were eating the little fish, one by one, the instant they popped out. And once again, no guilt!

To reinforce a key point: It's not simply that the turtle <u>didn't</u> feel guilt... the turtle <u>couldn't</u> feel guilt! As far as our science can tell us, turtles don't have the biological hardware required for the emotional experience of guilt.

With mammals came the capacity for care, for nurturing, for emotional attachment that was not present with the previous biological structures. Certainly this is important, as reptiles and fish come into the world much more prepared to "make a living" from the get-go than do mammals, most of whom are helpless at birth and require months and sometimes years of nurturing, physical contact and care.

Millions of years after mammals and the limbic system, the neo-cortex appeared in early human beings. With this, the possibility and invention of complex language, abstraction, planning, perception and self-perception arrived.

Why might this be important to us, living today? To start with, let's notice that evolutionarily speaking, emotions have been with us a great deal longer than language. So clearly, emotions have something to do with survival, something to do with keeping us alive.

Next, as we've discussed, one of our basic claims is that we human beings are fundamentally emotional beings. Have you noticed? There is no such thing as a non-emotional human. No matter what mood you're in, it's not nothing. In our interpretation, every one of us is a linguistic being, a biological being... and an emotional being. No exceptions, ever.

Today, we live in a world in which many of us believe that in order to make the best decisions and live our lives most effectively and wisely, we need to "take our emotions out of it" or be "rational" or always remain "calm and collected." In our understanding, this is simply impossible. Calm and collected is a mood. While we understand that making important decisions when we're very upset or super angry or even incredibly happy may not serve us well, we dispute the claim that our decisions can be made outside of and separate from our emotional states.

In *Descartes' Error*, author Antonio Damasio demonstrates clearly the physiological connection that exists between our limbic systems (moods and emotions) and our cortex (language and analytical reasoning). In cases in which accidents or surgery have separated these portions of the brain, some very interesting Results have ensued. Patients are still 100% capable of analyzing situations and coming up with viable options, but appear incapable of making "sound" or "good" decisions. They appear to retain complete analytical and linguistic functions, but the absence of emotions has the effect of drastically impairing their ability to choose. Choosing appears to be – inherently – an emotional response. It seems that our emotions are required – as opposed to being a liability – in order for us to make decisions that lead to balanced, successful, meaningful and effective lives.

4 Basic Moods

The following framework and set of distinctions is, in our view, one of the simplest and most powerful ways to understand four fundamental and very prevalent moodspaces, as well as practical approaches for "designing" more productivity and peacefulness into our lives. (For more information, explore the writings and coursework offered by Education for Living (Lake Charles, LA) and the Newfield Network (Boulder, CO). The writings of Julio Olalla and Rafael Echeverria have been particularly influential to us in these areas.)

The diagram below indicates that in our world, there are **Facts** (things we assess cannot be changed) and there are **Possibilities** (things we assess can be changed). And interestingly, how we human beings orient ourselves toward Facts and Possibilities – whether we **Accept** or **Oppose** them – yields four very basic "territories" of mood.

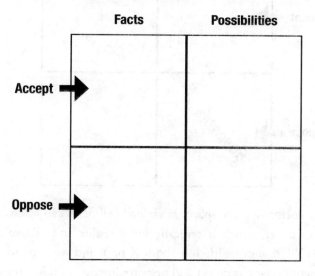

Let's start with the lower left – the quadrant of **Opposing Facts**. Let's say it's a fact that you are 5'11" tall. Question: Can you go through your life being opposed to your height? That is, can you live your life in opposition to your 5-11-ness? Well, of course you can. The question here is not "Can you <u>change</u> your height?" The question here is "Is it possible for you (or any of us) to live our lives in opposition to – being opposed to – our height?" Absolutely, and people do it all the time. While we can't change our individual heights, we can definitely live in opposition to them! This often sounds more like "I shouldn't be 5'11"... I should be 6'11"! I love basketball and my life would be so much different and so much better if I was taller. It's my parents' fault… it's not fair that I'm 5'11"… I would've gotten a scholarship if I was taller…"

How about being opposed to the in-laws that we have? Or being opposed to where we live? Or what we do for a living? Or who we work for? Or what we drive? Or that someone simply does or did a certain thing? Can you begin to get a sense for the "flavor" of the mood that seems to be present when we oppose what is so? What would you call this mood? Most of us have a sense that it has a "negative" flavor to it… we call it **Resentment**.

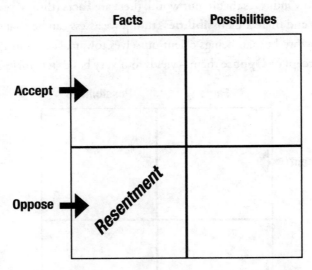

Resentment is a corrosive moodspace, as virtually all of us can attest. It's much less healthy than anger, which is typically quite visible and "above the table." With anger, it's: "I'm angry with you about X or Y and we need to talk about this." Resentment derives its power and negative impact from its non-disclosure. "What's wrong?" you ask. "Nothing" is the sullen response. When it's obvious that everything is wrong.

The relationship between moods and language allows us to linguistically "reconstruct" certain moods. Recalling the key Language Acts and their power, we can hopefully begin to see some new possibilities by taking a new look here. For resentment, the reconstruction may include:

- I assert that some Event has happened or is happening.

- I assess that this Event was bad and damaged me and limited or restricted my possibilities.

- I assess that this was or is not fair.

- I declare that I am the victim here.

- I declare "X" to be responsible for this ("X" being a person, a company, a government, a group of people…).

- I assess that there is nothing I can do now to make X repair the damage inflicted upon me or remedy the situation properly.

- I declare that this is not right, that it should be different than this.

- I declare that somehow, sometime… X will pay for this (I'll get even).

Let's now look at the lower right quadrant, that of **Opposing Possibilities**. This shows up when we dismiss out of hand even the possibility of some new Result being brought about. We dismiss out of hand even the possibility that things could change. A conversation with someone deep in resignation may look like this:

"I think we could improve the project team by re-staffing it with some of the newer hires and mixing them with the veteran guys. What do you think?"

"There's no way that'll work. The young guys are just not knowledgeable enough, and the older guys never come through with any mentoring…"

"I don't know… that approach seemed to work for the Jonesboro project, re-member? They even combined teams mid-stream and managed to come in under budget for the first time since…"

"I'm telling you, there's no way it'll work here. We have totally different types of guys in this district… Nobody here is willing to actually work 8 hours a day. They'll never change. They've always been this way and the sooner you get it through your head, the better off you'll be."

"Well, what if we changed the training program on the front end? Maybe if the team got more technical training before they actually had to work on the system in the field it could help with…

"No, I've thought of that already and the training programs out of corporate are too outdated to be of any use for this new system. And the trainers are terrible, anyway. They'd just make things worse..."

Most of us recognize this as a pessimistic mood, one that we will call **Resignation**. We've resigned, given up and have concluded that nothing we or anyone else can do has any hope of improving possibilities. This mood is often disguised as one being "realistic." A flavor of this can also show up as cynicism, a very caustic and damaging mood.

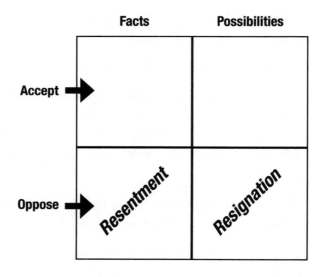

With resignation, it's:

- I assert that some Event or situation has happened (or is happening).

- I assess that this will continue to happen, no matter what Actions I do or do not take.

- I assess that this will continue to happen, no matter what anybody else does or doesn't do.

- I assess that the future is set in stone, and nothing anybody does will have any impact.

- I assess that I would like to change the situation.

- I declare that there is nothing I can do about this.

- I declare that there are no possibilities for me here.

- I declare that I will take no Action.

Turning now to the upper left, when we **Accept Facts**. This shows up when we declare acceptance for what is so. "I'm 5'11." "I've got the in-laws and parents I've got." "I drive what I drive… I may buy a new car tomorrow, but for now, this is what I drive." "I work where I work." And so on.

Let's be clear – to accept is not to "like". To accept is simply to declare that, for now, this is the way it is. What mood seems to accompany these types of declarations?

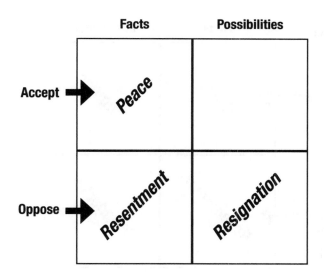

We call it **Peace**, and for many of us it's a "foreign" (not dwelt in very much) moodspace. Internal conversations in a mood of peace may include:

- I assess that there are things I don't like that I cannot change, and that there are things that I would like to do that I cannot. However, I still declare gratitude to life for what I have and what I can do.

- I declare that I am complete with my past, and that it is closed.

- I declare that I accept the present fully.

- I declare that I am open to and accept new, positive future possibilities.

And now, the upper right: **Accepting Possibilities**. This doesn't mean that we commit to everything, all the time; instead, it means that we can at least hold as possibilities the options and alternatives that future Actions represent. We can at least hold as possible that new Actions on our part or on the part of others can open opportunities, shift things, have an impact, make a difference. Here, we hold that the future is not set in stone, and that our orientations, our beliefs, our Actions and those of others can and do have an impact on how the future unfolds. We hold that tomorrow can indeed be different than yesterday and that possibilities do indeed exist for improving or changing what we'd like to improve or change. This mood we call **Ambition** (not blind ambition, where we harm others on our way "to the top", but ambition in the sense of being able to see possibilities where others in our exact same situation may not).

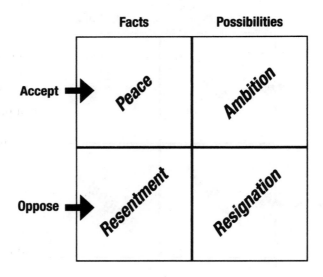

With ambition, it's:

- I see future opportunities and new possibilities for me (and/or others) here.
- I am open to learning more about what these possibilities may offer.
- I am committed to explore and possibly take Action in order to take full advantage of them.

Some degree of ambition is simply required for effective leadership, as leadership today has clearly shifted from command and control to inspire and enroll. And as a leader, what you're enrolling others in is your story, your story that is all about what you see that they don't! You're enrolling your employees and direct reports in the possibilities that you have accepted and that you see as attainable. You're enrolling your staff or your family in your vision of what could be and how you (collectively) could get there. You're enrolling your colleagues and anyone connected to your organization in the opportunities you see, the options and objectives and Actions that you see as necessary to achieve the goals and bring forth the vision.

So let's take a look at this grid and make a few points:

- This completed grid reminds many of us of something called the Serenity Prayer, which is: "God, grant me the serenity (peace) to accept the things I cannot change (facts), the courage (ambition) to change the things I can (possibilities), and the wisdom (Big Eye, new distinctions) to know the difference."

- If you look closely, you'll also see that the Serenity Prayer implies that the serenity (mood of peace) precedes and is what enables us to accept... while our generative understanding of language allows us to say that the declaration of acceptance produces or brings forth the experience of peace.

- If we stay in resentment long enough, we can often slide into resignation. Resentment and resignation seem to be "close cousins."

- Resignation often can be a spiral, where once we're in it, we continue to see fewer and fewer possibilities. (In our society, we often use the word depression instead of resignation here). And ultimately, if a person spirals downward long enough and deep enough to where they end up seeing no possibilities, zero possibilities... suicide can be the Result.

- Many people view peace as a mood of inactivity or non-Action. We offer that, on the contrary, it is a mood out of which truly effective Action is possible. By fully accepting what is so in this moment, we can turn our attention to Actions that will lead us to what we desire. Resentment, on the other hand, has us so preoccupied with "It shouldn't be this way, it's not fair that this has occurred, it's not right that things are the way they are..." that our ability to take effective Action to bring about positive change is greatly diminished.

- In our culture, peace is often mistaken for resignation. That is, we often confuse the ability to accept what is so, the ability to accept what cannot be changed... with giving up. This distinction is very important, as peace is a springboard for new Action while resignation is a profound predisposition to do nothing... since it's already been decided that no productive Action is possible in the first place. This being said, most of us can also tell very quickly whether a colleague, friend or loved one is peaceful or resigned by the content, tone and body language revealed in how they speak and how they listen.

- To reinforce – to accept is not to "like." What are two facts that all of us – especially those of us who live long lives – will ultimately encounter or experience? That people close to us pass away and that we, too, will pass away. We certainly don't like this... but can we accept it? These are very different questions. I believe that older people who have achieved a degree of peace in their lives have indeed come to this acceptance. And for many of them, complete acceptance of the facticity of physical death transforms how they live.

  Julio Olalla has said: *"The capacity to accept is the core of a healthy emotional life."* We agree wholeheartedly. And Carl Rogers puts it this way: *"The curious paradox is this – once I accept myself as I am, then I can change."* What a spectacular observation, one that can truly serve all of us – no exceptions.

Everyone we've worked with has spent time in all 4 of these moods, at one time or another. Haven't you? This being said, we still claim that you will produce far different Results in your life – and have a very different subjective experience while doing so – if you can spend more time in the top 2 and less time in the bottom 2, overall.

We say this: You're not responsible for the mood you wake up in, but you are responsible for staying there. So if you notice yourself in resentment or resignation – if your Big Eye is working well enough to recognize that you are indeed in one of these bottom 2 moodspaces – and you choose to shift out of them, what options do you have for moving into peace or ambition?

From Resentment to Peace

- <u>Make an effective request</u>. If the resentment stems from someone doing something – or not doing something – that we would prefer, then what is very available is to make an effective request. Often, our resentment stems from living in uncommunicated expectations of what others "should" and "should not" do… and then holding these uncommunicated and unfulfilled expectations as broken commitments!   We've heard it put this way: *Resentment is that which arises when you fail to honor a request I never made.* A key distinction for minimizing resentment is to be crystal clear that expectations un-met are not the same as promises broken. There are a great many people today walking around offended, and on the path to resentment, because people in their lives simply did not fulfill their unspoken expectations. It doesn't have to be this way.

  One word of caution here: As you think about making a request, beware of the internal conversation of "… *but I shouldn't have to ask you that! You should already know…* " This is a wonderful opportunity for us to stop, notice and ask ourselves: Do we want to be right or do we want to be happy? That is, do we want to be right or do we want to take Action that may actually lead to a new behavior on the other person's part? Do we want to be right or do we want to create a situation in which we're less resentful? Do we want to live in the certainty of how wrong the other person is or do we want to take Action that could actually change things? What are we willing to give up in order to be right? How we answer these questions, obviously, has a dramatic impact on the extent to which we will experience resentment in our lives.

- <u>Make a responsible complaint</u>. On the other hand, if the resentment stems from an actual commitment that was indeed not kept and not managed, a responsible complaint is a valid move to make. By definition, a responsible complaint is a conversational competency in which you initiate a conversation with the person who broke the commitment, not with any others. (The latter would be gossip, "recreational character assassination" or "trolling" – avenues guaranteed not only to not lessen the resentment, but also to not deal with the un-cleaned up broken commitment).

"I'd like to have a conversation with you about an agreement we had. When can we have this conversation? Did we or did we not have an agreement that you would do X by Y date? (Is it possible I misunderstood about having an agreement in the first place? If so, how can we prevent this from happening again?). Did you do what was promised? (It's possible that you did what you promised, but I just don't know about it... If this is the case, how can we prevent this from happening again?). If you did not do what was promised, let me share with you my assessments about the negative impact this has had, and declare that it's not acceptable... Here is my new request so we can renegotiate or create a new agreement ... or Let's revoke the agreement..."

- <u>Share more of your internal conversations with those close to you.</u> And share them as your internal conversations, your stories, your interpretations, your assessments... not as The Truth! Often, simply by shining the light of day on some of our previously-unshared thoughts, we can loosen the terminal certainty with which we may have been holding them and give ourselves the possibility of updating them or changing them – and by doing so, shifting our mood.

- <u>Change your mind.</u> We can simply declare that whatever it is, is now ok. We can come to see that in the grand scheme of things, it really didn't matter. We can choose to decide that other issues are more important and that we will manage just fine without any changes here. We can get some input and attempt to ground our assessments of unfairness or unjustness. What standards are we using? Do they appear reasonable to others we trust? Might we change or update them? What is the actual data or evidence? Is there any data or evidence that seems to point to different assessments? If so, what does this mean? We can get some input and attempt to ground our assessments of blame and responsibility and victimhood. Other Observers bring the possibility of seeing ourselves and our situations with new eyes, opening new opportunities and new avenues for "human becomings" to travel. A pop song by the group Sister Hazel captures this perfectly with the line: *"If you want to be somebody else, change your mind!"*

- <u>"Get over it" or "move on."</u> These familiar expressions point to the frustration that often arises when dealing with someone who appears "stuck" in the past, unwilling or seemingly unable to accept facts, to acknowledge that a situation or event is over, that the past is closed, that certain possibilities are closed... and move into the future. Getting over it and moving on are declarations of acceptance, of course, that have nothing to do with our legs and nothing to do with vehicles moving forward. They point instead to the generative power of language to shift both the quality of our journey and the dynamics of our interactions with others, in meaningful ways.

- Forgiveness. As we covered in Chapter 9, forgiveness is a powerful declaration, one that allows a chapter to close and another one to open. The other person may not even know, or need to know, about the Action of forgiveness. In this context, forgiveness is not for the other person. It's for the person doing the forgiving. For this is the person who is suffering. For example, can we benefit from forgiving people who are even deceased? The answer, of course, is yes.

Like all declarations, I Forgive You is highly generative and creative. And whether or not we forgive has a great deal to do with how we interpret forgiveness. Let's explore.

As we mentioned previously, forgiveness may be defined as a declaration in which we say: *What you have done to me caused me harm and damaged my possibilities. I do not condone this, and I do not give you permission to do this again. I choose to forgive you, to let go of these conversations. I now will focus my attention and my awareness in other areas, rather than continuing to live in these conversations about you and about what you did. I choose to move forward with my life. I revoke my promise to somehow, some way, get you back. I choose to move into some peace and out of this resentment.*

By forgiving, we bring one chapter to a close and open a new one. We are "moving forward" in a real (but non-physical) way. We are "shifting" out of something and toward something else. Has this been true for you? In cases in which you have forgiven someone, have you felt this? Many of us have. It's not physical, but it's real.

Now, what common interpretations or beliefs do we have about forgiveness that make it unlikely that we'll forgive someone? Said another way, what do we tell ourselves about the other person or about forgiveness that make it difficult or unlikely that we'll actually forgive? Here are some interpretations we've shared and learned in our work:

- "But I'm right"
- "They don't deserve to be forgiven"
- "If I forgive, that means I condone what he did"
- "To forgive is a sign of weakness"
- "To forgive means I'll forget, and I'll never forget…"
- "I won't forgive him because I want him to still suffer"
- "Forgiving her lets her off the hook"

Sound familiar? You can probably come up with others, too. We say that these interpretations are not very powerful. (This is key – notice how we're not talking about whether or not the above interpretations are "right" or "wrong." The focus here is on the Actions, interactions and Results these beliefs lead to). These beliefs need to be updated in order to serve as the starting point for different Actions. What's important to notice is that from the above interpretations (or beliefs, explanations or stories), the Action of forgiveness is not likely to occur. And because the Action of forgiveness doesn't occur, the Results (benefits) that come from forgiveness are not available, either.

One root word underneath forgiveness means "to refuse to hold." Beautiful – to forgive is to refuse to hold, to let go, and what we refuse to hold is our resentment toward someone or something, our personal, private promise to "somehow, someday get even." What we let go of are recurring negative assessments ascribing ill intentions and blame to others, and at the same time casting ourselves in the role of the victim. What we let go of is an orientation in which we're predisposed to withdraw, distrust, find fault and avoid intimacy. Resentment is an incredibly powerful and negative moodspace, one that we have all visited a time or two (or more). We believe that if more of us shifted our understanding of forgiveness, we'd be able to move through setbacks, suffering and difficulties in a healthier, more productive way.

Consider this: pain is biological, but suffering is linguistic. We don't need to have pain in order to suffer, and we can have pain without the suffering. Forgiveness deals directly with the suffering. The single most powerful tool that we have discovered for designing well-being in our lives is the declaration of forgiveness. It applies to our work and social lives as well as our home lives. A great many people in our workshops report the exact same thing, and for all of us it seems not to be a one-time thing. It's a process. It requires ongoing awareness, commitment and practice.

We can declare forgiveness, but we cannot declare forget-ness. That is, forgiveness is a conscious process involving new declarations on our part. Forgiveness is a choice. On the other hand, we cannot choose to "never remember" something! We cannot declare that a particular memory will not be "served up" from time to time, or that we won't be reminded of an event or situation occasionally, even when we're not consciously trying to have this happen. What we can do, however, is choose how we respond, how we react, how we move, what we do… what we declare.

Viktor Frankl brings this to our awareness with his incredibly powerful words, written from his experiences in a World War II concentration camp: *"In between stimulus and response there is a space. In that space is our power to choose our response. In our response lies our growth and our freedom."*

Forgiveness brings peace. It's just that simple. Show me a person in your life that you say is peaceful, and I'll show you someone who doesn't have a list of 10 people they haven't forgiven! Maybe, for non-hermits, there is no peace without forgiveness. And maybe our ability to forgive ourselves is at least as important as our ability to forgive others. In addition to bringing closure and a new context to our relationships with others, we say that forgiveness can also bring dignity, self-worth and self-acceptance into being. This is another key situation in which not being able to <u>say</u> a certain thing = not being able to <u>be</u> a certain way.

We've heard it put this way: *Resentment is the poison I drink, hoping you'll die.* And forgiveness moves us out of resentment, takes the cup from our hands and allows us to move forward with our lives in a fundamentally different way.

Don Miguel Ruiz, author of *The Four Agreements*, offers his perspective on the power of declaring forgiveness. He says:

"Forgiveness is the only way to heal. We can choose to forgive because we feel compassion for ourselves. We can let go of the resentment and declare "that's enough!"... I will no longer be the Victim."... That's the beginning of the free human. Forgiveness is the key."

Don Henley, in his song *The Heart of the Matter*, also speaks about the power of forgiveness. We agree that it really is the heart of the matter. He says:

"There are people in your life, who've come and gone
They let you down, they hurt your pride
You better put it all behind you, 'cause life goes on
You keep carrying that anger, it'll eat you up inside
I been trying to get down to the heart of the matter
But my will gets weak, and my thoughts seem to scatter
But I think it's about forgiveness, forgiveness
Even if you don't love me anymore."

From Resignation to Ambition

This movement can be especially difficult by ourselves. And as many of us — especially some men — have a version of the Lone Ranger syndrome, it's worth noticing so we can anticipate it and develop a strategy if it occurs. If a person is alone and deep in resignation, the last thing he will want to do is take any Action whatsoever, since he's already declared that nothing he or anyone else does can make a difference, anyway. The last thing she will want to do is enroll someone else in a conversation about this, since she's already decided that nothing the other person could possibly add could help the situation, anyway. So if your Big Eye is working to the extent that you do notice yourself in resignation, and you choose to move out of it, we offer three broad strategies:

- Before embarking on either of the paths below, start by doing something physical; that is, do <u>something</u> with your <u>body</u>. Take a bike ride, jog, take a walk, lift weights, exercise, go swimming, play tennis... do something that allows you to take advantage of the built-in connections among your body, your mood and your language. Simply do something to break a sweat or engage your body in some type of physical activity, as a starting point for other possible Actions.

- Just do it! Remember the Nike slogan? Here, the suggestion is simply to take some Action related to the desired outcome you're seeking. The suggestion is to take almost <u>any</u> Action, even if you don't believe it will work. (Remember, by definition, the mood of resignation is a profound pre-disposition to take no new Action). Do something, because some-times, the very act of moving and taking some Action provides an opening, a shift, a glimmer of hope that wasn't there before. Sometimes, just doing something is a very helpful and valuable thing to do.

- Enroll someone in what you're up to. Initiate a conversation with a trusted colleague, friend, spouse, partner… in which you share your resignation with them, as well as your desire to shift out of it and your willingness to listen to their perspective regarding future possibilities. Often these con-versations can lead to new possibilities being surfaced and embraced, new commitments to Action being made, feedback and accountability cycles being established and new Results being brought about.

- Also, let's be clear: We believe that there are times in which there is no substitute for finding competent medical care to address cases of severe, clinical depression. There is a multi-billion dollar pharmaceutical industry built around the fact that for many people in these sorts of situations, the right doctor, the right diagnosis and the right medicine can make a life-altering difference.

Moods, the Past and the Future

Many of us have found ourselves – or observed others – "living in the past" or "living in the future." Of course, we're always right here, right now. These are expressions, however, that point to very real experiences that have the Result of taking us away from the present moment, which we claim is the only place from which we can take Action.

Here, we are not referring to times in which we periodically find ourselves day-dreaming about future possibilities or reminiscing about happy past times or re-flecting on fond memories. There is, of course, nothing wrong with this. These experiences can bring enjoyment and even serve as a catalyst for new ideas and for opening opportunities. Instead, we refer to less helpful ways that certain moods can both trap us in the past as well as blind us to new future possibilities… all the while diminishing our ability to be present here and now, thereby diminishing our ability to take the Actions that lead to the Results we most desire.

Anxiety / Worry. Here we find internal conversations preoccupied with the uncertainty that the future holds (a fact), an unwillingness to accept this uncertainty, and ongoing and ungrounded assessments that the uncertainty is bad, negative and overly damaging. Worst-case scenarios are mentally played out repeatedly, and even seemingly positive or neutral events or situations are seen as "evidence" that the dire consequences are about to happen. This is totally different from healthy skepticism, a mood in which we are invited to take off the "rose colored glasses" and see potential pitfalls and obstacles ahead, so that we may anticipate them and devise ways to navigate around or through them. This is not the same as ignoring potential dangers or not taking adequate preparations for known or anticipated situations. Instead, strong moods of worry and anxiety center on not accepting that some uncertainty is simply a part of living in the kind of world we live in, and on persistent overly-negative assessments about the predicted impact of the uncertainty on our lives and/or the lives of those we care about.

There's an expression that comes to mind here: *What we resist, persists.* By spending too much time in these moods, we can actually take ourselves away from the present to such a degree that we inadvertently contribute to more negative consequences occurring than would have occurred otherwise!

Moving from anxiety or worry into more peacefulness includes declarations of acceptance, such as:

- I accept that the future always includes uncertainty, and that this uncertainty is simply part of living in the kind of world we live in.

- I declare that this uncertainty is not bad or negative in any way. It just is.

- I am beginning to see that I have lived in these future conversations long enough, and I now choose to live my life in the present, right here and right now.

- I am beginning to see that the uncertainty may instead hold great promise and great opportunities, and I declare my openness to embrace and explore these possibilities.

- I accept that I am a human being, and as such, I have the ability to learn what I need to learn in order to adapt, deal with and handle what circumstances the future may bring.

- I am gaining confidence that whatever the future may bring, I (or the person I was worrying about) have what it takes to be successful.

These are not descriptive statements; rather, they are profoundly powerful declarations. In 1776, it was not a factually true statement that "… these 13 Colonies are, and by right ought to be, free and independent States…". What that Declaration did, and what these do, is bring into being a new social reality. They establish a new orientation, a new context, a new place to stand and a new set of possibilities for the future. And given the connection between language and moods, and the claim that we are human becomings, this is important to understand.

Guilt / Shame. Here, the focus is on the past rather than the future. They include internal conversations in which we repetitively re-live events in which say we we violated our standards or the standards of our community. We blame ourselves, have a great deal of assessments in which we "should have" or "shouldn't have" done X or Y… and recurrently beat ourselves up because of what we did or didn't do. We assess ourselves as lesser human beings and declare that we should be punished. From a single past event, we can spend years in these conversations, years in guilt or shame.

These conversations may also include a declaration that we will never forgive ourselves, that what we did was so bad that nobody can or will forgive us… not even God. With shame comes the assessment that if you knew about what I did, you would not want to be with me. We assess that it dramatically, negatively impacts our public identity. If you knew about these dark secrets and how bad I really am, you would abandon me.

Moving from guilt/shame into more peacefulness may include making a sincere apology (a declaration) to the person our Actions or inactions have harmed or damaged. This is certainly possible and positive and is highly recommended, if it hasn't already occurred. But in a great many cases, the apology has long since taken place and the guilt or shame still remain. Here, what's needed includes the following additional declarations and commitments:

339

- I accept that my Actions or lack of Action violated some standard (mine or those of the community) and that I am sincerely sorry for this.

- I promise that I will not do this again.

- I accept that I am a human being, and I am also a human becoming. I am fundamentally good, and I have changed, grown and learned from that experience.

- I acknowledge that everyone makes mistakes. I am beginning to see that I have lived in the past and punished myself long enough. I now choose to live my life fully present, right here, right now.

- I am not broken or defective in any way. I am whole and complete and on a path of lifelong learning and growth.

- I am worthy of forgiveness, and I forgive myself.

- I accept myself for who I am and who I'm not.

- I love myself.

Three Broad Avenues for Designing Moods

Should you decide to more purposefully influence or design your own moods, we offer the following as three broad avenues available to you (once again, remember the 3-circle model and the inter-dependencies which exist among our moods, our bodies/biology and our language/internal and external conversations).

Biology	Body	Language
Medicine	Posture	Conversations with others
Caffeine	Walking	Conversations with self
Alcohol	Standing	Music
Nicotine	Breathing	Coaching
Drugs	Facial expressions	Enrolling others for support
Food choices	Exercise	Feedback
Nutrition choices	Dance	Noticing the tendency to "champion" our own moods

Sleep	Yoga	Sharing more internal conversations
	Meditation	
	Travel	

What are we more committed to?

For the examples above and countless others, we offer this: Should you choose to undertake a process of shifting out of any "negative" or unhelpful mood into something better, get ready to deal with the "I'm Right" conversation. Make sense? Get ready to deal with the internal conversation of "… but I'm right to be resentful!" or "… I'm right to be worried!" or "… I'm right to be resigned!" In these situations, we are confronted with a question about what we're more committed to – being right or shifting the mood. What are we willing to give up in order to be right? How we answer these questions, obviously, has a direct impact on whether <u>any</u> approach to designing and shifting moods will be effective.

Gratitude

Moods don't come about in random fashion, willy-nilly with no apparent connection to other moods. The mood of resentment isn't the predictable, natural jumping-off point for playfulness, for example. Instead, moods seem to show up in "clusters" and we can see certain themes ("positive"/helpful/open vs. "negative"/unhelpful/closed, for example) when we look at all the different types of moods. Certain moods seem to be related to and flow from certain other moods.

This brings us to the mood of gratitude, which many have claimed is the foundation of a healthy emotional life. We agree. And it's far more likely to be experienced by those who spend more time in ambition and peace than in resentment and resignation. In fact, it seems fairly predictable that if we spend significant amounts of time in the moodspace of peacefulness, we will find ourselves moving toward increasing degrees of gratitude.

Let's make a distinction between gratitude and thankfulness. Thankfulness may be understood as connected to transactions and agreements, and as an acknowledgement that someone has fulfilled their part of the arrangement. When we say (declare) "Thank you" to the person who has delivered the item we ordered, this is what is occurring. We may also say "Thank you" to acknowledge and show our affection for people who have taken Actions which are helpful, beneficial or kind to us or to those we care about. This may also be understood as a form of gratitude, of course, in which we are grateful for what they have done.

In a bigger and deeper way, however, gratitude may also be a way of living. It can be a permeating assessment that being alive is a privilege and that it's utterly worthwhile to be a part of this mystery. We can declare gratitude for simply being alive, for being here, or for no reason at all. Larger than thankfulness, gratitude can also be a pervasive state of mind that we can cultivate for ourselves, independent of any transactions or Actions others may or may not take. It was taught to us this way: Show me someone who has joy in their life, and I'll show you someone who's grateful for something. If you're looking for more joy in your life, begin by declaring gratitude.

We can notice that we're still here, alive, breathing. We can notice that we're able to read this book and reflect on new possibilities for how we'd like to lead and live our lives. We can notice that we have been offered options and ways of understanding to help us be, do and have what we most want to be, do and have… that many people living today are unaware of. We can notice that we have air to breathe, food to eat and water to drink, and the sun to warm our bodies. We can notice the incredible beauty of the natural world, of the mountains and canyons, oceans and rivers, forests and fields… as well as the unfathomable vastness of our universe. We can notice that we have certain unique capacities, abilities and talents. We can notice that many of our fellow human beings are living in conditions far worse than those we are experiencing now, and that in many cases they did nothing to "deserve" that and we did nothing to "deserve" this. (As many readers know and have experienced, one visit volunteering at a nursing home or one trip to an impoverished or war-torn area is often all it takes to bring much greater awareness to this). We can notice that we have a spouse or a partner or friends or children or parents or loved ones in our lives whose very presence – not anything they have to <u>do</u> – brings meaning and purpose, enjoyment and opportunity to our lives.

We can declare our gratitude for all of this, and we can declare gratitude "just because." We can say Thank You to God or to the Universe or to Nature or to

Life... for simply being here, for being alive, for the gifts and opportunities and relationships which exist in our lives. And when we find ourselves spending more and more time in gratitude, life changes – as virtually everyone who has experienced this has reported! In this mood, we are predisposed to give to others, to give back, to contribute, to serve. We are predisposed to see the best in others and in doing so, help others begin to see it in themselves, too. We are predisposed to be kind, patient and compassionate, with ourselves and others. We are predisposed to be open to new opportunities and new relationships. And in doing all of this, we end up creating (not simply "finding") a great deal of meaning and genuine, sustainable happiness in our lives.

A Gratitude Practice

We invite you to begin (if you haven't already) some form of gratitude practice. That is, to periodically pause, quiet your thoughts, reflect and declare gratitude. Whether you have a routine of weekly journaling 5 things you're grateful for or a daily practice of finding time to simply stop, close your eyes and say Thank You for whatever you choose to be grateful for... we invite you to explore the process and the power of bringing more gratitude into your life.

Gratitude – Additional Resources

There are a great many videos and books and materials of all types that do a wonderful job of exploring gratitude and helping us cultivate more of it into our lives. One of our favorites is a 10-minute TED talk by Louie Schwartzberg and it can be found at TED.com as well as:

http://www.youtube.com/watch?v=gXDMoiEkyuQ

Summary of Key Points

Moods and emotions are important not because leaders are interested in becoming psychologists, but because organizations are composed of unique Observers coordinating Action in order to produce Results... and these Observers (all of us) are by definition linguistic, physical and emotional beings. Moods and emotions are connected to Results, organizationally and individually.

Conversational, relational and emotional competencies are essential for effective leadership, excellent organizational performance and breakthrough Results, so learning something about moods and emotions is extremely helpful for leaders at all levels.

The increasing use of cross-functional teams and collaborative work processes increases the impact of workplace relationships on many types of organizational Results. And mutually-beneficial, productive relationships have a great deal to do with the ability to understand and "navigate" in the territory of our moods and emotions.

At a basic level, moods and emotions can both be understood as <u>predispositions for Action</u>. A key distinction we make is this: Moods are long-term predispositions for Action, lasting months to years to lifetimes. Moods are "already there" when events or circumstances arise, and dramatically influence how we interpret and respond to these events or circumstances. Because they are more in the background and last so much longer, they are often more difficult for us to see about ourselves.

Emotions, on the other hand, are short-term predispositions for Action, lasting moments to minutes to perhaps hours or days. By definition, emotions are triggered by some external event or circumstance and are therefore usually easier for us to see and acknowledge.

Human beings were emotional beings long before we were linguistic beings. Moods and emotions are totally normal and healthy and are part of how we connect and relate to our environment and survive.

Our bodies / biology are directly related to our moods and emotions. Physical movement can and does have the effect of shifting our moods, just as the moods we happen to be in show up in how we carry ourselves physically. Furthermore, the evolutionary development of certain biological "hardware" (limbic system) was required in order for mammals (including human beings) to have the experience of moods and emotions in the first place.

Learning in the area of moods and emotions is not the same as learning math or science, for example. This type of learning requires immersion, choice, reflection and feedback. It involves acquiring some new distinctions and practicing with others, having conversations and sharing observations. It has nothing to do with memorizing and categorizing data and information.

Everyone is always in one mood / emotional space or another. There is no such thing as a person in no mood. And whatever it is, it is shaping and influencing how we interpret, "see things," take Action and produce Results.

By examining how we accept or oppose facts and possibilities we can identify four basic moods: resentment, resignation, peace and ambition. While all of us visit all of these moods during our lives, we claim that by spending more time in peace and ambition we are able to dramatically improve our effectiveness as a leader, as well as the "quality of our journey," the nature of our most important relationships and even our own physical well-being.

Moods can be "reconstructed" linguistically, and the generative understanding of language allows us to actively design and shift our moods by inventing and living in different declarations, grounding our assessments more carefully, adopting new or different standards, updating certain beliefs, making new effective requests and entering into new commitments.

Moods clearly impact our language – our thinking and our external conversations, as well as our physical bodies. And our physical bodies and our language – our thinking and external conversations – clearly impact our moods. Any of these three domains can and does impact the coherency (Way of Being) that constitutes the Observer that we each are.

Forgiveness is a powerful declaration that enables us to "close a chapter", "let go" and "move on" out of resentment – one of the most corrosive and destructive moodspaces. Forgiveness, in this context, is not about the other person. It's always about the one doing the forgiving, for this is the person who is suffering.

Anxiety and worry are moods having to do with recurring, overly negative (and usually ungrounded and ungroundable) assessments and predictions about uncertainty and the future. Guilt and shame are more about the past, having to do with ongoing internal declarations of our unworthiness due to some long-ago violation of our standards or the standards of our community, even in cases in which we have apologized or made amends. These may also be coupled with the declaration that we do not deserve to be forgiven, by ourselves or others or possibly even by God.

Acceptance is the foundation of a healthy emotional life. The capacity to declare acceptance is an emotional competency which can be learned, strengthened and cultivated. To accept does not mean to "like" but instead, is an acknowledgement that now, this is the way things are. Moving out of resentment, resignation, worry / anxiety and guilt / shame all are connected with our capacity to declare acceptance, in one way, shape or form.

Gratitude and joy are connected, in that people who spend any time at all in joy have declared gratitude for something! We each have the ability to bring more joy and enjoyment into our lives by noticing, acknowledging and declaring gratitude. Establishing a gratitude practice is a practical, proven way to design and influence our own moods.

Application

1. A Gratitude Practice: We invite you to begin (if you haven't already) some form of gratitude practice. That is, to periodically pause, quiet your thoughts, reflect and declare gratitude. Whether you have a routine of weekly journaling 3 things you're grateful for or a daily practice of finding time to simply stop, close your eyes and say Thank You for whatever you choose to be grateful for... we invite you to explore the process and the power of bringing more gratitude into your life.

2. Look at others. Notice others' most prevalent moods. Notice the connections between their moods and their interpretations, their Actions, and the Results they produce (or don't).

3. Look at yourself. Notice your own prevalent moods, the ones that you tend to live in most of the time. Ask others to share with you what moods they experience you living in. Notice the connections between your moods and your interpretations, your Actions and the Results you produce (or don't).

4. When breakdowns occur, notice what within you gets triggered, what emotions you experience, how you tend to respond and what Results get produced. If they are not the Results you desire, consider the "gap" between stimulus and response, the choices you have available to you in that moment, and the connection between your choice of Actions and your desired Results. Share your thoughts and observations with your Accountability Partner(s).

CHAPTER 12
LOOKING AHEAD

"The future ain't what it used to be."

- Yogi Berra

N o one knows exactly what the future actually holds, of course. But we do know this: Our ability to continue learning and growing will be hugely important. This requires that we remain aware enough – and self-aware enough – to acknowledge our blind spots. It requires that we acknowledge that we don't already know everything there is to know... or more to the point, that we don't already know everything *of importance* that there is to know! It also includes a willingness to accept that whatever we do know is necessarily influenced by the way we see things, by a multitude of factors that have contributed to our perspective and have shaped the unique Observer that we each are.

Let's Spread the Word

We claim that the future of our organizations, societies and families can be greatly improved and enhanced by spreading the body of learning contained in this book (and in *Language and the Pursuit of Happiness*) as widely as possible. Our request to you is this: If you have found value within these pages, **please share these distinctions and ways of understanding with others!** It's been our direct experience, and the experience of many others, that these central tenets of:

- self-awareness
- self-responsibility
- choice
- the generative power of language
- the transformative power of second-order learning
- the impact and importance of context

- our capacity to impact the future, to actually bring about genuinely new quantitative and qualitative Results

- organizations (and societies) understood as networks of commitments

- the impact, importance and shapers of relationships

- the impact, importance and shapers of moods, emotions and culture

- the mutual causality among relationships, culture and execution

- the inherent subjectivity of the human experience

- looking at the world, ourselves, our relationships and our organizations through a "works/doesn't work" lens as opposed to a "right/wrong" lens

are part of an emerging new "common sense" that holds great promise, especially given the increasing globalization of our economies, the collaborative nature of our organizations and the inter-connectedness of our lives.

What We Believe and What We Offer

We believe these principles and ways of understanding can contribute to a world in which fewer of us are walking around being "terminally right," unable to see the ways in which our own perspectives are just that – our particular perspectives, shaped by the particular Observers that we are – and not The Truth.

We believe these principles and ways of understanding can support larger and larger groups of people being more able to explore the new possibilities that new explanations can open – rather than being trapped in older explanations that have no such power. We further believe that our organizations and our world will benefit greatly from these new explanations! The key, of course, is being able to see our old explanations as our explanations in the first place.

We believe that a middle school course called "Subjectivity and the Power of Language" and a high school course called "Self-Awareness, Self-Responsibility and Mutually-Beneficial Relationships in a Multi-Cultural World" would be hugely beneficial if widely established.

We believe these principles and ways of understanding can lead to more of us establishing and maintaining mutually-beneficial relationships – business relationships and personal relationships – with more and more people, from more and more places, on this planet. And this, to us, is a fundamentally positive step.

We believe we are human becomings, each of us in an active and ongoing process of learning, growing, changing and evolving in meaningful ways. And we further believe that this continual learning and growth is healthy and even necessary in order for us to craft a future that works for larger and larger numbers of human beings.

We believe that conversational, relational and emotional competencies are increasing in importance in our societies, organizations and relationships – and that they will continue to increase in importance in the years ahead. In fact, it's our view that improvements in these competencies need to advance lock-step with the obvious and rapid improvements in our functional and technical competencies.

We further believe that successful organizations, led by people equipped with these distinctions, frameworks and tools, are particularly well-suited to be at the forefront of very positive changes in the years ahead.

To this end, we offer a range of offerings for organizations of all sizes and shapes:

- **SOAR (Success through Observer – Action – Results):** This cutting-edge, cohort-based leadership and employee development program spans a 6-9 month timeframe and promises opportunities for transformational change. Focusing on conversational, relational and emotional competencies, SOAR is a journey in which new learning is embodied and breakthrough Results – in relationships, culture and execution – occur. Its cross-cultural impact resonates within organizations in the United States, Israel, the United Kingdom and India.

- **SOAR Train-the-Trainer (T3):** For the purpose of training experienced coaches and consultants to deliver their version of SOAR within organizations, this program includes virtual learning supported by experienced learning guides, access to SOAR program and facilitator materials, membership in a growing professional community, as well as a 3-day capstone session. It provides all the tools, templates and materials needed for transformational leadership and employee training. Coaches from the Georgetown Leadership Coaching program, Newfield Network, the George Mason Advanced Coaching Program and Coach Training Institute have been certified to-date. Sessions are held 2-4 times per year.

- **Leadership, Conversations and Results**: Half-day, full-day or two-day program designed to introduce these new frameworks, distinctions and tools to leaders at all levels.

- **Teamwork, Conversations and Results**: Half-day, full-day or two-day program designed to introduce these new frameworks, distinctions and tools to employees and teams of all types.

- **Relationship Teamwork**: Ideal for spousal retreats, this half-day, full-day or two-day program provides a powerful context, helpful distinctions and practical tools for building and sustaining our most important relationships.

- **Life Balance 101**: Ideal for spousal retreats or team events of all types, this half-day, full-day or two-day program provides a practical framework and powerful tools for designing and redesigning the most important domains of our lives.

- **Customized Programs**: We work with leaders and organizations to develop customized programs that tailor this powerful body of learning and new sets of tools to address your most important priorities and objectives.

- **Executive Coaching**: One-on-one coaching to support long-term growth and improvement in specific domains. Typically provided within the context of one of the above programs.

- **Licensing For Large Organizations**: Licensing of SOAR Program and materials for your internal use. Involves train-the-trainer programs for your HR or OD staff, and provides full sets of participant materials, facilitator guides and videos.

Organizations

If you have found value and benefit in this book, and would like to move further into this body of learning, we also invite you to explore these excellent organizations and programs that have had significant and positive impact on us and many of our colleagues:

- Newfield Network, Boulder, CO   www.NewfieldNetwork.com

- Education for Living, Lake Charles, LA   www.EFLseminars.com

- Georgetown University; Leadership Coaching Program; Washington, DC https://scs.georgetown.edu

- George Mason University; Leadership Coaching for Organizational Performance; Fairfax, VA   https://wellbeing.gmu.edu/leadership-coaching-for-organizational-well-being

- Columbia University, Coaching Certificate Program, New York, NY http://www.tc.columbia.edu/coachingcertification/

- The Coaches Training Institute (CTI), San Rafael, CA www.thecoaches.com

Furthermore, if you are a leader or business owner and would like to experience the power of a confidential leadership peer group, work on both business and personal challenges and opportunities and participate in a decidedly carefrontational space, we encourage you to explore Vistage – CEO Private Advisory Boards at www.Vistage.com.

Our Contact Information

- Chalmers Brothers, www.ChalmersBrothers.com, e: Info@ChalmersBrothers.com, p: 239-248-5000

- Vinay Kumar, www.leadingforbreakthroughs.com, e: vinay@leadingforbreakthroughs.com, p: 703-851-9466.

From Individual Change to Organizational Change

We began this book with a fundamental claim – that you cannot change another human being. We also claimed that we are not hermits; that is, we are dancing, metaphorically speaking, with our leadership teams, our colleagues, our customers, our significant others, our families. So while we can't change anyone else, what if we could become more powerful Observers of ourselves, acquire some new ways of understanding, new distinctions, new tools and frameworks... declare ourselves beginners at using the new tools, request feedback from those we trust about our new Actions… We make the first move, from the two-step to the waltz, in the dance we've been doing… And these new Actions on our part may be just the invitation that others need to step into change with us. How do you go from individual change to organizational change? **You go first**. It's a pull, not a push. As Mahatma Gandhi famously said: *"Be the change you wish to see in the world."*

Our Final Thought

We wish you only continued success, happiness, fulfillment and contribution. In closing:

When I was younger, I thought I could change the world.

I thought, "If I can just change the world, then that will change my country.
And if my country changes, then that will certainly change my city.
And if my city changes, then my family will have to change.
And if my family changes, then I will probably change.
Then I will be at peace.

Now, I'm a little older and I have come to realize,
Perhaps, if I had changed myself first,
Then my family may have noticed and changed a little too.

Then, if my family would have changed, their change may have brought about
a change in the way the people of my city treat each other.

Then, if the people of my city would have changed, they could have
changed the way my country interacts.

Then, if my country would have changed the way it interacts,
it may have changed the world.

Then, perhaps, my world would be at peace.

- Author Unknown

APPENDIX A:

REFERENCES

Language and the Pursuit of Happiness: A New Foundation for Designing Your Life, Your Relationships and Your Results, by Chalmers Brothers, New Possibilities Press, 2005, Naples, FL.

How Language Generates Your World and Mine, by Chalmers Brothers, TEDx, Boca Raton, FL 2014

Good to Great: Why Some Companies Make the Leap… and Others Don't, by Jim Collins, HarperCollins Publishers, 2001

How the Mighty Fall: And Why Some Companies Never Give In, by Jim Collins, HarperCollins Publishers, 2009.

The Essential Drucker: The Best of Sixty Years of Peter Drucker's Essential Writings on Management, by Peter Drucker; Harper Business; 2008.

Execution: The Discipline of Getting Things Done, by Larry Bossidy and Ram Charan; Crown Business; 2002.

Humans Are Underrated: What High Achievers Know That Brilliant Machines Never Will, by Geoff Colvin; Portfolio; 2015.

The Five Dysfunctions of a Team: A Leadership Fable, by Patrick Lencioni, Jossey-Bass Publishers, 2002.

The Advantage: Why Organizational Health Trumps Everything Else in Business, by Patrick Lencioni, Jossey-Bass Publishers, 2012.

Cultural Blueprinting Toolkit: A structured process for blueprinting your invisible architecture of core values, organizational culture, and workplace attitude; by Joe Tye, Values Coach, Inc., 2013

The Heart Aroused: Poetry and the Preservation of the Soul in Corporate America, by David Whyte, Random House Publishers, 1994.

What Got You Here Won't Get You There: How Successful People Become Even More Successful, by Marshall Goldsmith, Hyperion Publishers, 2007.

The 5 Languages of Appreciation in the Workplace: Empowering Organizations and Encouraging People, by Gary Chapman and Paul White, Northfield Publishing, 2011.

Start With Why: How Great Leaders Inspire Everyone to Take Action, by Simon Sinek, Penguin Books, 2009.

Executive EQ: Emotional Intelligence in Leadership and Organizations, by Robert K. Cooper and Ayman Sawaf, Berkeley Publishing Group, 1996.

The Thin Book of Trust: An Essential Primer for Building Trust at Work, by Charles Feltman, Thin Book Publishing Company, 2009.

Conversational Intelligence: How Great Leaders Build Trust and Get Extraordinary Results, by Judith Glaser, Bibliomotion, 2013.

Your Body Language Shapes Who You Are, by Amy Cuddy, TED Global, 2012.

How to Fly a Horse: The Secret History of Creation, Invention and Discovery, by Kevin Ashton, Random House Publishing; 2015.

The Triune Brain in Evolution: Role in Paleocerebral Functions, by Paul MacLean, Springer Publishing, 1990.

The Tree of Knowledge, by Humberto Maturana, Francisco J. Varela and Robert Paolucci; Shambhala Publications; ISBN: 0877736421; 1987; p. 27.

You Are What You Say: A Harvard Doctor's Six-Step Proven Program for Transforming Stress Through the Power of Language; by Matthew Budd, MD and Larry Rothstein, Ed.D.; Crown Publishers; 2000, p. 137.

Retooling On The Run: Real Change for Leaders With No Time, by Stuart Heller, PhD; Frog, Ltd.; 1995.

The Four Agreements: A Practical Guide to Personal Freedom; by Don Miguel Ruiz; Amber-Allen Publishing; ISBN 1-878424-31-9; 1997, p. 26, 63, 65, 69, 114.

The Power of Now, by Eckhart Tolle; New World Library, 1999, p. 128.

A New Earth: Awakening to Your Life's Purpose, by Eckhart Tolle, Penguin Group Publishers, 2005.

Conversations with God: An Uncommon Dialogue; Books 1, 2,and 3; by Neale Donald Walsch; G.P. Putnam's Sons Publishing; 1996.

The Fifth Discipline Fieldbook: Strategies and Tools for Building a Learning Organization; by Peter Senge, Richard Ross, Bryan Smith, Charlotte Roberts, and Art Kleiner; Doubleday / Bantam Doubleday Dell; 1994. p. 242.

Coaching to the Human Soul: Ontological Coaching and Deep Change; *Volume 1 – The Linguistic Basis of Ontological Coaching;* by Alan Sieler; Newfield Australia; 2003. p. 12.

The Expanded Quotable Einstein; by Alice Calaprice; Princeton University Press; 2000.

The Academic American Encyclopedia - Hoffer, Eric; New York: Grolier Electronic Publishing, Inc., 1993.

Expression and Meaning, by John Searle; Cambridge University Press; ISBN: 0521313937; November 1985

Linking Language to Action, by J.L. Austin; Cambridge University Press; 1962.

Merriam Webster's Collegiate Dictionary; Merriam Webster Editorial Staff; 1994.

Descartes' Error: Emotion, Reason and the Human Brain, by Antonio Damasio, Penguin Books; 2005

Leading Minds: An Anatomy of Leadership; by Howard Gardner; Basic Books / Harper Collins; 1995.

Leadership and the New Science, by Margaret J. Wheatley; Berrett-Koehler Publishers; 1992.

Diogenes Laertius: Lives of Eminent Philosophers, by Diogenes et. al.;Harvard University Press; 1938.

The End of the Innocence, by Don Henley; audio CD; 1989; Geffen Records.

Fortress, by Sister Hazel; audio CD; 2000, Universal Studios.

APPENDIX B:

INSPIRATION

The following books were not used directly as references in this project, but are works that have inspired us. We highly recommend them to you. To us, they are tremendous sources of wisdom, innovation and genuine optimism for tomorrow.

A Good Day: A Gift of Gratitude, by David Steindl-Rast and Louie Schwartzberg; Sterling Ethos; 2013

Integral Consciousness and the Future of Evolution, by Steve McIntosh, Paragon House Publishing, 2007.

Evolution's Purpose: An Integral Interpretation of the Scientific Story of Our Origins, by Steve McIntosh, Select Books Publishing, 2012.

Mindset: A New Psychology of Success, by Carol Dweck, Ballantine Books, 2007.

A Brief History of Everything, by Ken Wilber; Shambhala Press; 1996.

A Theory of Everything: An Integral Vision for Business, Politics, Science and Spirituality, by Ken Wilber; Shambhala Press; 2001.

Integral Psychology: Consciousness, Spirit, Psychology, Therapy; by Ken Wilber; Shambhala Press; 2000.

Boomeritis: A Novel That Will Set You Free, by Ken Wilber; Shambhala Press; 2003.

Mastery: The Keys to Success and Long-Term Fulfillment, by George Leonard, Plume, 1992.

Talks on the Gita, by Vinoba Bhave, The McMillan Company, 1960.

Living Buddha, Living Christ, by Thich Nhat Hanh; Riverhead Books / G.P. Putnam's Sons; 1995.

Conscious Evolution, by Barbara Marx Hubbard; New World Library; 1998.

Awaken the Giant Within: How to Take Immediate Control of Your Mental, Emotional, Physical and Financial Destiny, by Tony Robbins, Free Press, 1992.

The Cosmic Serpent – DNA and the Origins of Knowledge, by Jeremy Narby; Jeremy P. Tarcher / Penguin Putnam, NY; ISBN 0-87477-911-1; 1998.

Unfolding Meaning, by David Bohm; Routledge Publishing; 1985.

Ontologia del Lenguaje (*The Ontology of Language*), by Rafael Echeverria; Dolmen Edicion, Argentina.

Building Trust: In Business, Politics, Relationships, and Life, by Robert C. Solomon and Fernando Flores; Oxford University Press; 2001.

Understanding Computers and Cognition, by Terry Winograd and Fernando Flores; Addison Wesley Professional; ISBN: 0201112973; 1987.

Overcoming Organizational Defenses; by Chris Argyris; Allyn and Bacon; 1990.

The Web of Life, by Fritjof Capra; Doubleday; ISBN: 0385476760; 1997.

Conscious Business - Transforming Your Workplace (and Yourself) by Changing the Way You Think, Act and Communicate, by Fred Kofman; Sounds True Press; ISBN: 1564559319; 2000.

Seven Habits of Highly Effective People, by Stephen Covey; Simon & Schuster; 1989.

Emotional Intelligence: Why It Can Matter More Than IQ, by Dan Goleman; Bantam Books; ISBN 0-553-09503-X ; 1995.

Stopping by Woods on a Snowy Evening, by Robert Frost; Dutton Books – Reissue Edition; 2001.

Leading Minds: An Anatomy of Leadership; by Howard Gardner; Basic Books / Harper Collins; 1995, p. 14.

The Magic of Believing, by Claude M. Bristol; Prentice-Hall, Inc., 1948, p. 29.

Of Human Interaction; by Joseph Luft and Harry Ingham; Palo Alto, CA; National Press; 1969.

I Love You, You're Perfect, Now Change; audio CD; Varese Records; 1996.

The Times They Are A-Changin', by Bob Dylan; audio CD; Sony; original release 1964.

INDEX

A

acceptance 133, 142, 152, 182, 244, 246, 261, 313, 327, 329-330, 333, 338, 346

accountability 15, 26, 30, 35, 39, 41, 61, 76-77, 104, 150, 262, 280, 284, 286-290, 303-304, 309, 315, 337, 346

African proverb 268

agreements *see also* premises, commitments 69, 157, 251, 263, 268, 284-286, 291, 295, 307-308, 310, 335, 341, 354

ambition 63, 152, 169, 180, 184, 232, 328-330, 336, 341, 345

angle of inauthenticity 298

anxiety 169, 338, 345-346

apologies 243, 305

Argyris, Chris 14, 17, 20, 23, 92, 162, 358

Aristotle 11, 295

Ashton, Kevin 93, 354

assertions 191, 193-197, 199, 201-203, 205, 207, 209, 211-213, 215, 217-225, 253, 255, 257, 260, 263, 266, 289, 292

assessments 117, 121-124, 127, 144, 166, 175, 191, 193-225, 232-233, 235, 240-241, 246, 251, 253, 255-257, 260, 263, 266, 290, 292, 305, 332, 334, 338-339, 345

assumptions 59, 92, 159, 162, 168, 291, 306

attitude *see also* moods 130, 255, 299, 353

Austin, J.L. 355

authority 46, 135, 156, 170, 189, 207-208, 211, 225-226, 229-231, 235, 243, 250, 253-255, 257-258, 260, 292

awareness 1, 7, 86, 107, 118, 130, 138, 180, 210, 214, 219-220, 222, 249, 252, 301, 303, 308, 320, 333, 335, 342

enrolling others   34, 72, 178, 221, 259, 329

events   52-53, 57-59, 68, 73, 80, 84, 87-88, 93, 116, 166-167, 169, 173, 197, 202-203, 212-213, 226, 228, 243, 248, 256-257, 267-268, 314, 318, 338-339, 344, 350

exercise   10, 76, 79, 104, 142, 164, 174, 176, 184, 202, 240, 268-269, 271, 299, 336

expectations   211, 290-291, 304, 306, 331

F

Feltman, Charles   354

Fifth Discipline Fieldbook, the   92, 355

flexibility   5, 130, 178, 180-183, 185, 246

forgiveness   252, 261, 333-336, 340, 345

Four Agreements, The   157, 291, 335, 354

four basic moods   345

future action   263, 270, 272, 274-276, 279, 281, 294, 307-308

future, living in the   337

G

Gandhi, Mahatma   352

Glaser, Judith   354

Goleman, Dan   358

Good to Great   58, 67, 158, 353

gratitude   134, 177, 244-245, 261, 314, 327, 341-343, 346, 357

guilt / shame   339, 346

H

habits   73, 164, 174, 242, 312, 358

happiness   45, 88, 94, 98, 105, 205, 245, 290, 318, 343, 347, 352-353

heart of the matter, the   336

Heller, Stuart   93, 354

Henley, Don   336, 355

S